IRRECONCILABLE DIFFERENCES?

A Learning Resource for Jews and Christians

DAVID FOX SANDMEL

ROSANN M. CATALANO

CHRISTOPHER M. LEIGHTON

A Member of the Perseus Books Group

Copyright © 2001 by Westview Press, A Member of the Perseus Books Group

Published in 2001 in the United States of America by Westview Press, 5500 Central Avenue, Boulder, Colorado 80301-2877, and in the United Kingdom by Westview Press, 12 Hid's Copse Road, Cumnor Hill, Oxford OX2 9JJ

Find us on the World Wide Web at www.westviewpress.com

Westview Press books are available at special discounts for bulk purchases in the United States by corporations, institutions, and other organizations. For more information, please contact the Special Markets Department at The Perseus Books Group, 11 Cambridge Center, Cambridge MA 02142, or call (617) 252-5298.

A CIP catalog record for this book is available from the Library of Congress.

ISBN 0-8133-6568-6

The paper used in this publication meets the requirements of the American National Standard for Permanence of Paper for Printed Library Materials Z39.48-1984.

10   9   8   7

Contents

Acknowledgments

The Institute for Christian & Jewish Studies is deeply grateful to the following individuals and foundations who share our vision and have generously provided the funding that has enabled the ICJS to produce this book. We especially wish to thank Suzanne F. Cohen; the Nathan Cummings Foundation; the Stella and Charles Guttman Foundation, Inc.; the David and Barbara B. Hirschhorn Foundation, Inc.; the Children of Harvey and Lyn Meyerhoff Philanthropic Fund; Charles H. Revson Foundation; Mr. and Mrs. Arnold I. Richman; Ben and Esther Rosenbloom Foundation, Inc.; Mr. and Mrs. Sidney Silber; the Alan B. Slivka Foundation; and the Aaron Straus & Lillie Straus Foundation, Inc. In addition, we wish to thank Dr. Emil Bendit; the Caplan Family Foundation, Inc.; Mrs. Lois Blum Feinblatt; Mr. Benjamin K. Greenwald; Mr. and Mrs. George Hess; Mr. LeRoy E. Hoffberger; the Ann and Sam Kahan Philanthropic Fund; Herbert M. Katzenberg Fund of the Baltimore Community Foundation; the Robert and Lois Klein Family Foundation, Inc.; the Irving Kohn Foundation, Inc.; the Abraham and Ruth Krieger Family Foundation, Inc.; the Zanvyl and Isabelle Krieger Fund; the Lilly Endowment, Inc.; the Mandel Family; the Bernard Manekin Family Fund, Inc.; the Toby and Mort Mower Philanthropic Fund; Dr. and Mrs. H. Alexander Munitz; the Morton B. and Tamara S. Plant Foundation, Inc.; the Judy and Michael Steinhardt Foundation; and the Harry and Jeanette Weinberg Foundation, Inc.

Rabbi Samuel K. Joseph, Ph.D., of the Hebrew Union College–Jewish Institute of Religion in Cincinnati provided invaluable advice and assistance in the crafting of the discussion questions.

We also want to thank the members of the ICJS's Christian and Jewish Educators Study Group, whose insight and constructive criticism has been invaluable to us: Dale Balfour; Geoffrey Basik; Sr. Kate Bell, RSM; Rev. Christa Burns; Fr. Richard J. Bozzelli; Dina

Burt; Hasia Cohen; Sr. Mary Jeremy Daigler, RSM; April Dietrich; Rachel Glaser; Nelda Goergen; Rabbi Jay Goldstein; Beryl Gottesman; Joseph Jensen; Janis Koch; Margie Meyers; Barbara Miller; Fr. Joe Muth; Jeanette Parmigiani; Rena Rotenberg; Nancy Saarlas; Rev. Roberta Scoville; Margie Sullivan; and Rabbi Stuart Weinblatt.

Finally, the editors express our thanks to the staff of the ICJS without whose tireless effort none of this would have been possible: Judi Mellendick, Finance Manager; Sharon Rabb, Director of Development; Laura Riger, Director of Programs and Administration; and Thomas Varner, Program Associate.

Abbreviations

Tanach

Gen.	Genesis
Ex.	Exodus
Lev.	Leviticus
Num.	Numbers
Deut.	Deuteronomy
Jos.	Joshua
Jud.	Judges
1 Sam.	1 Samuel
2 Sam.	2 Samuel
1 Kgs.	1 Kings
2 Kgs.	2 Kings
Is.	Isaiah
Jer.	Jeremiah
Ezek.	Ezekiel
Hos.	Hosea
Obad.	Obadiah
Jon.	Jonah
Mic.	Micah
Nah.	Nahum
Hag.	Haggai
Zech.	Zechariah
Hab.	Habakkuk
Zeph.	Zephaniah
Mal.	Malachi
Ps.	Psalms
Prov.	Proverbs
Qoh.	Qohelet
Lam.	Lamentations

Est.	Esther
Dan.	Daniel
Neh.	Nehemiah
1 Chr.	1 Chronicles
2 Chr.	2 Chronicles

New Testament

Mt.	Matthew
Mk.	Mark
Lk.	Luke
Jn.	John
Rom.	Romans
1 Cor.	1 Corinthians
2 Cor.	2 Corinthians
Gal.	Galatians
Eph.	Ephesians
Col.	Colossians
1 Thes.	1 Thessalonians
2 Thes.	2 Thessalonians
1 Tim.	1 Timothy
2 Tim.	2 Timothy
Tit.	Titus
Heb.	Hebrews
Jam.	James
1 Pet.	1 Peter
2 Pet.	2 Peter
1 Jn.	1 John
2 Jn.	2 John
3 Jn.	3 John
Rev.	Revelation

Rabbinic Sources

M.	Mishnah
T.	Tosefta
B.	Babylonian Talmud
TJ	Palestinian Talmud
R.	Rabba (e.g., Gen. R., Ex. R., etc.)

Tractates

Ar.	Arakhin
ARN	Avot d'rabbi Natan
AZ	Avodah Zarah
BB	Baba Batra
Bekh.	Bekhorot
Ber.	Berakhot
BM	Baba Meßi'a
BQ	Baba Qamma
Dem.	Demai
Eduy.	Eduyot
Er.	Eruvin
Git.	Gittin
Hag.	eagigah
Hor.	Horayot
Hul.	eullin
Kel.	Kelim
Ker.	Keritot
Ket.	Ketubot
Kid.	Kiddushin
Mak.	Makkot
Meg.	Megillah
Men.	Menafot
Mid.	Middot
Miq.	Miqavot
MQ	Mo'ed Qatan
M. Sh.	Ma'aser Sheni
Naz.	Nazir
Ned.	Nedarim
Neg.	Nega'im
Nid.	Niddah
Ohol.	Oholot
Pes.	Pesafim
RH	Rosh Hashanah
Sanh.	Sanhedrin
Sem.	Semafot
Shab.	Shabbat
Shev.	Shevuot

Sheq.	Sheqalim
Sof.	Soferim
Sot.	Sota
Suk.	Sukkah
Tam.	Tamid
Ta'an	Ta'anit
Tem.	Temurah
Ter.	Terumot
Yev. (Yeb.)	Yevamot
Yom.	Yoma
Zev.	Zevafim

I

Speaking Theologically . . . Together

Loving God with All Your Mind

ROSANN M. CATALANO AND

DAVID FOX SANDMEL

Why Did We Write This Book?

The purpose of this book is to help Jews and Christians explore fundamental beliefs that lie at the core of each tradition and thereby to equip them to talk with each other about what distinguishes Judaism and Christianity and what these traditions have in common. Getting Jews and Christians to talk with one another has proven an effective way to increase understanding and reduce prejudice, in and of itself a worthwhile goal, but there is an additional benefit. When Jews and Christians learn about each other *in each other's presence,* the outcome is often a deeper sense of self-understanding and an invigorated commitment to one's own tradition. Jews become stronger Jews, and Christians become stronger Christians; through the encounter with the "other," we come to know ourselves better.

Jews and Christians have been in relationship with one another since the beginning of Christianity. Much of that relationship has been tragic; there are wounds that have not yet healed. There is distrust, ignorance, fear, and even hatred. At the same time, encounters between the two communities—and they have not all been tragic[1]—have been integral in shaping what both Judaism and Christianity are today.

In the years following the Shoah and the founding of the State of Israel, there have been dramatic changes in the relationship between the Jewish and Christian communities. Some Jews and Christians have embarked on a concerted effort of reconciliation, of facing history and looking for new ways to relate to one another. Scholars have produced an increasingly sophisticated portrait of the history of Judaism and Christianity. The roots of prejudice and its consequences have been examined and have led Christians and Jews to confront the past directly and in conversation with one another. Some Christian theologians are taking a close look at anti-Judaism as part of the Christian tradition and are reconstructing a Christian theology that respects and affirms Judaism. And Jews are beginning to take a new look at Christianity. They are acknowledging the changes taking place and as a result are thinking about Christianity as something more than a monolithic and dangerous enemy that is not worthy of consideration and should be avoided.

The impetus for the project of which this book is part came from a group of Jewish scholars working under the auspices of the Institute for Christian & Jewish Studies in Baltimore. These scholars believe that it is in the best interest of the Jewish community to find a way to talk about Christianity from a Jewish theological perspective. This endeavor entails a serious consideration of the religious claims of Christianity: of how Jews might understand and evaluate them, learning where the traditions agree and where they do not. Equally important, this endeavor entails learning about Judaism in a new way. To begin that process, the Jewish scholars, who worked for five years with the Institute for Christian and Jewish Studies, issued "Dabru Emet: A Jewish Statement on Christians and Christianity" on September 10, 2000. This brief statement, written by Tikva Frymer-Kensky, David Novak, Peter Ochs, and Michael Signer and endorsed by over 200 rabbis and scholars from across the Jewish religious spectrum, appears at the end of this chapter. In addition, the scholars produced *Christianity in Jewish Terms* (Westview Press, 2000), a collection of essays that explore in detail the core theological concepts that both unite and divide Jews and Christians. *Irreconcilable Differences? A Learning Resource for Jews and Christians* is written to facilitate study of the issues raised in "Dabru Emet" and *Christianity in Jewish Terms*. The Institute for Christian & Jewish Studies has supported the work of the Jewish scholars and the production of this book and has embarked on a project to engage Jews and Christians in the study of these resources. The institute will continue to offer an educational forum in which the challenges of religious diversity can be explored.

The positive developments in Jewish–Christian relations noted above have occurred at a time when both Jews and Christians have become increasingly concerned about the future. Before the Shoah, there were 18 million Jews; now there are 14 million. In most parts of the world outside Israel, Jewish communities are shrinking because of low birth rates, assimilation, and interfaith marriages. As American society has opened up to Jews, the traditional social and religious boundaries that used to maintain community cohesion have broken down. The demographic projections give Jews ample cause for concern; Jewish continuity has become the first priority for many Jewish leaders and institutions. Some Christians (to the surprise of many Jews) also believe they are facing a crisis. Religions other than Christianity and Judaism are growing in strength and in influence, an inevitable outcome of the growing diversity within our culture. The greatest threat, however, comes from a secular culture that devalues religious experience and mistrusts any expression of religious values or motivation in the public arena. No religious community is immune from secular influence. Yet, at the same time, there is a great hunger in our society for spiritual fulfillment and community.

Both Jews and Christians are compelled to respond to the challenges and opportunities such an environment presents. Both communities have recognized that education is the most effective way to preserve and strengthen religious identity, to defend against communal deterioration, and to enable individuals to experience the spirituality they seek within the religious community to which they already belong.

We believe that the encounter between Jews and Christians that this volume strives to nourish is an essential, and profoundly rewarding, component of contemporary religious education. This encounter can deepen and strengthen the current programs of education within individual Jewish and Christian communities and thus serve the twin goals of reducing prejudice and promoting the ongoing vitality of each community.

How Did We Write This Book?

In order to write this book, in March 2000, a group of Jewish and Christian educators came together under the auspices of the Institute for Christian & Jewish Studies. Working together, Jews and Christians composed responses to the following questions, responses that instruct Jews and Christians about themselves and about each other, and that encourage conversation, discussion, and further study.

- Do Christians and Jews worship the same God?
- How do Jews and Christians read the Bible?
- How do Jewish and Christian ethics differ?
- What is the meaning of Israel for Jews and Christians?
- How do Judaism and Christianity respond to suffering?
- How do Jews and Christians understand sin and repentance?
- What do Jews and Christians believe about redemption, salvation, and life after death?
- Are there irreconcilable differences between Christians and Jews and, if so, are these differences a blessing, a curse, or both?

In order to carry out this assignment, the educators entered into the very same conversation that this book strives to promote among its readers. We started the process with a two-day working meeting, during which the authors taught each other about their particular topic according to their own religious tradition. They asked questions of each other and read sacred texts together. And they also spoke from their personal experience as participants in living, worshiping religious communities. The creative and searching exchange continued over months as the authors and the ICJS scholars composed the chapters. Each chapter, then, is an opportunity to join in a conversation between Jews and Christians and to continue the study and discussion that begins here.

Can Jews and Christians Talk to Each Other About God?

It is not always easy for Jews and Christians to talk to one another about religion, due in part to the reality of the history of Jewish–Christian encounters. Jews and Christians have talked at each other and past each other for centuries; only in the past two or three generations have some Jews and Christians started talking *to* one another. We are still learning to trust one another. We are still learning to understand each other's religious language; as the questions above demonstrate, both traditions use many of the same key terms (God, worship, Israel, sin, redemption, Messiah, etc.) even though in many instances we define them differently.

A second problem makes it difficult for Jews and Christians to talk about religion. One of the most basic assumptions of the Jewish–Christian encounter is that Christians do theology; Jews study texts. The study of sacred texts, taken almost exclusively from the Jewish Tanach/Christian Old Testament, has thus come to occupy center stage in the dialogue between Jews and Christians because biblical texts are thought to provide a neutral ground upon which both Jews and Christians can safely stand. Ask any long-term participant of the dialogue, and they will tell you that interfaith text study works an intoxicating magic. It teaches Jews and Christians what they can learn in no other setting: that the other brings to the study of a particular text ways of seeing and hearing, ways of listening and learning that illumine portions of the textual terrain that otherwise remain in darkness. Having glimpsed facets of a text previously hidden from our view, who among us would want to settle for a partially lit text.

Yet, the decision to focus—almost exclusively—on sacred texts as the subject matter of interfaith learning is based on at least two erroneous assumptions that seriously compromise the goal of such study. The first of these assumptions is that the playing field created by biblical texts is a theology-free zone. If Christians can reign in their impulse to "do theology," the text itself will provide a common language that both Jews and Christians can speak. But no study of texts is devoid of theological interpretation. No one, neither Jew nor Christian, comes to the text as a theological tabula rasa. Whether they know it or not, whether they admit it or not, both Jews and Christians approach a biblical text with eyes, hearts, and minds molded by a living tradition of interpretation.

The second erroneous assumption focuses on the character of theology itself. On the Christian side, theology is mistakenly assumed to be the exclusive domain of academics who reside in ivory towers far removed from the hopes, fears, and longings of ordinary people. Theology is thought to be what philosophers and theologians do when they ramble on about the number of angels on the head of a pin. For folks in the midst of the fray of life, theology may dazzle with its erudition, but it is judged to be fundamentally irrelevant to all but residents of other towers.

Jews, on the other hand, mistakenly assume that theology is synonymous with dogma, an arcane and peculiarly Christian grammar that is both foreign to and considered suspect by Jewish sensibilities precisely because it is judged as far removed, if not completely detached, from the study and interpretation of sacred texts. Christian theology is seen as a misguided effort still under the influence of Greek philosophy that focuses on abstractions such as "faith" and "belief." It is abstruse and systematic, with little, if any, connection to practice.

The consequences of such erroneous assumptions about theology pose a serious threat to the vitality of the Jewish–Christian encounter. Because theology is judged as either irrelevant or suspect, Jews and Christians rarely venture down paths of mutual learning that are open to them only when they risk speaking theologically. To limit interfaith conversations to the study of sacred texts is thus dangerous on two counts. First, both Jews and Christians are deprived of learning that can enrich, guide, and support them in their everyday lives as they strive to live in accord with God's commands. Second, both Jews and Christians risk the loss of conversations vital to the well-being of their respective communities and to their mutual enrichment, because they are without a language with which to speak. If they cannot speak theologically, neither Jews nor Christians can access their respective traditions. Deprived of the wisdom borne by synagogue and church, Jews and Christians become disconnected from a particular way of living in the world.

Both communities are then consigned to secular solutions, and the society in which they live is deprived of critical religious voices. Thus, one of the primary educational tasks facing both the Jewish and Christian communities is to equip their members with the skills needed to reclaim their particular tradition, to articulate their unique spiritual identities, and to share that richness with each other and with the world. The question is: What are the skills that will best serve this end?

Characteristics of Theological Speech

Perhaps the most important skill both Jews and Christians need to acquire is the ability to speak theologically together. This kind of theological speech has three key characteristics: it is *self-conscious,* it is *self-critical,* and it is *modest.*

Self-conscious speech entails knowing that you are speaking theologically. It means that you are aware that you are engaging in theological discourse whenever you put into words that which gives your life enduring meaning and value. Jews and Christians speak theologically whenever they *knowingly* strive to articulate the ways in which their lives serve the Holy One of Israel, as mediated through Torah or Jesus Christ.

Self-critical speech entails the ability to ask yourself questions about what you believe and about the moral consequences that flow from those beliefs. It means that you intentionally engage in the *content* of your belief. Not satisfied to say, "I believe . . . and that is enough," the self-critical person asks: "What do I mean when I say I believe that . . ." For example, one of the core affirmations of Judaism is that God gave the Torah to Moses on Mt. Sinai. But it is one thing to say "I believe that God revealed the Torah" and quite another to articulate a coherent understanding of what I believe that revelation to be and what difference it makes in how I live? Are the answers I give myself credible to me? Do *I* believe what I say? Do *I* understand what I believe? To be theologically self-conscious and self-critical is to run completely counter to the bumper sticker that reads: "God said it; I believe it; and that's enough for me!"

The third, and perhaps most important, characteristic of theological speech is often in short supply, namely, modesty. Modesty makes room for doubt. Although the notion of doubt may seem, on first hearing, to run counter to faith, theology puts doubt in the service of faith. Making room for doubt requires a profound awareness that no single articulation of the mystery of God can exhaust the meaning of who God is and what God requires of us. Jews and Christians alike are commanded to love God with all their hearts, all their minds, and all their strength (Deut. 6:4; Mt. 22:36; Mk. 12:29; Lk. 10:27). When they admit the limits of every theological concept and foundation, Jews and Christians may well learn better how to love God more fully with all their minds.

If speaking theologically is the skill most needed to access one's own tradition for the good of the self, the other, and the society in which one lives, if the skills required to speak theologically are the ability to be self-conscious, self-critical, and modest about one's beliefs and practices, then interfaith study offers an extraordinary opportunity. No other setting is better suited to help sharpen one's ability to speak theologically, because when Jews and Christians, in the presence of one another, try to put into words what they believe, they are more likely to be asked what their beliefs mean, and how those beliefs make them more righteous people. For example, it is one thing for a Roman Catholic to talk about what the Eucharist means with a group of other Catholics, but nothing is more disarming, more challenging, or more humbling than when a Jew turns to them and says, "What is the Eucharist?" In no other setting are we more self-consciously aware of what it means to speak theologically, because the religious other has the uncanny ability to "ask the obvious" and open up unacknowledged assumptions. Speaking theologically together makes us better Christians and better Jews precisely because in one another's company we are more compelled and inspired to give an account of what most shapes our religious identity.

Theology, Faith, and Revelation

What, then, is the subject matter of theology? The primary focus of theology is the religious dimension of human experience in our everyday lives. Both Jews and Christians claim that God has spoken a word in history, a word that is directed first and foremost to how we are to live in the world. The greatest challenge to the word of

God emerges when our experiences of life conflict with what our religious traditions teach us.

Human experience often confronts us with hard questions—questions of purpose, of meaning, of pain, of hope: Am I making of my life all that it can be? Why isn't the meaning of things clear? Why do we keep asking *why*? Why do the innocent suffer? In what do I place ultimate hope? Is it worthy of my trust? Our responses to these questions are theological when we self-consciously, self-critically, and modestly frame them in the context of our religious tradition. To speak theologically at such times is to put oneself in the company of countless generations of women and men whose questions are our own, and in such company we may well find wisdom and comfort. The power of both Judaism and Christianity lies in their respective abilities to give life meaning that *endures.* The challenge is this: As we struggle to live lives faithful to Torah or to the gospel, can our faith withstand our questions and sustain our hope? In its broadest and most basic sense, theology is what we do when we respond within the context of our faith tradition to the questions life poses. It is what we do when we seek to understand the meaning, coherence, and truth of what our faith teaches and what we most fundamentally believe and trust.

Theology ought to accomplish several important tasks. First, it ought to make a statement about life that is intelligible to us; second, it ought to sustain our questions; third, it ought to help us make sense of our lives; fourth, when we cannot make sense of our lives, theology ought to sustain us in hope; and last, it ought to assist us in the critical task of distinguishing "good" theology from "bad" theology. "Good" theology is self-conscious, self-critical, and modest religious thinking that leads us to actions and behaviors that enhance life both corporately and individually. It is life-giving, life-affirming, and in accord with God's command to repair and redeem the world. "Bad" theology is religious thinking that fills our heads and hearts with ideas that ultimately lead us to live lives unworthy of the One in whose image we are created.

A last word about the relationship between theology, faith, and revelation: We have put forth the notion that theology is a self-conscious, self-critical, and modest way of thinking about God, about what God requires of us, and about how we are to bring our human experience into dialogue with what our religious traditions teach us. To make a decision to do theology is to make a conscious commitment to move from naïve faith to critical faith, from faith that does not ask itself questions about what it believes and does not contemplate the implications of believing it to faith that is able to engage critically what it believes and in whom it trusts, faith able to confront and embrace both our questions and the questions that life itself poses.

As such, theology follows faith and is at its service. It is faith seeking understanding, a self-conscious, self-critical, and modest articulation of what one believes. But the faith to which both Jews and Christians are committed and that they seek to understand is not some vague, amorphous feeling. In both Judaism and Christianity, faith is first and foremost faith *in* God. Thus, in both our traditions, God is always in the midst of our thinking. Furthermore, faith is related to and committed to what God has revealed to our respective communities. For both of our traditions, faith is always and ultimately committed to God's revelation and intrinsically tied to God's actions at Sinai or on Calvary. Revelation precedes, sustains, and evokes faith just as faith precedes, sustains, and evokes theology. Revelation is the starting point of faith just as faith is the starting point of theology. Revelation, faith, and theology are not simply related to each other. They are inseparably bound together, intrinsically and essentially connected one to the other. This being the case, Jews and Christians cannot escape doing theology because both are in covenant with the God of Israel. The only question is: Are we going to do good theology or bad theology?

The essays that make up this learning resource are an attempt to do good theology. They are self-conscious, self-critical, and modest exercises in which a Jew and a Christian do theology together by putting into their own words something of their faith. As you read and study each chapter you will hear the authors speak words that capture, however partially, something of what is at the heart of the mystery of our lives with God and with one another. These essays have been collected for two reasons: first, so that you may learn something more about the content of Jewish and Christian self-understanding; and second, so that you may use them as examples of how to go about the essential task of bringing to speech what *you* understand, what *you* believe, and what *you* practice.

The mandate to get our stories straight, both the ones we tell about ourselves and the ones we tell about the other, beckons us beyond where we are. The commitment to create together a new and better future, one that is free from the hateful entanglements of our tragic pasts, requires both courage and humility. With sacred text in one hand and flashlight in the other, Jews and Christians stand together at the edge of a path barely trod and hardly visible. As such, we may be fulfilling Isaiah's dream of creating a new highway to the One in whose image we are both created. If that is so, perhaps the words of the Spanish poet Antonio Machado are equally apt: *Caminante, no hay camino se hace camino al andar*: Walker, there is no road; the road is made by walking.

Notes

1. See Robert Chazan, "Christian–Jewish Interactions over the Ages," in *Christianity in Jewish Terms,* ed. Tikva Frymer-Kensky, David Novak, Peter Ochs, David Fox Sandmel, and Michael Signer (Boulder, Colo.: Westview Press, 2000), 7–24.

Dabru Emet:
A Jewish Statement on
Christians and Christianity

TIKVA FRYMER-KENSKY, DAVID NOVAK,
PETER OCHS, AND MICHAEL SIGNER

In recent years, there has been a dramatic and unprecedented shift in Jewish and Christian relations. Throughout the nearly two millennia of Jewish exile, Christians have tended to characterize Judaism as a failed religion or, at best, a religion that prepared the way for, and is completed in, Christianity. In the decades since the Holocaust, however, Christianity has changed dramatically. An increasing number of official church bodies, both Roman Catholic and Protestant, have made public statements of their remorse about Christian mistreatment of Jews and Judaism. These statements have declared, furthermore, that Christian teaching and preaching can and must be reformed so that they acknowledge God's enduring covenant with the Jewish people and celebrate the contribution of Judaism to world civilization and to Christian faith itself.

We believe these changes merit a thoughtful Jewish response. Speaking only for ourselves—an interdenominational group of Jewish scholars—we believe it is time for Jews to learn about the efforts of Christians to honor Judaism. We believe it is time for Jews to reflect on what Judaism may now say about Christianity. As a first step, we offer eight brief statements about how Jews and Christians may relate to one another.

Jews and Christians worship the same God.   Before the rise of Christianity, Jews were the only worshipers of the God of Israel. But Christians also worship the God of Abraham, Isaac, and Jacob; creator of heaven and earth. Although Christian worship is not a viable religious choice for Jews, as Jewish theologians we rejoice that through Christianity hundreds of millions of people have entered into relationship with the God of Israel.

Jews and Christians seek authority from the same book—the Bible (what Jews call "Tanakh" and Christians call the "Old Testament").   Turning to the Bible for religious orientation, spiritual enrichment, and communal education, we each take away similar lessons: God created and sustains the universe; God established a covenant with the people Israel, God's revealed word guides Israel to a life of righteousness; and God will ultimately redeem Israel and the whole world. Yet, Jews and Christians interpret the Bible differently on many points. Such differences must always be respected.

Christians can respect the claim of the Jewish people upon the land of Israel.   The most important event for Jews since the Holocaust has been the reestablishment of a Jewish state in the Promised Land. As members of a biblically-based religion, Christians appreciate that

Israel was promised—and given—to Jews as the physical center of the covenant between them and God. Many Christians support the State of Israel for reasons far more profound than mere politics. As Jews, we applaud this support. We also recognize that Jewish tradition mandates justice for all non-Jews who reside in a Jewish state.

Jews and Christians accept the moral principles of Torah. Central to the moral principles of Torah are the inalienable sanctity and dignity of every human being. All of us were created in the image of God. This shared moral emphasis can be the basis of an improved relationship between our two communities. It can also be the basis of a powerful witness to all humanity for improving the lives of our fellow human beings and for standing against the immoralities and idolatries that harm and degrade us. Such witness is especially needed after the unprecedented horrors of the past century.

Nazism was not a Christian phenomenon. Without the long history of Christian anti-Judaism and Christian violence against Jews, Nazi ideology could not have taken hold nor could it have been carried out. Too many Christians participated in, or were sympathetic to, Nazi atrocities against Jews. Other Christians did not protest sufficiently against these atrocities. But Nazism itself was not an inevitable outcome of Christianity. If the Nazi extermination of the Jews had been fully successful, it would have turned its murderous rage more directly to Christians. We recognize with gratitude those Christians who risked or sacrificed their lives to save Jews during the Nazi regime. With that in mind, we encourage the continuation of recent efforts in Christian theology to repudiate unequivocally contempt of Judaism and the Jewish people. We applaud those Christians who reject this teaching of contempt, and we do not blame them for the sins committed by their ancestors.

The humanly irreconcilable difference between Jews and Christians will not be settled until God redeems the entire world as promised in Scripture. Christians know and serve God through Jesus Christ and the Christian tradition. Jews know and serve God through Torah and the Jewish tradition. That difference will not be settled by one community insisting that it has interpreted Scripture more accurately than the other, nor by one community exercising political power over the other. Jews can respect Christians' faithfulness to their revelation just as we expect Christians to respect our faithfulness to our revelation. Neither Jew nor Christian should be pressed into affirming the teaching of the other community.

A new relationship between Jews and Christians will not weaken Jewish practice.   An improved relationship will not accelerate the cultural and religious assimilation that Jews rightly fear. It will not change traditional Jewish forms of worship, nor increase intermarriage between Jews and non-Jews, nor persuade more Jews to convert to Christianity, nor create a false blending of Judaism and Christianity. We respect Christianity as a faith that originated within Judaism and that still has significant contacts with it. We do not see it as an extension of Judaism. Only if we cherish our own traditions can we pursue this relationship with integrity.

Jews and Christians must work together for justice and peace. Jews and Christians, each in their own way, recognize the unredeemed state of the world as reflected in the persistence of persecution, poverty, and human degradation and misery. Although justice and peace are finally God's, our joint efforts, together with those of other faith communities, will help bring the kingdom of God for which we hope and long. Separately and together, we must work to bring justice and peace to our world. In this enterprise, we are guided by the vision of the prophets of Israel:

> It shall come to pass in the end of days that the mountain of the Lord's house shall be established at the top of the mountains and be exalted above the hills, and the nations shall flow unto it . . . and many peoples shall go and say, "Come ye and let us go up to the mountain of the Lord to the house of the God of Jacob and He will teach us of His ways and we will walk in his paths. (Isaiah 2:2–3)

2

Jewish–Christian Relations in Historical Perspective

CHRISTOPHER M. LEIGHTON AND

DANIEL LEHMANN

Christians and Jews learn to stand in their respective traditions with a blind eye toward the other. Most of us were taught to read and interpret our sacred texts, to think and act without any sustained attention given to the beliefs and practices that define the other. Those of us who are religious professionals, educators and clergy, have been particularly reluctant to scale walls and leave the comforts of home. Rarely have we ventured beyond our familiar surroundings and faced the disorienting affirmations of our religious neighbors. When our practiced isolation is critically challenged, our anxieties are triggered and we reactively wonder: Why should we teach about the other's tradition when the people in our midst know so little about their own? How can we venture onto alien theological turf without leading our people astray? It is easy to get lost in a morass of conflicting religious claims. Interfaith dialogue seems to blur vital distinctions, confuse the uninitiated, and erode the integrity of each community. So, most Christian and Jewish professionals insist that religious revitalization depends upon education that turns us inward, connects us more firmly to our own foundational stories, and enables us to retrieve our own distinctive voices. An educational task has increasingly emerged as a top priority for both Jews and

15

Christians: to reclaim our separate spiritual identities and to affirm the irreducible singularity of our religious allegiances.

The authors of this book recognize that both Christians and Jews stand before pressing educational imperatives. No less than the coherence and integrity of our traditions are at stake. We both find ourselves in the midst of a dominant culture that consistently ignores, trivializes, or domesticates religious questions. In the midst of contrasting, if not conflicting, religious claims, the tendency is to see religion as a private matter that reflects the idiosyncratic tastes and opinions of the individual. According to the prevailing ethos, it does not matter if you are Christian or Jewish or Muslim, believer or agnostic, as long as you are sincere and tolerant. In such a climate, religious affiliations are interchangeable and generational loyalties disposable. Unless and until Christians and Jews can articulate the distinct wisdom that emerges in the light of their specific communities, unless and until they can access the traditions, the stories, and the practices that give the spiritual imagination its particular texture and moral engagement its specific direction, their religious moorings will become no more than anachronistic attachments, no more than empty ancestral ties. If Christians and Jews are defined by the drift of secularism, they will soon discover that they have little to say and less to do.

To meet the bewildering challenges that face religious communities today will require a renewed commitment to learning. Without the rigors of sustained study and disciplined reflection, neither Christians nor Jews can navigate the depths of their traditions. Among the many educational experiments that need cultivation, we are convinced that one avenue of exploration is worthy of considerable attention, namely, an inquiry into the Jewish–Christian encounter. However counterintuitive this proposal first appears, our experience over the years is that Christians who dare to learn about the dynamics of Judaism become better and more knowledgeable Christians. Jews who risk engagement with Christianity develop deeper and firmer grounding in Judaism. The Christian–Jewish entanglement runs far deeper than most of us have acknowledged, and the tangled interplay of our communities requires unraveling. Each of our traditions has defined itself over and against the other. Whenever we teach our own heritage, we wittingly or unwittingly form perceptions of the other. As we will review in this chapter, the distortions within the Christian tradition have reverberated with deadly results in the Jewish community, and nothing remotely comparable has unfolded from Jewish attitudes of Christianity. Nonetheless, both Jews and Christians lug around misshapen portraits of the other that have been used to bolster excessive claims about their own superiority. If Jews and Christians fashion their own distinctiveness on caricatures of others, the images mirrored will prove dangerously distorted. Traditions that are unwilling or unable to correct their misperceptions ultimately prove untrustworthy. This book is written in the conviction that overcoming these stereotypes not only will free us from unfair judgments, but also will sharpen and deepen the awareness of our own individual particularity.

If Jews and Christians are to develop a textured awareness of their distinctive religious identities that can flourish amid the pushes and pulls of a religiously diverse society, then they must acquire a vocabulary and grammar that enable them to speak to one another about their foundational beliefs and practices. The bulk of this volume is devoted to the acquisition of a theological language that will better equip Jews and Christians to discover wherein their singularity lies. Yet, creative exchange also necessitates an awareness of the collective experiences that we both bring to the table. Jews and Christians cannot find our rightful place without attending to the wanderings of our ancestors who brought us here. We carry a great many memories and become hopelessly lost without their company. An indispensable task that confronts both Christians and Jews is learning to read and interpret the past through the lens of the other. This chapter will briefly outline a few key historical moments that will help orient readers and that will suggest new possibilities for further exploration.

The Origins of Judaism and Christianity

The pages of our history are doors behind which reside unsuspected surprises. Nowhere are we Christians and Jews likely to find hidden treasure more abundantly than at the threshold of our origins. Christians and Jews both excavate their Scriptures to unearth their distinct foundational stories. Both communities trace their ancestry

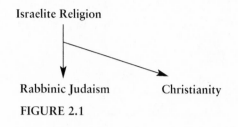

FIGURE 2.1

to Abraham, and both see themselves as the true inheritors of Israelite religion. Jews maintain that the covenant forged between God and Abraham continued through the patriarchs and matriarchs, came to fuller realization through Moses, and flows organically from the times of the priests, kings, and prophets through the rabbinic sages into our own time. The prevailing view in the Jewish tradition holds that Jesus was a Jew who veered from the normative observances of the community. The trajectory initiated by Jesus deviated far more radically under the direction of Paul, who is often credited not only as the real founder of Christianity but also as the principal architect of anti-Judaism. Figure 2.1 illustrates an often unspoken view among many Jews about the beginnings of rabbinic Judaism and Christianity.

The story of Christian beginnings is understood quite differently when framed within the context of the church. Jesus is positioned in continuity with God's people, and the line extends through Jesus and his disciples to Paul and the early Christian community. According to this rendering of the past, attempts to restore the covenantal relationship between God and the people of Israel were rejected. Inclusion of Gentiles and acceptance of the marginalized and dispossessed was thought to run counter to the legalism and tribalism of Judaism. By rejecting Jesus, the Jews deviated from God's plan of salvation. This historical formulation undergirds a displacement theology known as supersessionism and is charted in Figure 2.2.

In recent decades, Jewish and Christian scholars alike have challenged the assumptions that have dominated both communities. Jesus and his earliest followers are increasingly situated within the context of a Judaism far more variegated than once imagined. First-century struggles between rival Jewish factions were compounded and intensi-

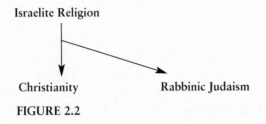

FIGURE 2.2

fied by a range of reactions to Roman occupation and the cultural pressures to assimilate Hellenistic mores. The pivotal moment for both the followers of Jesus and the progenitors of rabbinic Judaism came with the destruction the Second Temple by the Romans in 70 C.E. This catastrophe left Jews bereft of the national center of their religious life, and adaptation to this loss demanded a radical realignment in religious sensibilities among the followers of Jesus no less than the sages of rabbinic Judaism. Rather than play off an analogy that posits Judaism as the parent and Christianity as the child, scholars such as Alan Segal maintain that the relation of siblings functions as a more fitting metaphor for the historical development of the two traditions. The shift that has emerged in recent scholarship yields a revised schematic, as shown in Figure 2.3.

The complexities of this development, frequently referred to as the Parting of the Ways, cannot be squeezed into a tidy summation. However, a shift in our historical paradigms may prove essential if

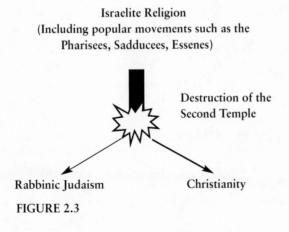

FIGURE 2.3

there is to be a new and searching inquiry that brings Christians and Jews into meaningful conversation. The traditional practice of setting Jesus and his followers over and against Judaism belies the historical record and invariably reinforces the one-dimensional images Jews and Christians have of one another. What begins as a family quarrel mutates into an embittered separation that finally culminates in a systematic attempt to sever the links of a deep theological connection. This fragmentation is the result of multiple areas of divergence that unfolded over a period of time. To fathom this process of estrangement, scholars have attempted to reconstruct a sharper and more historically reliable picture of the Jewish context leading up to the first century in the common era. This scholarly initiative has paid particular attention to the growth of popular religious movements, notably the group that the New Testament pictures as polemical adversaries of Jesus: the Pharisees.

Although efforts to trace a clear path from the Pharisees to rabbinic Judaism require speculative leaps, there can be little doubt that the religious reforms found along this path show evidence of innovative genius. These reforms were revolutionary because they radically altered the structures of organization and the exercise of power, thus making way for rabbinic Judaism.

1. *The Oral Torah.* The crystallization of the Oral Torah enabled Jews to interpret and reinterpret the Written Torah with far greater flexibility and creativity. The Oral Torah, subsequently redacted into the Mishnah and the Talmud, enabled the Jewish community to adapt and respond dynamically to the issues of the day. Although this literature is extremely difficult to date, the tradition of reinterpreting the Hebrew Scriptures led to new ways of embodying the Torah and most certainly became a disciplined dimension of Jewish life well before the time of Jesus.

2. *Table fellowship.* Not only did the Oral Torah allow for theological affirmations of concepts such as the resurrection, it also manifested itself in the development of central practices, notably the development of table fellowship. Traditions once confined to the Temple and limited to priests were reinterpreted and applied to conduct within the home. The maintenance of a household governed by dietary regu-

lations extended religious observance to members throughout the community. Every home could function as a reflection of the Temple, a sacred locus from which holiness flowed and from which the sanctification of life could find expression in daily routines. In a sense, the dinner table was transformed into an altar, and the fellowship of family and friends constituted a new priesthood.

3. *The rabbinate.* The democratization of religious life evident in table fellowship is also reflected in the emergence of the rabbinate. In contrast to regulations that made eligibility to the priesthood dependent on pedigree, any male Jew could become a rabbi in virtue of his mastery of the tradition and his halachic dedication.

These three developments, along with the emergence of the synagogue, enabled rabbinic Judaism to take shape in the aftermath of the destruction of the Second Temple, not only enduring the cataclysm but finally thriving.

The spiritual innovations wrought by the Pharisees not only laid a foundation upon which rabbinic Judaism was constructed, but also may have provided an indispensable religious framework for the teachings of Jesus and, thus, for the development of the early church. E. P. Sanders maintains that almost every argument in the Gospels falls within the spectrum of Jewish debate, and that Jesus is best understood when closely aligned with the Pharisees. But if Jesus was a Torah observant Jew and if his teachings can be situated within the diverse spectrum of first-century Jewish interpretations, then how are we to account for the splintering of the tradition?

The followers of Jesus experienced the revelatory presence of God in the life, death, and resurrection of Jesus. To find meaning and direction from the disorienting course of events, they sought understanding from the only Scriptures they knew and trusted, namely, the Hebrew Scriptures. However, the trajectory of their interpretations increasingly pressed the envelope at several critical junctures. According to the New Testament scholar James Dunn, the movement that eventually became Christianity explicated its understanding of Jesus in three ways that undercut the traditional pillars of Palestinian Judaism.

1. The Temple transposed. The power and sanctity of the
   Temple was increasingly transposed and applied to Jesus
   Christ, whose very person was seen as its new embodiment.
   Jesus became the sacrifice to end all sacrifices, and the trans-
   formative power of forgiveness was recapitulated in the
   communion meal known as the Eucharist, which maintained vital linkages with the dynamics of Temple sacrifice
   (see chapters 7–10 in the New Testament's Epistle to the
   Hebrews).

2. The redefinition of communal boundaries. A crisis among
   the followers of Jesus emerged in the wake of missionary activity, for the greatest success did not occur among Jews but
   among Gentiles. At issue were the terms of inclusion, and
   the criteria for membership were sharply debated. Some
   maintained that one could not be a follower of Jesus without being Torah observant. Others, most notably Paul, argued that the covenantal requirements of the past no longer
   held for Gentile converts. The obligations that once made
   membership inseparable from ritual practices such as circumcision and dietary regulations simply did not apply to
   Gentiles. This position was developed at the same time that
   rabbinic Judaism was tightening the boundaries to consoli-
   date the community and better equip it to resist the drift
   into the dominant Hellenistic culture. In short, the followers
   of Jesus extended the conditions of communal membership
   to be more inclusive of Gentiles and in the process became
   increasingly estranged from the direction charted by rabbinic leadership. The communal boundaries of the early
   church were increasingly defined on the basis on belief in Jesus Christ and the rejection of ritual practices that differentiated Jews. These changes led to different, indeed incompatible, conceptions of "election" or "chosenness."

3. Monotheism reformulated. Early Christians were convinced
   that in his life, death, and resurrection Jesus Christ manifested God's presence. A rich vocabulary to describe this
   dynamic was developed, and much of it grew out of first-
   century Judaism. For example, the immanence of God was
   frequently described in the Jewish literature of the time as
   Wisdom. By the time the Gospel of Matthew was crafted

(ca. 85 C.E.), Jesus was identified not simply as divine Wisdom's messenger but as the embodiment of Wisdom herself. Although Jews understood God's holiness as particularly manifest in the Temple and in the Torah, the ensuing formulations of Jesus as God's incarnation broke open the prevailing boundaries and were seen by Jews as the corruption of monotheism.

The Battle for the Bible

The process of separation was far more confused than this sketch suggests. There is ample archeological evidence to demonstrate that the interplay of Jews and Christians did not unfold uniformly in time or place and that tensions were compounded by political, social, economic, and religious rivalries. However, there is no doubt that the early clash between Jews and Christians engendered considerable rancor. This rancor is evident in polemics throughout the New Testament and mutated into a more virulent strain of rhetoric in subsequent centuries. Family feuds are rarely exempted from impassioned name-calling and incrimination, and this divorce was no exception. At a time when claims to antiquity were used to establish authority and credibility, Jews and pagans alike dismissed Christianity as a "new religion." To combat the accusation, Christians maintained that they were the true interpreters of the Hebrew Bible and that their reading of the Scriptures established them as the authentic people of God. The church fathers argued that they could penetrate the literal meaning of the Bible and discover its inner logic. Their methods of study were said to disclose God's salvation plan, namely, that the ancient promises point to fulfillment in Christ. The purposes of God are no longer realized in the synagogue among the Jews but come to fruition exclusively in the church among faithful Christians. Thus, the battle for the Bible began almost from our earliest beginnings, and over the centuries it has proven far more costly than most of us recognize.

The allegorical interpretation of the Cain and Abel story (Gen. 4:1–16) developed by the most influential of the church fathers, Augustine (354–430), serves to illustrate the point. In his tract *Reply to*

Faustus the Manichean (Book 12), Augustine develops a typological or symbolically representational reading of Genesis 4. He equates Abel with Christ and identifies Cain with the Jews. Just as Cain murdered Abel, so the Jews killed Christ. Cain is banished from the land and doomed to wander, and, Augustine argues, a corresponding punishment should determine the destiny of the Jews. Like Cain, they are to be maintained in a degenerate condition, for their degradation provides eloquent testimony to the consequence of rejecting Christ. Augustine nonetheless sets a limit to the logic of Christian supersessionism. The "negative witness" of the Jews serves a divine purpose, and like Cain they are to be protected from attacks that imperil their existence.

This typological interpretation exemplifies a disturbing dynamic: The church generated a reading of the Scriptures that provided a theological platform used to sanction the humiliation of the Jewish people. At various times and in various places, the protection offered by Augustine's formulation collapsed under the strains of political, economic, and religious upheavals. The atrocities visited upon the Jews during the Crusades and the Inquisition, the recurrent patterns of expulsions throughout Christendom, and the eruption of violent pogroms indicate the precarious condition of the Jewish people, especially after the thirteenth and fourteenth centuries. The church collaborated intimately with the state in the formulation of legal codes that situated Jews on the margins of society. The policies of exclusion were sustained by anti-Jewish caricatures that migrated from the portals of cathedrals to popular folklore. Indeed, the depth and breadth of these stereotypes are etched into the art, the literature, the music, the philosophy, and the theology of Western culture's greatest luminaries. However radical changes wrought by the Reformation, the inflammatory polemical assaults and the practices of discrimination endured and in some cases even intensified. Luther's vitriolic outbursts in his infamous pamphlet *Concerning the Jews and Their Lies* (1543) are among the worst, for this work advised civil authorities to burn synagogues, confiscate rabbinic texts, and expel those Jews who refused to convert.

Although the breadth and depth of anti-Jewish prejudice is well-known within the Jewish community, most Christians were raised on historical accounts that ignored or avoided all questions of the church's ongoing complicity. The realization that many of the church's most illustrious thinkers and leaders over the centuries have placed the gospel in the service of hate and indifference administers a severe jolt to the Christian imagination. The imperative to neutralize this legacy of contempt requires a willingness to examine the most basic assumptions in the church and in the culture at large. The magnitude of this endeavor is only beginning to dawn on Christians, and we will turn to this task in our conclusion.

The task within the Jewish community is to move beyond a conception of history that freezes Jews into the passive role of victim and envisages Christians as incurable agents of oppression. In a series of lectures delivered at Chautaqua and subsequently developed into a highly readable volume, *Moments of Crisis in Jewish–Christian Relations*, Marc Saperstein asks how our history would have differed if Constantine had converted to Judaism rather than Christianity. Although the question invites wild speculation, Saperstein advocates a reading of the past that engenders an aptitude for self-criticism on all fronts. The coupling of religious conviction with political power has repeatedly generated noxious consequences, and no religious community can place itself beyond the temptations of zealotry. Furthermore, Saperstein and other Jewish historians remind us that the history of the Jewish–Christian encounter not only includes pogroms and disputations but also encompasses creative adaptations to the challenges posed from without. The interplay with Christians led Jews to develop a varied repertoire of responses simultaneously resisting and accommodating the dominant culture.

Two examples offered by Saperstein illustrate the complex dynamic between Judaism and Christianity in the premodern era. In the area of biblical studies, medieval Christian scholars studied with learned Jews to discover more about the original text of the Hebrew Scriptures. Similarly, medieval Jewish scholars developed a four-tiered exegetical system patterned on structures developed centuries earlier by Christian commentators. Even more striking, the Hasidei Ashkenaz, German Jewish pietists in the twelfth century known for their anti-Christian rhetoric, introduced a new practice of "individual confession of sins to a sage who instructs the penitent about the appropriate acts of penance." This religious innovation in Jewish religious practice occurs at the same time that the Roman Catholic Church is requiring confession to the priest.

In the seventeenth and eighteenth centuries, the predicament of Jews in western Europe appeared to improve as the engineers of social and political reform struggled to dispel the enchantments of religious zealotry. To disarm the bloody passions of Protestants and Roman Catholics, western European nations began to march beneath the banner of universal "tolerance." The rhetoric and the logic of the Declaration of the Rights of Man issued by the French National Assembly (August 26, 1789) supplied a new approach to "the Jewish Question," namely, the possibility of Jewish participation within the body politic as equal citizens. Christian Wilhelm Dohm advanced an argument for Jewish emancipation that was echoed by other "enlightened" political reformers.

> Let us concede that the Jews may be more morally corrupt than other nations, that they are guilty of a proportionately greater number of crimes than Christians; that their character in general inclines toward usury and fraud in commerce, that their religious prejudice is more antisocial and clannish; but I must add that this supposed greater moral corruption is a necessary and natural consequence of the oppressed condition in which they have been living for so many centuries.[1]

The dominant culture had grown accustomed to a fantasy that had demonized the Jewish people. While the chimera of the misanthropic Jew seeped into almost every crack of the popular imagination, the advocates of emancipation insisted that these so-called character flaws were not innate but the consequences of a landless and disenfranchised condition inflicted on the Jewish populace by an abusive and oppressive society. Since "the Jew is even more man than Jew," the liberal reformers maintained that Jews would become indistinguishable from the rest of the population once released from the confines of the ghetto. To facilitate the process of assimilation, Jews were required to relinquish those communal practices—social, political, economic, and religious—that had long sustained the community as a self-governing "state within a state." The logic behind Jewish emancipation secularized the religious expectations of an earlier era and bequeathed the modern nation-states of western Europe with an ominous dream. In both the medieval and modern scenarios, a time was envisioned when "the Jewish problem" would find resolution through the absorption of the Jews into the larger society and their eventual disappearance as a distinct people.

After the Shoah

When Jews refused to blend into the nation in the terms defined by the champions of emancipation, resentments mounted and the more extreme policies of anti-Semitism gained momentum. The new predicament signaled a far more precarious condition. When "the Jewish problem" was construed as religious, conversion remained "a solution"—and this spiritual transformation ultimately depended upon the return of Christ at the end of days. When "the Jewish problem" was defined by the genetics of an immutable national identity, a far more radical solution was demanded. The pseudoscientific theories of social Darwinism left people intoxicated with grandly malevolent visions of racial purity. The health of nations depends upon the willingness of its citizens to expel or eliminate foreign substances from the body politic. Diseases are not cured by benign neglect and compassionate accommodation. The cold logic of eugenics was coupled with a mythology of utopian perfection in Nazi Germany, and the ideological fallout magnified and intensified the vulnerabilities of the Jewish community.

All attempts to find a comprehensive explanation for the "Final Solution" falter under the enormity of the destruction. Scholars will continue to debate the extent to which the Shoah depended upon the accumulated animus of Christian anti-Judaism. Yet, there is no way around the fact that the massive failure of the churches calls into question the moral and spiritual credibility of Christianity. The gravity of this challenge has pressed many Christians to reckon with the underbelly of their history and to identify those facets of its tradition that can be used to sanction hate or indifference. The single most important document to advance a dramatic reversal in the teaching of contempt was a short declaration issued at Vatican II in October 1965 and known as *Nostra Aetate*. The document teaches that Jews and Christians share a common spiritual ancestry, and it insists that the death of Jesus "cannot be charged against all Jews, without distinction, then alive, nor against the Jews today." Yet, the most fundamental reorientation is reflected in the assertion that "Jews should not be presented as rejected or accursed by God, as if this followed from the Holy Scriptures."

Within the sixteen sentences that compose paragraph 4, the Roman Catholic Church initiated a shift in thought that is still revolutionizing Christian understandings of the Jewish people and Judaism. Judged by the standards that now prevail within the Roman Catholic Church, *Nostra Aetate* may appear timid and flawed. Neither the Holocaust nor the birth of the Israel is mentioned, and the need to embark upon a long and arduous process of repentance remains unacknowledged. Yet, what in hindsight might appear as a small turn of the rudder has altered the course of history, and the momentum begun by *Nostra Aetate* has acquired greater force and focus through subsequent publications. Many mainline Protestants have also begun to confront prejudices deeply rooted within their traditions and have issued their own statements.

The guilt that animates many of the churches' official statements not only serves as a painful acknowledgment of past complicity; these pronouncements also disclose the difficulties in imagining a new and mutually beneficial partnership. As a result, the haunting legacy of the Christian–Jewish encounter may induce a fatalism that leads both the Jewish and Christian communities to abandon hope that any new project can make a genuine difference. Paradoxically, the Holocaust both impels an unflinching accounting from Christians and constricts the terms for creative engagement with the larger Jewish world. If a new and creative relationship is to emerge that deepens religious understandings within and between both Christian and Jewish communities, the shared venture may hold special promise in the North American context.

The American experience has differed sharply from the encounter between Jews and Christians in Europe. The separation of church and state in the Unites States has created an environment in which Jews can interact with Christians as equals before the law. The powerful link between Christian dogma and governmental policy has been broken by the development of a secular state. Indeed, Jews and Christians have often become allies in the struggle for religious freedom in an age of secularity. In addition, the immigrant history and the multicultural character of American society have enabled Jews to assert their cultural equality with Christians. This American experience has contributed to an environment in which Jews and Christian enjoy a relationship of mutual respect unparalleled in the history of these two religious communities.

The North American context simultaneously poses unique possibilities and challenges to the Jewish–Christian encounter. The deeply rooted religious pluralism of American culture challenges the traditional structures that have governed the Jewish view of Christianity. No longer can Jews claim to be tolerant of other faiths merely based on Noahide laws. The Noahide laws, a rabbinic construct in which monotheistic, non-Jewish religion is given legitimacy as a human striving for religious expression, no longer speak to the very specific and intimate relationship between Jews and Christians. Jews need to develop a theological space in which Christians can stand in their particularity and be recognized by their distinctive, covenantal claims. The view of Christianity as the force of oppression or as a corrupted version of Jewish messianism will be unable to propel us forward in an age of religious tolerance, mutual respect, and cultural assimilation. A new paradigm must emerge that can speak to a generation that does not feel threatened by the presence of the other and is searching for ways to define the other as a partner. At the same time, the syncretistic merging of religious traditions and the secularization of public life demand an approach that maintains communal boundaries and individual religious identity. The difficult balance between particularism and pluralism is at the heart of the Jewish–Christian relationship in America.

Beyond the American setting, the creation of the State of Israel has also significantly altered the familiar dynamic between Judaism and Christianity. Judaism's reemergence into the realm of political statehood has created a new, more even playing field for the Christian–Jewish encounter. Jews today have a renewed confidence that comes only from experiencing themselves as defining a majority culture. The sense that Jewish destiny is not determined by Christian power has freed Jews to see Christianity in ways not governed by the patterns of cultural, political, and religious hegemony that have characterized the encounter for centuries. Christianity has also been faced with the theological challenge of a resurrected Jewish polity that has asserted its claim to the land. The Jewish connection to the land and the creation of Jewish political autonomy raise fundamental questions about supersessionist theologies and the relationship between universal messianism and the particularity of unredeemed history. Israel's very existence can serve as a catalyst for shaping a new type of relationship in which the other can be seen as fully embodied in history.

Conclusion

Christians and Jews have reached a critical juncture in their history. They can no longer retreat into isolated enclaves and remain oblivious of the other's tradition, nor can they recapitulate the ancient and enduring patterns of contempt that enshrine fear, distrust, and ignorance. Both strategies betray the religious mandates to repair the world's fractures. If Christians and Jews simply follow the scripts handed to them from the past, they will fail to respond to the new possibilities inherent at this time and in this place. In a religiously plural democracy, withdrawal from an honest and probing encounter will undermine their full participation in the society at large and will deprive the wider public of the invigorating wisdom that each of these traditions has to offer.

A new moment has arisen, and the relational character of the future will turn on the responses. Jews and Christians need to develop beyond the sibling rivalries that have polarized and antagonized them in the past. The paradigm-shattering historical events of the twentieth century and the blossoming of democracy and pluralism demand a more sophisticated approach to the Jewish–Christian encounter. Theological creativity must propel both communities to envision new ways to construct a relationship that is both true to the particular religious experience and open to the presence of the other's religious claims. In textual exegesis and in the formation of religious communities, we must hear the voice of the other as we create distinctive forms of religious life. The challenge is not to untangle the intertwined history of these two great religious traditions. Instead, it is to develop a new narrative that will provide a religious framework for greater reciprocity and mutual blessing.

Notes

1. *Concerning the Amelioration of the Civil Status of the Jews* (Berlin: 1781). Reprinted in *The Jew in the Modern World,* ed. Paul R. Mendes-Flohr and Jehuda Reinharz (New York: Oxford University Press, 1980), 27–34.

3

Do Christians and Jews Worship the Same God?

PHILIP A. CUNNINGHAM AND

JAN KATZEW

The question we face presupposes that different Jews worship the same God and that different Christians do likewise. It is a highly problematic presupposition. Two Jews may not believe in the same type of God. One may believe that God wrote the Torah, making it a perfect document. Another may believe that God inspired human beings to write the Torah, making it a holy document. Another may believe that human beings wrote the Torah, making it a historical document. There are similar positions in the Christian world in regard to God and the Bible. As a consequence, there is a diversity of Jewish and Christian beliefs in God, a diversity that makes this essay very personal, even though the word "I" may rarely appear in it. This essay reflects a conversation between a Jew and a Catholic who share an educational premise: We need to learn more about, from, and with each other. Our goal is theological harmony, not homogenization. We seek what we share and acknowledge where we differ. It is written in the spirit of dialogue, a learning tool, certainly for its authors and, we hope, for its readers.

There is a fundamental asymmetry between Jewish and Christian theology. God-belief in Judaism is not the focus of Jewish learning; that distinction belongs to Torah. There is no Jewish counterpart to the creedal statements of the church. Even though eminent teachers of Torah have articulated basic principles of Jewish thought, there is no dogma accepted by all Jews that proclaims the essence of Jewish belief.[1] Christianity, on the other hand, has tended to emphasize the necessity of correct belief in doctrinal statements. Ironically, the central affirmation of God—"Hear O Israel: YHWH is our God, YHWH is One" (Dt. 6:4)—has been interpreted as a point of both divergence and convergence between Judaism and Christianity.

In the second century C.E., a bishop named Marcion tried to persuade other Christians that the God of Israel was a different deity than the God revealed by Jesus Christ. This notion was firmly rejected by Christians, and down to the present day all Christians understand that they worship the One God of Israel.

Jews have understood the oneness of God to refer both to divine unity and to divine uniqueness. Consequently, the debate about God has revolved around the Christian claims of a triune, incarnate deity. Rabbi Abahu, in third-century Cæsaria, commented on the verse "I am the first, and I am the Last, and beside Me there is no God"(Is. 44:6) as follows: " 'I am the first,' for I have no father; 'and I am the last,' for I have no son; 'and beside Me there is no God,' for I have no brother" (Ex. R. 29:5). The Jerusalem Talmud (450 C.E.) refutes the claim that three Hebrew names for God—El, Elohim, and YHWH—justify a triune understanding of God (Ber. 9:1). This rejection of the Christian claim that God is one but also three led Maimonides, the twelfth-century authoritative commentator, codifier, and philosopher, to hold that Christians practiced idolatry (Mishneh Torah: Hilchot Avodat Kochavim 9:4, inter alia). As a practical matter, Jews should not enter into business relationships with Christians because they would be required to take an oath to establish the contract. An oath sworn to some other deity would constitute idolatry (B. Sanh. 63b).

This polemic was crystallized in a fourteenth-century text entitled *The Refutation of Christian Principles* by Hasdai Crescas.

The Christian says God, may He be blessed, has three separate attributes, which he calls Persons, and the Jew denies this; the Christian believes that God, may He be blessed, has an attribute called son, generated from the Father, and the Jew denies this; the Christian believes that God, may He be blessed, has an attribute which proceeded from the Father and the Son called Spirit, and the Jew denies this. The Christian believes that the Son took on flesh in the womb of the virgin. . . . The Jew denies . . . this."[2]

However, since the twelfth century, an alternative Jewish theological voice has emerged—one that tolerates, accepts, and appreciates the Christian claim to worship the God of Israel. Commenting on the same passage in the Babylonian Talmud, Sanhedrin 63b, that led some interpreters to circumscribe relations between Jews and Christians, Rabbi Isaac argued that worship of the Trinity was idolatry for Jews but not for Christians. Concurrently, Rabbi Menachem Ha-Me'iri of Provence concluded that Christians believe in God's existence and, therefore, were not idolaters.[3] In the eighteenth century, Rabbi Yeuhuda Ashkenazi argued: "In our era . . . when the gentiles in whose midst we dwell . . . [speak of God], their intention is directed toward the One Who made Heaven and Earth, albeit that they associate another personality with God."[4]

Although we acknowledge the history of polemic and the real differences that exist between Jewish and Christian theology, it is in the spirit of Rabbi Ashkenazi that we affirm the claim that Jews and Christians worship the same God. Although not a novel assertion, it is a significant one to make now, as our communities seek to move beyond disputation and debate toward dialogue, and beyond tolerance toward mutual enrichment. We intend to seize this opportunity to learn about, from, and with each other what we share in worship of God. From this starting point, we will consider three questions: (1) How does God become known? (2) What kind of God have we come to know? and (3) How do we respond to this God? In each case we will draw authority and inspiration from sacred texts and commentaries in an attempt to make relevant that which our respective traditions understand to be authoritative.

How Does God Become Known?

I am YHWH your God, who brought you out from the land of Egypt, from a house of serfs. You are not to have any other gods before my presence. (Ex. 20:2–3)[5]

Jews read these verses as the first two of the Ten Commandments, whereas Christians read them as a single commandment. However counted, they represent a singular event, the revelation at Mount Sinai, the most public divine disclosure. Generally in the Bible, God chose an individual to receive an intimate glimpse of the divine— Abraham, Sarah, Hagar, Isaac, Jacob, Moses, Manoah, Hannah, and Solomon. But, according to Jewish tradition, these two verses were directed to the entire people.[6]

This is the essence of revelation, that is, God revealing God. God initiates the process; God searches for us and defines the terms of our relationship. In this theophany, a manifestation of the divine, God's presence was announced with thunder and lightning; a cloud of smoke enveloped Mount Sinai; the mountain itself trembled, and the shofar blasted. All of the senses were engaged in anticipation of the revelation. Other revelatory moments had their own unique character, but on Mount Sinai, God's power over nature, God's supernatural essence, was revealed for all to see, hear, smell, taste, and feel. The opening words of the revelation at Sinai established divine authority. They were not legislative; they were historical and covenantal. The first clear mitsvah, commandment, is the absolute rejection of polytheism. God prescribes loyalty and proscribes idolatry. If the first statement is one of historical context, the second is one of theological content. God is known to us through historical experience, and as a result of that experience Jews are called to accept that God as the one and only, the foundation for ethical monotheism.

The contents of this revelation make an essential point about our shared religious understanding of God. Our belief in God's existence is not the consequence of philosophical argument but of historical experience. The first of the Ten Commandments is not really a command at all. It is a statement of relationship, of covenant. We need to accept the authority of the Divine Commander before we can accept the commandments. How many of us can recall the words "because I am your mother" or "because I am your father" in response to a question about why we could or could not do something? Here we have a revelation that effectively begins with the statement, "Because I am your God, you will do what I ask of you."

Even though the revelation at Mount Sinai was public, it was also personal. Each of the people who saw and heard God perceived God uniquely. The Jewish prayer par excellence, the core of every worship service, begins with these words: "Praised are You, Lord our God, and God of our ancestors, God of Abraham, God of Isaac, and God of Jacob, and (some of us add) God of Sarah, God of Rebecca, God of Leah, and God of Rachel . . ." Why, the sages asked, was it necessary to write "God of" in front of each person? The words are necessary, the sages replied, to illustrate the individual nature of a relationship to God. The ancestors worshiped the same deity, but their relationships were private, personal, and unique. So it is with each one of us.

Christians agree with the Jewish experience that God is met in history and that such meetings generate relationship. Roman Catholics and many other Christians hold that God's self-disclosure to human beings is at essence an interactive process. To put it another way, although God is revealed through events in human history and experience, human beings must decide to interpret particular, concrete events as manifestations of the divine. In the words of Pope John Paul II, revelation comes to people "as a gift . . . set within the context of interpersonal communication."[7] Different people can witness or experience the same events or series of occurrences, but only some of them might conclude that God's activity has been revealed. For instance, different people might observe a sunset. Some will take note that this astronomical event indicates a certain time of the day. Other observers might be struck by the beautiful colors and grand vista. Still others might feel a brush with the Transcendent One who sustains all of existence. The same historical phenomenon is witnessed, but only some witnesses conclude that a disclosure of the divine has occurred. Likewise, not everyone who participated in or witnessed the escape of forced laborers from Egypt would conclude that God had chosen these refugees for special purposes; nor would everyone who noticed that a tomb was empty judge that a corpse had been transformed to new life. Revelation is relational. It is a two-way street.

This relational understanding of revelation is visible in Luke 24:28–35, a passage known as the Emmaus story and found in one of the Christian Gospels. In this scene, two disciples of Jesus are returning to their homes in Emmaus. They are grief-stricken and disillusioned after the execution of Jesus. On their way an unknown stranger joins them. He shows them ways of reading the Scriptures of ancient Israel to explain why Jesus died:

As they came near the village to which they were going, he walked ahead as if he were going on. But they urged him strongly, saying, "Stay with us, because it is almost evening and the day is now nearly over." So he went in to stay with them. When he was at the table with them, he took bread, blessed and broke it, and gave it to them. Then their eyes were opened, and they recognized him; and he vanished from their sight. They said to each other, "Were not our hearts burning within us while he was talking to us on the road, while he was opening the Scriptures to us?" That same hour they got up and returned to Jerusalem. They found the eleven and their companions gathered together. . . . Then they told what had happened on the road, and how he had been made known to them in the breaking of the bread.

Here, the disciples of Jesus experience a revelation that leads them to conclude that their crucified friend has been raised from death to a new kind of life. They have an extensive conversation with a stranger whom they fail to recognize. Only when they have a meal with him, just as they had eaten numerous fellowship meals with Jesus before, do they come to perceive that it is Jesus who is with them. This story is probably Luke's way of conveying that especially when they gathered for memorial meals Jesus' friends felt his abiding presence. Luke also shows that the Jewish followers of Jesus read Israel's Scriptures in new ways that explained and confirmed their resurrection experience. Transcendent encounters are mediated through concrete experiences.

One cannot empirically prove that some experience is a manifestation of the divine. It requires a decision to interpret certain occurrences as revelatory. Matthew 28:17 provides another quick example of this. The crucified Jesus is described as manifesting his resurrected self to his disciples: "When they saw him, they worshiped him, though some doubted." Persons confronted with a transcendent experience must choose how they will comprehend it. As the Pontifical Biblical Commission has expressed it, the principle that revelations of God require human affirmation

must be applied in a special way to the resurrection of Christ, which by its very nature cannot be proved in an empirical way. . . . [It is not] as if any historian, making use only of scientific investigation, could prove it with certainty as a fact accessible to any observer whatsoever. In this matter there is also needed "the decision of faith" or better "an open heart," so that the mind may be moved to assent.[8]

Conceiving of revelation as relational clarifies why experiences of God cannot be "proven"; this conception of revelation can also be very helpful for understanding the relationship between Judaism and Christianity. Since it is God who initiates interpersonal revelation, it is reasonable to wonder if such disclosures are divinely aimed or targeted. Not only must divine self-disclosure be mediated through the created world and interpreted as such by human beings, but it is conceivable that God selects the recipients of particular disclosures. To use the metaphor of a radio transmission, God's revelatory broadcasts do not have to be omnidirectional. God can choose to reveal Godself only to particular people at particular moments through particular means. This diversity of revelatory experience does not compromise God's oneness. It exalts divine sovereignty. Although it would be a violation of the oneness of God for God to impart contradictory revelations, that does not mean that every act of divine self-disclosure must or could be shared by everyone. Moreover, mortal engagements with the Transcendent One are necessarily only partial glimpses of the divine.

Revelatory experiences can be both unshared and complementary. The reality that Jews and Christians have different sets of defining revelatory experiences should not be understood as leading to inevitable conflict between the two traditions and communities. Christian and Jewish experiences of God are distinctive; therefore, they can also be sources of mutual learning, respect, and appreciation.

What Kind of God Have We Come to Know?

YHWH came down in a cloud; stood with him there and proclaimed the name YHWH. YHWH passed before him and proclaimed: YHWH! YHWH! A God compassionate and gracious, slow to anger, abounding in kindness and faithfulness, extending kindness to the thousandth generation, forgiving iniquity, transgression, and sin; yet

God does not remit all punishment, but visits the iniquity of parents upon children and children's children, upon the third and fourth generations. (Ex. 34:5–8)

This description of God provides an ethical portrait. It also addresses a widespread misconception that the God of the Jews is a God of justice in contrast to the Christian God of love. There are passages in the Tanach that speak of a jealous, zealous God, that emphasize the divine pursuit of justice and right. But that perception is incomplete, more of a caricature than a characterization of God. One telling rabbinic anecdote notes that the Torah begins and ends with acts of God's love—the clothing given to Adam and Eve when they become conscious of their nakedness and the opportunity for Moses to see the land of promise before his death. With these and other demonstrations of *chesed shel emet,* true kindness without the hope of recompense, God reveals boundless love. Put succinctly, though not simply, without God's love, we would not exist. These Exodus words of revelation paint a picture of a God who cares about people, whose kindness is infinite, but whose punishment is finite. Jewish tradition interprets these verses as defining thirteen attributes or qualities of God.[9] Each of these qualities is ethical, and each of them represents an ideal worthy of our inspiration, aspiration, and, above all, our imitation.[10]

The biblical context for these verses helps us understand their significance. The children of Israel had worshiped a molten calf while Moses was on Mount Sinai meeting with God. When Moses returned and witnessed the children of Israel engaging in idolatry, he broke the tablets on which the Ten Commandments were inscribed. After successfully pleading for God to forgive the children of Israel, Moses returned to God to repair the covenant, physically and spiritually. He asked to see the divine presence and learned that "you cannot see My face, for a human may not see Me and live" (Ex.33:21). However, Moses was allowed to see God's goodness, God's ethical presence, that is, divine grace and compassion. God had inscribed the first set of tablets; Moses would carve the second set. The partnership between divine and human was literally set in stone. It is instructive to note that according to rabbinic tradition both the broken tablets and the intact second set were placed in the

Holy Ark together. The broken tablets were still holy, a reminder to each of us who may feel that our spirits are "broken." Like the "broken" tablets, each one of us retains an essential sanctity, a reflection of the divine image.

Christians and Jews reading this moving Exodus passage can understand it to be a remarkable synthesis of centuries of ancient Israel's experiences and interactions with God. It is a profound declaration that the God that the children of Israel know is a God of surpassing generosity, compassion, loyalty, and friendship. It was precisely its faith in *this* God that set ancient Israel apart from other peoples. When other cultures worshiped cruel, capricious deities who stood behind despotic and authoritarian leaders, the people of Israel were covenanting with a God who championed the weak, the widow, the orphan, and who insisted that human beings treat one another with dignity and mercy.

Since he was Jewish, Jesus' relationship to God was shaped by such texts. As Pope John Paul II has noted, "He nourished his mind and heart with them, using them in prayer and as an inspiration for his actions."[11] It is not remarkable, then, to discover the same ethical principles articulated in parables attributed to Jesus in the Christian Gospels:

> Then Peter came and said to him, "Lord, if my brother or sister sins against me, how often should I forgive? As many as seven times?" Jesus said to him, "Not seven times, but, I tell you, seventy-seven times. For this reason the kingdom of heaven may be compared to a king who wished to settle accounts with his slaves. When he began the reckoning, one who owed him a huge amount was brought to him; and, as he could not pay, his lord ordered him to be sold, together with his wife and children and all his possessions, and payment to be made. So the slave fell on his knees before him, saying, 'Have patience with me, and I will pay you everything.' And out of pity for him, the lord of that slave released him and forgave him the debt. But that same slave, as he went out, came upon one of his fellow slaves who owed him a much smaller amount; and seizing him by the throat, he said, 'Pay what you owe.' Then his fellow slave fell down and pleaded with him, 'Have patience with me, and I will pay you.' But he refused; then he went and threw him into prison until he would pay the debt.

When his fellow slaves saw what had happened, they were greatly distressed, and they went and reported to their lord all that had taken place. Then his lord summoned him and said to him, 'You wicked slave! I forgave you all that debt because you pleaded with me. Should you not have had mercy on your fellow slave, as I had mercy on you?' And in anger his lord handed him over to be tortured until he would pay his entire debt. So my heavenly Father will also do to every one of you, if you do not forgive your brother or sister from your heart." (Mt. 18:21–35)

Parables by definition have a startling twist to them. Here, the astonishing mercy of the lord who pardoned an absolutely astronomical debt is contrasted with the lack of mercy of the one who had been pardoned. Jesus' reply to Peter was that forgiveness should be extended an unlimited number of times. Why? Since the God of Israel was a God of infinite mercy, God's people must imitate this graciousness in their lives.

Not surprisingly, Jesus' teachings are consistent with Israel's experience of God as generous, merciful, and forgiving. So what is distinctive about Christian understandings of God? How did such distinctiveness originate, and is it utterly antithetical to Jewish understandings?

Specifically "Christian" ideas arose in the aftermath of Jesus' execution. His Jewish friends had religious experiences, subjective revelations, that convinced them God had restored Jesus to transcendent life. This perception of the crucified one as raised is the origin and heart of the singularly Christian religious perspective. The Jews who shared this experience naturally reflected upon and spoke about their unprecedented understandings according to the concepts, texts, and traditions of Israel. Over the next few decades, joined by Gentile allies who came to share their experience of the crucified and raised one, they adapted current Jewish rituals and prayers, most notably by sharing memorial meals to celebrate the ministry, death, and new life of Jesus. They revised songs about the Wisdom of God who comes into human life to reveal God and is rejected, and they applied them to Jesus. They began to pray to God in the name of Jesus. At some point they began to address Jesus with the divine title of "Lord." These Jews did not understand themselves to be violating their tradition's emphasis on God's holiness and transcendence by concluding that God had been met in the human being Jesus. They grounded their experience in Israel's equally ancient, if paradoxical, claim that the Transcendent One was encountered in human history.

During the following centuries, an increasingly Gentile church pondered all these things. Church thinkers grappled with the paradox of a God who is both supremely transcendent and yet encountered in the physical life, death, and resurrection of Jesus. They also sought to relate their firm belief in the oneness of God to their equally firm conviction that this One God could be invoked "in the name of the Father, and of the Son, and of the Holy Spirit" (Mt. 28:19). Using the prevailing Greek philosophical categories of their time and culture, they formulated the Christian doctrine that the One God of Israel is a triune God, a Trinity.

The classical articulation of this doctrine is that in the One God there are three "persons." This formulation can be quite perplexing to people living today, Jew and Christian alike, because we do not think in the same conceptual categories as its authors. In particular, the use of the word "person" has certain connotations in our psychologically minded age. To us "person" means an individual with a self-aware consciousness. When folks today hear about "three persons" in God, they inevitably imagine three individual deities, which is precisely the polytheistic understanding that early Christian thinkers wanted to avoid.

A different, current perspective on what constitutes "personhood" may be helpful. The human person is a unique, unrepeatable, surpassingly precious reality that has been shaped by innumerable relationships with other persons during his or her life. To be human is to engage in relationships. To be unable to relate interpersonally with others is a diminution of one's personhood. The less-than-human behavior of those rare children who were raised in the wild and deprived of contact with other human beings or the tragedies of people who suffer from physical and psychological disorders that inhibit interaction with the outer world demonstrate how essential human relationships are to the full realization of human potential.

This relational character of personhood lies at the heart of the Christian doctrine of the Trinity. Both Israel and the church know

God to be a personal God, one with whom their respective faith communities interact personally. The doctrine of the Trinity helps Christians understand that for God to be personal means that God is innately and infinitely relational.

Thus, Christians are in relationship with a God who is experienced simultaneously as continuously creating and sustaining all that exists, as constantly revealing Godself and extending invitations to enter into relationship, and as perpetually empowering the perception, acceptance, and vitality of that relationship. When Christians bless themselves in the name of the Father, the Son, and the Holy Spirit, they are testifying that they are immersed in an eternal interaction with One who is eternally sustaining, inviting, and enabling. For Christians, God's constant invitation to relationship is incarnated and experienced in the felt presence of Jesus, a crucified Jew.

Christians do not worship three "Gods." They understand themselves to be linked in relationship, through God's actions in Christ, with the God of Israel—a God who is infinitely relational both in Godself and in all of God's activities. This relationship imparts to Christians a responsibility for the world that parallels Israel's understanding of its duties before God. Thus, although Jews and Christians do not conceive of God in the same way or feel that their encounters with God have been through an identical set of events, their common conclusion is that they must live lives patterned after the same ethical principles. We have come to know God in a variety of ways, but we have come to know the same God.

How Do We Respond to This God?

Whereas some Jews believe that divine revelation was limited to the Torah, written and oral, others believe that revelation is ongoing and progressive. In this latter view, Torah is a process, not a completed product of our encounter with God. God addresses us through Torah, and we respond through *tefillah*, most commonly translated as "prayer." The Psalms contain some of the most sublime examples of human communication with God.

I turn my eyes to the mountains; from where will my help come? My help comes from YHWH, maker of heaven and earth. (Ps. 121:1–2)

YHWH, who may live in Your tent, who may dwell on Your holy mountain? One who lives without blame, who does what is right, whose heart acknowledges the truth; whose tongue is not given to evil, who has never done harm to another, or borne reproach for [actions toward] a neighbor . . . (Ps.15:1–3)

After the Tanach was completed, the authoritative teachers of Torah, the rabbis, developed a formula for blessing, called a *berachah*, which expressed, and continues to express, the essence of the relationship between God and the Jews. This formula makes the ordinary extraordinary and transforms the natural into the supernatural. Within these words lives the heart of Jewish theology—a heart, according to Jewish tradition, with many chambers.

Baruch atah YHWH Eloheynu Melech ha-Olam asher kidshanu b'mitsvotav v'tsivanu . . .
   Praised are You YHWH, our God, Ruler of the Universe, who has sanctified us with commandments and commanded us to . . .

Let us examine the different components of this formula.

Baruch.   The opening word of the formula is derived from the Hebrew word for "knee" *(berech).* It is an immediate reminder that our status is that of servants to God. As much as we may think we are in control of our lives, when we praise God, we acknowledge that we are all students of the same divine teacher. The blessing formula begins with a prescription for humility. We depend on God.

Atah.   The relationship between a person and God is direct and personal. "You" is written in the singular. This beautifully juxtaposes the ultimate and the intimate. There is no intermediary agent, no honorific title, just a dialogue.

YHWH.   This divine address seeks access to the God who gives and forgives, who loves, who is dominated by mercy and compassion.

When Moses sought to know God intimately, face to face, YHWH revealed only goodness to Moses. When we invoke this name of God, we link our petition to that of Moses, and we hope to see a portion of the goodness he saw.

Eloheynu.   Our God. This word introduces the communal element of the relationship to God. Although we each have a personal connection with the divine, we share a covenant, a contract that binds us to each other and to God. Each individual Jew dances with God as a member of a community that stretches across time and space.

Melech ha-Olam.   Sovereign of the Universe. God is not mine, or even ours. I am God's. We are God's. The universe is God's. God rules everyone and everything, that is, God is transcendent, wholly other. God does not equal all existence. Rather, all that exists is subject to the will of God.

Asher kidshanu.   Who has sanctified us. Jews have a unique, differentiated responsibility in relationship to God. The Jewish experience of God is distinctive, separate, and apart from others but not elevated above or superior to others. God has made the first move— separating and sanctifying the Jews—but like any marriage, the relationship between God and the Jewish people depends on the mutual acceptance of the partners.

B'mitsvotav.   With commandments. The God of all has separated a few by issuing specific orders, making explicit demands, and holding the Jewish people particularly accountable. By observing commandments, the Jewish people express belief in God.

V'tsivanu.   And commanded us to. These words are typically followed by dedicated actions, and if we recite the words without the accompanying action, it is as though we did not say the words at all, or even worse, that we said the words in vain. Jewish distinctiveness is dependent upon belief that is expressed through action.

The berachah, the blessing formula, epitomizes Jewish theology—a complex, even seemingly contradictory, symphony of motives that yields the basic contours of Jewish thought and practice. It sets Jews apart from others in the world, yet it requires that Jews be part of the world.

Christianity's debt to the prayer traditions of Israel is plainly seen in the church's central prayer, often called the Lord's Prayer. This is the longer form of the prayer from the Gospel of Matthew 6:9–13:

> *Our Father in heaven, hallowed be your name.*
> *Your kingdom come.*
> *Your will be done, on earth as it is in heaven.*
> *Give us this day our daily bread.*
> *And forgive us our debts,*
> *as we also have forgiven our debtors.*
> *And do not bring us to the time of trial,*
> *but rescue us from the evil one.*

By addressing God as "Father," Christians continue the practice of Jesus and other first-century Jewish holy men and women who prayed to God with the Aramaic "Abba." This term denotes a very personal relationship, a bond of covenantal love uniting God and the person praying.

The phrases "Your kingdom come," "Your will be done ... ," and "Give us this day our daily bread" (or "the bread for the morrow") are all making the same basic petition. O God, may your Reign come to full reality in our world! May the Age to Come dawn! These entreaties indicate humanity's utter dependency on God. They also show the Christian realization that the redemption of the world is not yet fully accomplished, despite how highly Christians exalt what God has done through Christ. Every day Christians pray for the full achievement of God's will. The prayer for the forgiveness of debts is also a pledge that Christians will seek to imitate God's boundless mercy. But the prayer concludes with a recognition that human beings will fail to live up to God's standards, and so it beseeches divine deliverance.

Jews and Christians have similar ideas about God's characteristics of love and mercy and about the human requirement to respond to God by pursuing love and justice and forgiveness. These similarities can be seen in the central prayers of both traditions.

Conclusion

Do Jews and Christians worship the same God? We realize that
some Jews and Christians believe that our differences are unbridge-
able, that dialogue is undesirable, and that the definitive answer to
this question is "No." We do not share their view. We acknowledge
differences in the ways that Jews and Christians have come to know
God, in our interpretations of God, and in our prayerful relationships with God. Despite our efforts to compose a coherent essay, we
not only write differently because we are two different people, but
we write about God differently because we are a Jew and a Christian. However, we refuse to allow these differences to distract us any
longer from our common task of mending the world. We share a belief in One, Good God. That makes us ethical monotheists. The way
we describe the qualities of God, the ethical responses that God requires, and the prayers that are central to Judaism and Christianity
give us a shared foundation of belief and action, a hope that differences derive from our limited, mortal perspectives of the Transcendent One.

We conclude with a poem by Judah Halevi, arguably the preeminent medieval Hebrew poet, whose life wrapped around the cusp of
the twelfth century (1075–1141) and who died on the way to the
land of Israel where his soul awaited him. His prayerful poetry captures the balance, the rhythm of divine mystery—the One who is Always Present but Never Fully Seen. Halevi reminds us that God is
both intimate and ultimate. God defies human description and human logic—thank God.

> Lord, where shall I find You? Your place is lofty and secret. And
> where shall I not find you? The whole earth is full of Your glory!
>
> You are found in man's innermost heart, yet You fixed earth's
> boundaries. You are a strong tower for those who are near, and the
> trust of those who are far. You are enthroned on the cherubim, yet
> You dwell in the heights of the heaven. You are praised by Your hosts,
> but even their praise is not worthy of You. The sphere of heaven can-
> not contain You; how much less the chambers of the Temple!
>
> Even when you rise above Your hosts on a throne, high and exalted,
> You are nearer to them than their own bodies and souls. Their mouths

attest that they have no Maker except You. Who shall not fear You? All bear the yoke of your kingdom. And who shall not call to You? It is You who give them their food.

I have sought to come near You, I have called to You with all my heart; and when I went out towards You, I found You coming towards me. I look upon Your wondrous power with awe. Who can say that he has not seen You? The heavens and their legions proclaim Your dread—without a sound.

But can God really dwell among men? Their foundations as dust— what can they conceive of God? Yet You, O Holy One, make Your home where they sing Your praises and Your glory. The living creatures, standing on the summit of the world, praise Your wonders. Your throne is above their heads, yet it is You who carry them all![12]

Discussion Questions

1. Is belief in God integral to being Jewish? Why/why not? Is belief in God integral to being Christian? Why/Why not?
2. How does the core revelation of God in your religious tradition come alive for you today? What does it mean for your life and daily actions?
3. How does being in a relationship with God distinguish you from someone who is not?
4. What can those in relationship with God expect from God? Does God have any obligations?
5. How do you understand the relationship between the Jewish (and Christian) claim that God is revealed in history, especially in the history of the People of Israel, and the Christian belief that God is embodied in Jesus, a particular first-century Jew?
6. The authors write, "We have come to know God in a variety of ways, but we have come to know the same God." Do you agree that Jews and Christians worship the same God, the God of Israel?
7. Jews tend to emphasize the utter uniqueness and otherness of God even though God is met in human history. Chris-

tians, with their Trinitarian understanding, prefer to think of God as close at hand, seeking relationship with people, even though they acknowledge God's transcendence. How would you describe these views? Contradictory? Contrasting? Complementary? How does your own view of God relate to these views?

8. In the light of your answers to the previous questions, do you think it is possible for Jews and Christians to share meaningful prayer experiences together?

Notes

1. See, for example, Solomon Schechter, *Some Aspects of Rabbinic Theology* (1909; reprint, New York: Schocken Books, 1969).

2. Hasdai Crescas, *The Refutation of Christian Principles,* trans., with an intro. and notes, Daniel Lasker (Albany: State University of New York Press, 1999), 25. Cf. David Ellenson, "A Jewish View of the Christian God: Some Cautionary and Hopeful Remarks," in *Christianity in Jewish Terms,* ed. Tikva Frymer-Kensky, David Novak, Peter Ochs, David Fox Sandmel, and Michael Signer (Boulder, Colo.: Westview Press, 2000), 72–74.

3. See Ellenson, "A Jewish View of the Christian God."

4. Ibid., 74.

5. Everett Fox, *The Five Books of Moses* (New York: Schocken Books Inc., 1983, 1986, 1990, 1995).

6. In Hebrew, the letters in the alphabet, or alephbet, represent numbers. The letters in the word *Torah—Tav-Vav-Resh-Hey*—add up to 611. There are 613 mitsvot, or commandments, in the Torah. How can we explain the discrepancy? Six hundred eleven commandments were given through Moses to the people of Israel. The other two were revealed directly to the people—"I am YHWH your God, who brought you from the land of Egypt, from a house of serfs. You are not to have any other gods before my presence."

7. Pope John Paul II, *Fides et Ratio,* in *Origins* 28, no. 19 (October 22, 1998): 317–348, sec. 13.

8. Pontifical Biblical Commission, "Bible and Christology," in Joseph A. Fitzmeyer, *Scripture and Christology* (New York: Paulist Press, 1986), pt. 1, sec. 2, 6.2.

9. Nahum Sarna, *Exodus: The Traditional Hebrew Text with the New JPS Translation* (Philadelphia: Jewish Publication Society, 1991), 216; Tosafot to B. RH 17b; also S. D. Luzzato, *Commentary on the Pentateuch* (Hebrew) (Tel Aviv: Dvir, 1965), 386–387.

10. "You shall be holy for I, YHWH, am holy" (Lev. 19:2). Our ultimate ethical aim is imitation of the divine. For example, "Just as God is compassionate, so

should you be compassionate." Sifra on Leviticus 19:2; Baruch Levine, *Leviticus: The Traditional Hebrew Text with the New JPS Translation* (Philadelphia: Jewish Publication Society, 1989) 256–257.

11. Address to the Pontifical Biblical Commission, April 11, 1997.

12. T. Carmi, ed. and trans., *The Penguin Book of Hebrew Verse* (New York: Viking Press, 1981), 338.

4

How Do Jews and Christians Read the Bible?

AMY GROSSBLAT PESSAH,

KENNETH J. MEYERS, AND

CHRISTOPHER M. LEIGHTON

The Bible is the bedrock on which Jews and Christians stand. In the Bible, Jews and Christians find ancient memories and grand expectations that ground their communities. Yet, the Bible offers a world that is strange and mystifying. The extravagant claims, the implausible tales, the ponderous legal material, and the unpronounceable genealogical records do not speak in a familiar language. However confusing or even intimidating the Bible may be, Christians and Jews cannot avoid this encounter. Historically, Judaism and Christianity have both maintained that the sacred Scriptures provide access to the living word of God. By learning to read the Bible, Jews and Christians learn distinctive ways to make sense of the world around them. Those who study the Bible in the context of the Jewish or Christian traditions find themselves surrounded by an intergenerational community of readers, and they discover the horizons of responsibility clarified and enlarged—to self, neighbor, and the larger creation. All these obligations are situated in the context of a relationship with the God of Israel, who calls them into covenantal partnership.

There is no access to the God of Israel except through the Bible. Christians and Jews both insist that reason, personal experience, and encounters with the world can be understood only in conversation with the Bible that lives in their respective traditions. The Bible becomes a living word intimately connecting past and present when Jews and Christians test its assumptions, question its content, and argue with its directives. Jews and Christians of every generation have noted that sacred Scriptures require disciplined engagement, and only after listening to and contending with the Bible's many voices can they discern its truthfulness, its authority, and its relevance.

We begin with a paradox: The Scriptures that bring Jews and Christians together also set them apart. The book that each tradition calls the Bible is not one book but many; the many books are not the same, nor are they ordered in the same sequence. Each community makes sense of the Bible in the light of a living tradition (replete with massive libraries of commentaries) that continues to unfold in new and surprising ways. The central task of this essay is to map the distinctive ways that Christians and Jews read the Bible and live in the light of its wisdom.

The Content, Order, and Language of the Bible

Jews refer to the Bible by its acronym, Tanak or Tanach, in which each consonant ("t," "n," and "k") stands for one of its three constitutive parts. They are: (1) *Torah*, here designating the Pentateuch (Greek for "five") or the Five Books of Moses; (2) *Nevi'im*, referring to the "early" prophets (Joshua–Kings), the "later major" prophets (Isaiah–Ezekiel), and the "minor" (as regards length) prophets (Hosea–Malachi); and (3) *Ketuvim* or writings, including Psalms, Proverbs, Job, the Five Scrolls (Song of Songs, Ruth, Lamentations, Ecclesiastes, and Esther), Daniel, Ezra, Nehemiah, and Chronicles. Each year, as part of regular Sabbath worship, the entire Torah is read from beginning to end in a sequence of weekly portions. In addition, a specific selection from the Prophets (or occasionally from the Writings), called the *haftarah*, is read. The haftarah is related thematically either to the weekly Torah portion or to the season of the year. Students becoming bar or bat mitsvah demonstrate their learning by chanting from the weekly Torah portion and the haftarah.

The Christian Bible includes all the books of the Tanach in what Christians traditionally call the "Old Testament." However, the order of the books in the Old Testament is different from the Tanach. The significance of this difference is apparent when the last verses of each are compared. In the Tanach, the concluding verse is 2 Chronicles 36:23, an allusion to the return to the land of Israel and the rebuilding of the Temple. In contrast, the Old Testament ends with the prophet Malachi proclaiming the coming of Elijah and the divine judgment known as the Day of the Lord (Mal. 4:5–6). The ending of the Tanach is rooted in the hope of returning and rebuilding the land of Israel. The Old Testament concludes with a prophetic oracle that anticipates the coming of the Messiah, setting the stage for a new and unique collection of writings, namely, the New Testament.[1]

The New Testament begins with the four Gospels (Matthew, Mark, Luke, and John) that the early church claimed as authoritative accounts of the life, death, and resurrection of Jesus. These narratives are followed by the book of Acts, a story that chronicles the developing church, written by the author of Luke's Gospel. The letters or epistles of Paul, followed by the epistles of other authors, were written to address the struggles of emerging Christian communities. The New Testament concludes with the book of Revelation. Although liturgical practices vary enormously among Christians, passages from both the Old and the New Testaments are generally read at worship services. Many Christian denominations have created their own collections of readings, known as lectionaries, that pair selections from the Old and New Testaments. These lectionaries serve to bind worshiping communities far and near to the same biblical texts.

Before turning to the relationship between the Old and New Testaments, a few words on translations are in order. The Tanach was written in Hebrew (with a few passages in Aramaic) over the course of a thousand years. Beginning in the third century B.C.E., Greek-speaking Jews translated the Tanach, and this translation became known as the Septuagint. *Septuagint* means seventy and refers to a Jewish legend that seventy-two scribes, working independently, arrived at an identical translation. This legend conferred divine authority on this translation. Not only did the Septuagint make the Hebrew Scriptures accessible to Jews who were insufficiently literate in Hebrew; it was also the version upon which the early church de-

pended. The New Testament was originally composed in Greek during the later half of the first century C.E., and its authors built their
own narratives on the foundations of the Septuagint. This point
may initially appear pedantic, but it leads to a more important ob-
servation: Every translation is also an interpretation. The significance of this truism becomes plain when considering a well-known
illustration. In the Hebrew text of Isaiah 7:14, the prophet delivers
the following oracle: "Behold, an *almah* shall conceive and bear a
son and shall call his name Immanuel."

The Hebrew word *almah* means "young maid." It is translated in
the Septuagint with the Greek word *parthenos*. This word is laden
with an added meaning, for the Greek term assigns the young maid
the status of virgin. This allusion then finds expression in the
Matthew 1:23 and Luke 1:27, and these verses become the scriptural basis for the doctrine of Jesus' conception. What is promised
in the Old Testament is said to find confirmation in the virgin birth
of a son who Christians believe makes manifest God's very presence.

The problems of translation and interpretation raise fundamental questions about the meaning and truth of sacred Scriptures. If
the Bible can support only one meaning, then either the Jewish or
the Christian reading is right. The other must be wrong. The battle
for the Bible thus flows out of the different ways in which Jews
and Christians engage their sacred texts and define the acceptable
field of meanings for their respective communities. The battle for
the Bible is waged not only between our respective communities
but also within them, and so there is no escape from a struggle
that faces every generation. Each community must determine the
boundaries of interpretation, that is, the range of meanings and
truths that each tradition can welcome without compromising its
own integrity.

The Interpretation of the Bible

The Bible provides a narrative framework that gives shape and
meaning to the decisive moments in the life of the individual and the
community. From birth to death, from winter to spring, in sickness
and in health, Jews and Christians have traditionally taken their
bearings from the Bible.

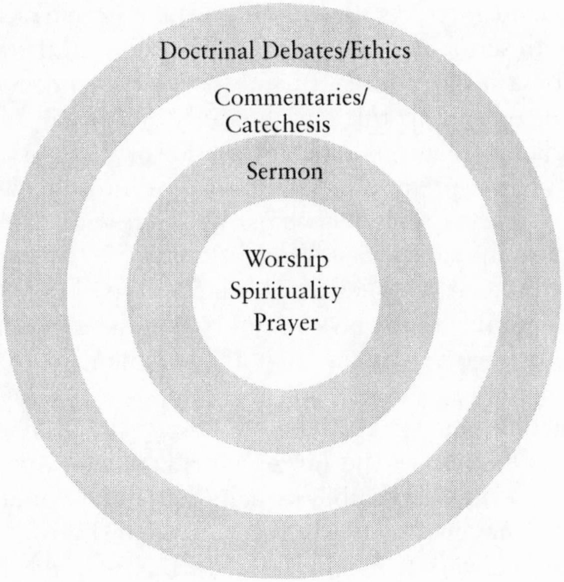

Doctrinal Debates/Ethics

Commentaries/
Catechesis

Sermon

Worship
Spirituality
Prayer

FIGURE 4.1

The most formative encounters with the Bible for Christians occur in the context of worship. Although many Christians may analyze the Bible as literature or examine it in terms of history and archeology, the deepest meaning of the Bible comes into view through the rhythms of personal and communal prayer. The Bible provides the language and the grammar that enables Christians to speak with God. It offers indispensable instruction, modeling when and how to turn to others and to God, when and how to give praise and thanks, when and how to cry, to grieve, and to lament.

To understand and appreciate the centrality of the Bible in the life of Christian faith, Frances Young, the Christian theologian and historian, offers a helpful diagram, which we have adapted for our purposes (see Figure 4.1).[2] Worship, spirituality, and prayer define the innermost core of Christian life, and these disciplined practices of turning to God are all formed and maintained through ongoing engagement with the Bible. As Christians are educated and initiated into the life of the larger community, they discover that their sacred

stories demand interpretation, and so the core narratives are surrounded with sermons. This homiletical layer of oral commentary is
encircled by a larger library of interpretation, and, ideally, Christians are introduced to this vast literary tradition in the process of
their catechesis (religious education). Through the study of these
traditions of interpretation, Christians are introduced to previous
generations of Christians who have wrestled with the same stories
and on whose shoulders they frequently stand. In the next circle, the
Bible is used to clarify issues of doctrine and to illuminate questions
of ethics. The Bible thus plays a vital role in the explication of what
Christians believe and what they are commanded to do. Here is
where the community calls upon its Scriptures to translate its worship into action, and here is where Christians give concrete expression to their beliefs in the larger world. At the outermost ring,
Christians call upon the Bible to help define the boundaries of the
community. They invoke the Bible to distinguish insiders from outsiders, true believers from the false. In this way the Bible orients
Christians to the non-Christian world, and it equips the community
to explain and defend its faith, and to discredit its competitors and
opponents. This deployment of the Bible is at the farthest remove
from the core of worship because the community's gaze is directed
to the threats posed by neighbors rather than devotion to the divine.
Although Christians have often employed their Scriptures to wage
polemical battles, the impetus to protect the religious borders of the
church emanates from the commitment to worship God in the light
of the revealed truth entrusted to it. Unless the integrity of the faith
is preserved, the center cannot hold.

In the telling and teaching of the Bible, Christians discover how to
pattern their lives in accord with their Scriptures. The Christian way
of living is discerned in the light of Jesus who is seen as the embodiment of the core teachings of the Old Testament. In other words,
Christians discern in their Bible a "lifestyle," a moral and spiritual
guidebook.

The Torah stands at the center of Jewish life, and the encounter
with Scripture is integral to Jewish worship. Jews attach quotations
from Torah to the doorposts of their homes, and during daily worship
some Jews adorn themselves with leather boxes, called *tefilin*, containing scriptural citations. Equally important for Jews, however, is
the study of the Tanach and its commentaries. Indeed, in Judaism,

study itself is an essential form of worship that shapes the inner character of both the individual and the community. By learning to enter into debate with commentators ancient and contemporary, Jews fulfill an essential sacred obligation. This disciplined encounter with Torah provides the platform on which ritual practice, ethical deliberation, and moral action are built. Thus we read in M. Peah 1:1:

> These are things the benefit of which a person enjoys in this world, while the reward is reserved for him in the world to come: honoring father and mother, righteous deeds, and bringing peace between a man and his fellow. But the study of Torah is equal to them all [because it leads to them all].

When Jews study Tanach in a traditional manner, it is always through the lens of commentary. In almost every synagogue, the version of the Torah found in the pew contains the Hebrew text, at least one translation, and at least one commentary. Studying the biblical text along with its commentaries is an invitation to join in the discussion (or the argument, since one commentator will often disagree vociferously with another) and, in the process, to become an interpreter oneself! Most bar/bat mitsvah students compose a *dvar torah* (literally: a word of Torah) in which they offer their own interpretation of the texts they have just read aloud to the congregation. This ability to engage the text and to delve into the commentaries is deemed as essential as learning the skills necessary to lead the congregation in worship and to read from the Torah scroll. Indeed, Jewish tradition teaches that everything one needs to know can be learned by studying Torah and its interpretation:

> Turn it [Torah] over and over for everything is in it, and grow old and gray in it, and do not turn away from it, for there is no better rule for you than it. (M. Avot 5:35)

In the life of Christians and Jews, the Bible plays a dynamic function, and through sustained engagement with their Scriptures, the distinct religious identities of our two communities are formed. We now turn to the specific ways that Jews and Christians have learned to live out of their Bibles, and we will then examine some of the challenges that demand attention in a modern democratic society.

Rabbinic Interpretation

Rabbinic Judaism emerged as the authoritative form of Judaism in the centuries after the destruction of the Second Temple in 70 C.E. Whereas before the destruction, Judaism was centered on the Temple and its rituals of animal sacrifice, rabbinic Judaism made the word of God, Torah, its focal point. When the rabbis speak of Torah in its broadest sense, they refer to something much larger than just the Five Books of Moses. Torah encompasses both the Written Torah *(Torah she-bichtav)* and the Oral Torah *(Torah she-be'al peh)*.

These terms can be confusing, since both now exist as written documents. Written Torah is, first and foremost, the Pentateuch, but by extension, the entire Tanach. Oral Torah is the entire tradition of rabbinic interpretation of the Written Torah. The Oral Torah (comprising the Mishnah, the Gemara, and the midrashic literature) was originally meticulously memorized and passed from one generation to the next. The various documents of the Oral Torah were eventually written down in order to preserve and disseminate them. The key point for understanding the status of Written and Oral Torah, or Torah in its broadest sense, is that the rabbis insisted that both the Written and Oral Torah were given to Moses on Sinai, and therefore they are co-equal in divine origin and authority. This claim is prominently embedded in M. Avot 1:1:

> Moses received Torah at Sinai and handed it on to Joshua, Joshua to elders, and elders to prophets. And prophets handed it on to the men of the Great Assembly [who passed in on to] Simon the Righteous, [who] was one of the last survivors of the Great Assembly.... Antigonos of Sokho received [the Torah] from Simon the Righteous. Yose b. Yoezer of Seredah and Yose b. Yohanan of Jerusalem received [it] from them.... Joshua b. Perahiah and Nittai the Arbelite received [it] from them.... Judah b. Tabbai and Simeon b. Shatah received [it] from them.... Shemaiah and Abtalion received [it] from them.... Hillel and Shammai received [it] from them. Rabban Gamaliel [received it from them]. ... Simeon his son [received it from him].... Rabban Simeon b. Gamaliel [received it from him] .... Rabbi [received it from him].

In this passage, the rabbis draw a straight line from Moses and Sinai to "Rabbi," that is, Rabbi Judah the Patriarch, who is credited with publishing the Mishnah itself, the foundation document of rabbinic Judaism. This rabbinic genealogy posits an unbroken chain of tradition and established the rabbis themselves (and no one else!) as the authoritative interpreters of Torah.

The rabbis further claim that God's direct revelations stopped after the destruction of the First Temple in Jerusalem in 586 B.C.E. Thereafter, God's presence is discerned through the Jewish community's encounter with Torah, as mediated by the authoritative interpreters of Torah, the rabbis.

By linking Moses to the rabbis, divine authority is invested in the entire Torah, both Written and Oral. This chain of transmission connects interpreters of the past with those who continue to interpret the Torah. All past and future interpretations are claimed by the tradition to have been given to Moses at Sinai. The following story illustrates this point. Moses descends from heaven and sits in the back of a lesson taught by Rabbi Akiba, one of the greatest rabbis of the Talmud, who lived more than a thousand years after Moses:

> Moses . . . saw a house full of students, sitting at the feet of a master who was explaining to them the secrets and mysteries of the Torah. Moses heard their discussions, but could not follow them and was greatly grieved. Thereupon he heard the disciples asking their master, "Whence do you know this?" and Rabbi Akiba replied, "What I have told you has already been explained to Moses the son of Amram, on Mount Sinai." When Moses heard these words, he was content. (B. Men. 29b)

The Jewish sages claimed that the Tanach could not be understood unless filtered through the lenses of the oral tradition. This approach opened the door to new and creative insights. For example, there is little support in the Tanach to uphold and authenticate the concept of resurrection. Yet, the Oral Torah provides elaborate readings and rabbinic debate that establish resurrection and the afterlife as a core affirmation grounded in Tanach.

Once the Mishnah, a digest of rabbinic legal interpretations of the Written Torah, was codified, it became the subject of study and debate. The body of interpretation of the Mishnah was preserved in oral form in the rabbinical academies for several centuries. During the sixth century, it, too, was written down and came to be known as the Gemara. Mishnah and Gemara together form the Talmud, the primary compendium of Jewish law. Over the centuries, rabbis and scholars have continued to generate biblical commentary and legal interpretation.

The approaches to interpretation that emerged within rabbinic Judaism continued to evolve and in the Middle Ages crystallized into a system known as *Pardes,* a word that means "orchard" in Hebrew. Like Tanach, Pardes is an acronym and represents four distinct levels of meaning: *peshat* (simple or literal), *remez* (hint), *drash* (interpretation), and *sod* (secret). Together, the levels create an "orchard" full of meaning and richness. The peshat level is the most basic, simple reading of the text. It is the meaning that resides on the surface of the text or the level of the literal. Remez provides hints about another textual dimension, often arrived at through numerology or other ways of "playing" with the text. Drash entails interpretation that enables the reader to relate the text to our own lives. Finally, sod holds secret or mystical meanings that are accessible only to the adept who has mastered the disciplines of advanced Torah study. It is at this level that the initiated gain access to hidden mysteries of God's form and glory and are given glimpses of the end of days.

These strategies of interpretation enabled Jews to penetrate multiple layers of the text and in the process address the ambiguities and conflicting assertions found in the Bible. The interpreter's job is to identify what lies behind an apparent contradiction or gap in the text, for the problem could not possibly emanate from the Tanach itself. The Scriptures were thought to have been revealed by God, and therefore they embody an unparalleled perfection. The Torah is nothing less than an extension of divine speech. If the Bible seems to support mutually exclusive claims, the problem is that the interpreters have not dug deep enough to expose the hidden meaning. This orientation gave rise to the talmudic affirmation that the Torah has seventy faces or, according to one medieval mystic, 600,000, one for every Israelite present at Mt. Sinai. Differences of interpretation inevitably surface. The community over and over again must adjudicate the conflicts and decide which interpretation will be binding. Yet, there is a profound recognition that minority voices deserve respect and that the preservation of their dissenting arguments is the way to honor their memory. In the long run, the minority view may prove instructive and may even become the authoritative guide when the community finds itself in different circumstances.

With the evolution of modern biblical criticism (see below) and the emergence of the Reform and Conservative movements in the nineteenth century, some within the Jewish community began to reassess the belief in *Torah mi-Sinai,* the divine transmission of all of the Written and the Oral Torah at Mt. Sinai. As a result, some Jews began to question the authoritative and binding nature of rabbinic halachah, or Jewish law.

For Conservative Judaism, halachah remains binding, but at the same time, halachah is viewed as a flexible system that must be able to respond as times change. Legal decisions, therefore, may be modified due to ethical considerations, technological advances, sociological changes, or the needs of the time. Questions such as "Are organ transplants permissible by Jewish law?" or "Can one drive to synagogue on the Sabbath and holidays?" are directed to the Committee on Jewish Law and Standards. Although the process it uses to determine the new law is the same process that has been used over the centuries, the committee has the authority to modify an existing law. In short, the Conservative movement makes its legal decisions by simultaneously working within the framework of halachah and balancing the realities of modern day life.

The Reform movement began in nineteenth century Germany, in part as a reaction against what it perceived to be the narrowness of traditional halachah. The movement proclaimed that halachah is not divine in its origin but human and, therefore, not divinely authoritative. Reform Judaism emphasized the ethical teachings of Judaism, while rejecting the authority of halachah, especially as it related to religious practice that served to separate Jews from the larger society: dietary regulations, strict Sabbath observance, traditions about special modes of dress, and so on. More recently, the Reform movement has moved toward a greater appreciation of distinctive Jewish practice and of halachah as a source of guidance in matters of both ritual and ethics. Nonetheless, the movement has chosen to make its decisions in consultation with, but not under the

authority of, halachah. "Personal autonomy" is stressed; each individual, after careful study, has the freedom to make his or her own
decision in terms of accepting or rejecting a particular halachah.

The major movements in Judaism approach biblical interpretation
differently, yet all would agree that Torah and the study of the
Torah are the heart and soul of Judaism. Each movement continues
to study the traditional commentaries and to produce new commentaries of its own as it seeks to define its path in a changing world.
Thus the Torah remains a living and authoritative document within
the various denominations of Judaism.

Christian Interpretation

The Christian practice of interpretation was forged in the heat of
conflict. From its inception, the followers of Jesus disputed with
Jews who claimed the same Scriptures but read them differently.
They also contended with Hellenists who dismissed the Bible as little
more than a primitive myth devoid of philosophical substance.
Perhaps even more arduous was the struggle to resolve conflicting
attitudes toward the Scriptures that bubbled up within the ranks of
the early church. The most challenging of contestants was Marcion,
a second-century leader and a deeply committed champion of the
apostle Paul's message of God's unconditional love. Marcion attempted to resolve the problems of biblical interpretation by means
of radical surgery. In his opinion, the Hebrew Scriptures have no
place among the followers of Jesus, and he advocated their removal
from the Christian congregation. The excision was deemed imperative because the god portrayed in the "Old Testament" was perceived as a vindictive deity who has entrapped people in the physical
world that he created. To escape the material confinement of this
world, the Christian was exhorted to reject the Creator, namely, the
God of the Old Testament. Instead, Marcion urged his followers to
pledge allegiance to another, higher power, the God of love and forgiveness. This is the God who truly redeems humankind, is made
known in Jesus, and is expounded in the writings of Paul.

The early church declared Marcion's dualistic interpretation of
Paul totally mistaken, his repudiation of the Hebrew Scriptures dangerous, and it condemned him as a heretic. The attempt to drive a

wedge between the divine activities of creation and redemption effectively removed God from the entanglements of human history. Despite the unequivocal rejection of Marcion's teachings, his legacy casts a shadow that continues to cloud the Christian imagination. Whenever Christians maintain that they worship a God of love not a God of wrath, whenever they describe themselves as "New Testament" rather than "Old Testament" people, they recapitulate the teachings of Marcion and give fresh expression to an ancient and noxious idea.

The rebuttal of Marcion not only defined attitudes toward the Hebrew Scriptures but also profoundly influenced Christian perceptions of Judaism and the Jewish people. Marcion's strongest critic, Tertullian, and subsequently many other notable church fathers, argued that the problem of sin did not stem from the God of the "Old Testament." In contrast to Marcion, who saw evil as having its source within the Creator, the church fathers argued that the failure to realize God's purposes stemmed from the people with whom God entered into a covenantal partnership. The failure to redeem the world was traced to the "stiff-necked" and "hardhearted" Jews. As even the Hebrew Scriptures noted over and over again, the Jews failed to remain faithful to the covenant, and therefore God took a more radical step to redeem the world and entered history in a radically new way—becoming flesh in the person of Jesus of Nazareth.

The affirmation of God's unprecedented intervention raises a serious issue for Christians about the meaning and relevance of their Bible. If the decisive moments in the redemption of the world revolve around the life, death, and resurrection of Jesus, then why do Christians need the Hebrew Scriptures? The responses to this query are varied, but two brief comments will underscore their indispensable function in the life of the early church. First, the early followers of Jesus were Jews and thus relied upon the Hebrew Scriptures, the only Scriptures available to them, to make sense of their experiences—both the trauma of crucifixion and the elation of resurrection. They called upon these Scriptures to frame the story of Jesus and to help them develop a pattern of life that would uphold God's presence in their midst. The connections established between Jesus and the Scriptures enabled the Christian community to sustain hope, which even death and persecution could not shatter.

Second, as previously noted, critics of this messianic movement tried to undermine its validity by classifying Christianity as a "new" religion, which therefore had no legitimate authority. Without a pedigree that could establish the antiquity of the Christian faith, all claims to authenticity rang hollow. Nothing was regarded as trustworthy or venerable that had not withstood the test of time. Christians rebuffed these accusations by noting that their own claims were grounded in the Hebrew Scriptures. Indeed, Christians argued that they were the true inheritors of the biblical promises.

These strategies of interpretation, however, had a profoundly negative impact on Christian perceptions of Judaism and the Jewish people. Christians countered the heresies of Marcion and the Hellenists by reclaiming the God of the Bible. Yet, the reclamation was accomplished at the expense of the Jewish people. A supersessionist habit of reading the Bible thereby took hold in the Christian tradition, and a theology of replacement developed that displaced the synagogue to make room for the church.

The practice among Christians that has historically dominated the church is to read the "Old" Testament as a collection of promises. The glorious hopes of the Hebrew Scriptures find fulfillment in the "New" Testament in the person of Jesus Christ. The church fathers consistently mined the Hebrew Scriptures in search of texts that prophesied the coming of Christ, and they found "evidence" everywhere they looked. The ingenuity of the early church is reflected in its interpretations of the Suffering Servant passages in Isaiah (42:1–9; 49:1–6; 50:4–11; 52:13–53:12). Less obvious passages were utilized to substantiate key doctrinal affirmations. Thus, the proclamation in Genesis 1:26 where God declares "Let *us* make humankind in *our* own image" is enlisted to demonstrate the Trinity. The tendency to read the "Old" Testament as a prologue to the "New" remains a fixture in the liturgical life of the church, and the depth of this habit is easily detected by reviewing the lectionary readings for Advent (the period leading up to Christmas) and Lent (the time leading up to Good Friday and Easter).

In its struggle to establish its own legitimacy, the early church developed a polemical posture toward the Jewish people. The church caricatured the Jews as blind to the truth of their own Scriptures. Some Christians maintained that the Jews did recognize the spiritual treasure buried within their Scriptures but refused to accept it because they were in league with the devil. This process of laying claim to the Bible either dispossessed Jews of their Scriptures by writing them out of their own story or it demonized them as adversaries of biblical truth.

The church fathers shaped the lenses of interpretation that enabled Christians to see the Old and New Testaments as a coherent whole. Church authorities nonetheless recognized that the Bible could be manipulated and put in the service of almost any ideological agenda. To curtail the proliferation of heretical readings, Tertullian maintained that the Bible should be considered the sole property of the church. The Bible belongs under the care of the official church, and it must be guarded from the intrusive meddling of outsiders and the misguided innovations of its own members.

The Protestant Reformation was in large part a protest against a tradition that had moved the Bible out of the public's reach. Protestants insisted that the wisdom of the Bible was accessible to the common believer, and the emergence of the printing press played a decisive role in the advancement of their cause. The motivation to disseminate the Bible sprang from the desire to anchor its revolutionary vision in the Scriptures. By returning to the Bible, the Protestant Reformers argued that the organizational and dogmatic structures supporting the Roman Catholic hierarchy had corrupted the simplicity and purity of the early Christian church. The Reformers used the Bible as a blueprint for the restoration and reconstruction of what they considered the golden age of the early church. In other words, the Reformers attempted to retrieve the pristine character of the early church. This renewal depended upon the recovery of the foundational biblical truth, untarnished by the layers of corruption that the Protestants associated with the Roman Catholic tradition.

In large measure, the Reformation emphasized an approach that privileged the literal interpretation of the Bible, and this orientation still influences many Protestants. However, the return to the Bible did not challenge the well-established supersessionist assumptions or the liturgical practices of their churches. The new habits of reading the Bible left the old portraits of the Jews intact. Even when the antagonisms between Roman Catholics and Protestants intensified and erupted in deadly battle, the warring factions continued to share a common contempt for their archetypal enemy, the Jews.

As Protestants and Roman Catholics pursued their polemical debates and wrote each other's epitaphs in blood, a philosophy celebrating the powers of reason and identified with the overconfident title "the Enlightenment" was designed to neutralize or at least constrain unruly religious passions. One of its most notable champions was Benedict de Spinoza (1632–1677), and the development of new strategies of biblical interpretation was pivotal for his larger philosophical project. Living in the aftermath of the Thirty Years War, Spinoza was keenly cognizant of the manipulative powers of religion. He noted that the gifts of theologians were deployed "to wring their inventions and sayings out of the sacred text and to fortify them with Divine authority . . . compelling others to think as they do" (*Tractatus Theologico-Politicus,* chap. 7, 1). Spinoza argued that the passionate excesses of religion demanded a new discipline of reading. His proposal anticipated the systematic analysis of "historical criticism," which rested on the conviction that the Bible must be treated like any other ancient literature and scrutinized with methods as rigorous as those used by the scientist who studies nature.

Not only did Spinoza demarcate many of the core features of historical criticism; his proposal also anticipated a separation of religion from the public sphere and the toleration of religious differences. The affairs of religion are associated with "sincerity of heart," and they "stand outside the sphere of law and public authority." In other words, religion thrives in the realm of the irrational, the unruly world of passions. To domesticate the excesses of religion we need to invest individuals with the authority to interpret Scripture for themselves and then to consign their findings to the purely private and personal. Our religious attachments then become subjective expressions of taste, mere opinion—nothing to fight over.

The Enlightenment gave rise to new habits of mind and heart that are often associated with modernity. Their impact on the study of the Bible has proven considerable in both Jewish and Christian communities. New and important insights continue to emerge from the disciplined methods of study that restore the text to its original setting and reacquaint readers with the tensions and struggles of the historical context in which these documents were written. It is no simple task to hurdle thousands of years of tradition, to bracket our own assumptions, and to hear an author or editor's own voice.

Despite its claims to objectivity, the techniques of modern scholarship have not neutralized the prejudices of earlier generations. The complicity of scholarship in the anti-Semitism of the larger culture is etched into nineteenth- and much of twentieth-century biblical study. Over and over again, modern scholars, most of them Protestant, delivered a portrait of Jesus who stood over and against a Jewish legalistic piety that was spiritually vapid, politically xenophobic, and morally bankrupt. That trajectory, which began in the early church, has remained a fixture in Western culture that not even the most revolutionary religious and intellectual movements have overturned.

This historical sketch of Christian interpretation has revolved around a challenge that many Christians might relegate to the fringes of their life with the Bible. As noted earlier, the definition of boundaries occurs at the edges of the tradition. The deployment of the Bible to wage polemical battle is often a lamentable misuse of the Scriptures and should be regarded as antithetical to the core business of worship. Our focus on this problem reflects a strong conviction: The ways Christians use the Bible to define their relationships to non-Christians, most especially the Jewish people, have a profound impact on the character of Christian worship. These habits of reading are deeply anchored within the Christian tradition, and they continue to ground many liturgical practices of the church. Christians therefore find themselves confronted with two critical questions: (1) Can they live out of the depth and beauty of their Bible without simultaneously denigrating their Jewish neighbors? (2) Can Christians make room for other understandings of the Bible and continue to affirm its authority as divinely given?

The prospects of developing a nonsupersessionist reading of the Bible will emerge when Christians recognize and affirm that their interpretation of the Bible does not exhaust the truth of the Scriptures. There are ample resources within the Bible to correct ancient Christian distortions of Judaism, and they all begin with the insistence that God remains faithful to God's promises: God's covenant with the Jewish people is for all time. The next steps will surely follow. Not only are Jewish understandings legitimate, they may also prove instructive for the church.

A New Challenge for Judaism

After devoting so much energy to exploring the legacy of supersessionist Christian biblical interpretation, the question arises whether there is a parallel history of Jewish biblical interpretation that focuses on the denigration of the other. The answer to this question is not a simple one; there are both theological and historical factors that must be considered.

From the theological perspective, neither Christians nor any other specific group or tradition occupies a place in Judaism similar to that of Jews and Judaism in Christianity. The challenges posed to the early church by the Jewishness of Jesus and the relationship of Christianity to Jewish tradition and practice find no parallel in Judaism. There is evidence in the Tanach of competition, even warfare, between the ancient Israelites and their neighbors, as well as of religious division among the Israelites themselves. The rabbis used biblical interpretation to respond to the challenges of internal sectarian deviations. They also stressed aspects of Jewish tradition such as dietary regulations that served to insulate Jews from the rest of society. Their other great concern was with whoever held political power over the Jews, which changed from year to year and place to place. The rabbis did make distinctions between Jews and Gentiles as a whole, and there are ample citations that reflect a negative view of the non-Jew. The picture that emerges from a comprehensive examination of Jewish views of the other, however, is one of a complicated relationship marked by a tension between the recognition of the commonality of all humanity on the one hand and self-pride and xenophobia on the other. Rather than focus on Christians or Moslems or any other specific group, the rabbis tended to identify these groups with traditional biblical enemies, such as Pharaoh or Haman. In rabbinic literature, Esau (or Edom, as he is also called), the brother of Jacob, becomes the archetype of the enemy of Israel. In the period following the destruction of the Temple, Edom was equated with the Roman Empire. Later, when Christianity emerged as the dominant power in Europe in the Middle Ages, it, in turn, became identified as Edom.

Another important difference within Judaism is that the boundary between Jews and Gentiles is based primarily on birth rather than

on matters of belief. This boundary is based on the biblical understanding of Israel as a people, a nation descended from a common
ancestor. One is a Jew because one is born a member of the Jewish
people (in rabbinic law, this was defined as being born of a Jewish
mother) or because one is adopted into the Jewish family through a
ritual of conversion. According to Jewish tradition, what one believes does not itself preclude one from being considered a Jew,
though certain behaviors can, especially those involving idolatrous
worship. Furthermore, the obligations and responsibilities of the
Jew are not incumbent upon others; therefore, the impetus to convert Gentiles to Judaism, though not absent from Jewish history,
never assumed the importance it did in Christianity. (Whatever Jewish inclinations toward proselytizing existed before the rise of Christendom were quashed by harsh restrictions against conversion to Judaism, to the point that Judaism for all intents and purposes ceased
to be a missionary religion.)

In addition to these theological issues, historical circumstances
have also determined Jewish views of, and behavior toward, others.
Christianity was the dominant political and social force in Europe
and other parts of world for much of the last 2,000 years. This marriage of religion and politics enabled the church to use the power of
government to further its theological goals. This fact had particularly tragic ramifications for the Jews. In comparison, Jews have
been, until quite recently, a people in exile and an oppressed minority, unable to exercise power over others. Whatever potential there
may be in Judaism for denigration and oppression of others was
kept in check by its powerlessness.

Thus, we find an asymmetry between Judaism and Christianity.
Both history and theology have shaped how Jews have interpreted
their Scriptures regarding the spiritual worth and basic humanity of
those who are not Jewish. In the past, Jews have had to respond to a
Christianity that is essentially hostile. However, in recent decades,
Christianity has presented a different face to its Jewish neighbors.

Based on a new reading of Christian Scriptures, some Christians
have declared that God's covenant with the Jews is eternal and have
affirmed the spiritual legitimacy and integrity of Judaism. The challenge to Jews is whether this recognition of Judaism is a one-way
street. Is it necessary or even appropriate for Jews to acknowledge

the covenant that Christians claim to have with the God of Israel through Jesus Christ? Can Judaism find biblical warrant to recognize the spiritual legitimacy and integrity of Christianity?

These are hard questions for Jews, in part because the legacy of Christian anti-Semitism, as well as its persistence in some parts of the Christian world, make it difficult for Jews to consider thinking differently about Christians and Christianity. The courageous Christian theological reevaluation of the past few decades still represents a vanguard within the Christian world. Most Jews are leery of granting too much to Christianity lest it encourage those who retain traditional anti-Jewish prejudice or break down walls that have protected Jews from assimilation and interfaith marriage. But the challenge remains; indeed, it lies at the heart of the work that inspired this book.

The Future of Jewish and Christian Biblical Interpretation

In the course of preparing this essay, we found that each community has lavished a great deal of time and energy over the centuries reading, studying, and praying with their Bibles. Because Christians and Jews see the Scriptures from such different angles, they have something important to offer one another. In the encounter with the Bible, both communities may discover that God can speak through the same sacred text and deliver a distinctively different truth to each. Does this mean that Christians and Jews must accept each other's truth claims? Does this set both communities down Spinoza's path, leaving us dangling with the notion that every interpretation is a subjective opinion, and therefore anything goes?

To be sure, Christians and Jews cannot live out of each other's truths. The Christian reading of the Bible will revolve around the person of Jesus Christ, and the Jewish reading will center on the Torah. Both communities will continue to struggle to define the range of interpretations that will advance their covenantal commitments to God and their communities. Both communities will continue to engage their Bibles to retrieve the ethical and spiritual resources needed to mend the world.

In addition, Christians and Jews face a common challenge from the secular world. Modern scholarship has left both our faith communities with a book largely emptied of its authority, its mystery, and its spiritual power. Biblical critics have made it clear: It is difficult to cut into a sacred text without draining the words of their life. Modern critical scholarship will continue to yield important new insights, most especially in helping us navigate the vast terrain that separates the ancient past from the present. Nevertheless, Jews and Christians are now confronted with the challenge of gaining access to a transcendent reality that history cannot contain. Biblical interpretation that remains fixated on the occurrence or nonoccurrence of historical events offers insufficient traces of God's presence, and the academy all too often leaves no room for the responses of faith.

As Abraham Joshua Heschel, one of the greatest Jewish scholars and philosophers of the twentieth century, noted:

> If God is alive, then the Bible is His voice. No other work is as worthy of being considered a manifestation of His will. There is no other mirror in the world where His will and spiritual guidance is as unmistakably reflected. If the belief in the immanence of God in nature is plausible, then the belief in the immanence of God in the Bible is compelling.[3]

If Jews and Christians are to engage in the hard work of reading their sacred Scriptures and interpreting them in the light of the distinct traditions to which they belong, they do well to bear in mind that this process of participatory discernment will enable them to hear many voices of ancestors once lost and forgotten. Behind these choruses of ancestors, they may hear different melodies rising up from unfamiliar places. Whether all these chants come together to create a contrapuntal music depends upon our aptitude to listen and learn from one another and from the One who calls us forth to a grand and elusive promise.

Discussion Questions

1. Both Jews and Christians have historically viewed the Bible as the word of God. How do you understand this view from your tradition?

2. "There is no relationship between the Tanach and the New Testament." "There is a profound relationship between the Old Testament and the New Testament." What is your reaction to these statements?
3. How do you use the Bible for guiding your life?
4. If you had to tell the story of the Bible in but two or three sentences, what would say? What place does the other have in that story?

Notes

1. Roman Catholic and Orthodox Christians also include the Apocrypha in their Bibles.

2. Frances Young, *Biblical Exegesis and the Formation of Christian Culture* (Cambridge; New York: Cambridge University Press, 1997), 220.

3. Abraham Joshua Heschel, *God in Search of Man* (New York: Farrar, Straus, Giroux, Inc., 1955), 245.

5

Where Do Jewish and Christian Ethics Differ, and Where Do They Overlap?

LAWRENCE W. FARRIS AND

ISAAC SEROTTA

Within our two faith traditions, we take ethics as having to do with the discernment of what is good and just behavior in and by the human community. Jews and Christians approach ethical decision-making from different starting points and through different methods. Sometimes they reach virtually identical decisions, sometimes quite different ones. This chapter seeks to set forth the two traditions' methods of making ethical decisions and to delineate an ethical issue of common concern.

The Jewish View of Ethics

There are many different kinds of Jews in the world today. We often think of Judaism's main movements: Reform, Conservative, Orthodox, and Reconstructionist. It is equally important to recognize the differing traditions of Ashkenazic Jews (Jews of eastern European descent), Sephardic Jews (Jews of western Europe, Asia, and North Africa), and Beta Israel (Jews of Ethiopia). Further, one of the hallmarks of Judaism is a healthy and vigorous debate on issues of importance (and sometimes on issues of no importance). And yet with all this diversity, there are some basic similarities that cut across the Jewish community when it comes to ethics. These similarities may be summarized in the following three principles: (1) Jewish ethics come from the Torah; (2) the Torah must be interpreted to be truly understood; and (3) Jewish ethics progress over time by virtue of this interpretation of Torah.

Jewish Ethics Come from the Torah

For Jews, the starting place for ethics and the source to which we continually look for ethical guidance is the Torah. The ancient Israelites had no word for religion. They called themselves either a nation or a people. This fact is important to the understanding of ethics in Judaism. The Torah is not so much a set of laws as it is a guide to leading a life of holiness. When we think of the Torah only as law, we are apt to forget that the goal of Torah is to help us emulate our Creator. Jewish ethics are not about following the law as much as they are about recognizing that we have been given a guidebook to lead a holy life.

Judaism believes that we are born pure. No doubt we all make mistakes and sully our spotless souls as we go through life, but when we aim at holiness, indeed, we can feel a touch of the holy in our lives.

As an example, let us look to the most repeated mitsvah (obligation) in the Five Books of Moses: "Do not oppress the stranger." The text often continues with the phrase "remember you were slaves in the land of Egypt," but there are other formulations as well. We are at times reminded that we "know the heart of the stranger." Is this a law? A commandment? It seems to be something altogether more spiritual. Some form of this statement appears thirty-six times in the text. By weight of sheer repetition, we must infer that it is a bedrock principle of Jewish ethics. The requirement to be tolerant and even supportive of others is one of the most compelling ethical ideas in all of Judaism.

Have we always lived up to this obligation as individuals? As a community? I wish we had, but the mistakes we've made do not diminish the beauty and the centrality of the concept. Indeed, an entire way of life can be drawn just from this statement. The Torah does not allow this statement to remain a generalization about tolerance; it also governs such particulars as why we must use fair weights and measures, why we should take care of the widow and orphan, and why we should abide by all the other everyday mitsvot written in the Torah. The goal is living a holy, ethical life every day. "You shall be holy, because I, the Lord your God, am holy" (Lev. 18:1).

Our Jewish ancestors did not have a word for religion because Judaism could not be relegated to the place that religion holds in some people's lives. It was not something to be left in church or synagogue or mosque but rather a set of principles by which to live each and every day. Even now, when Jews need to make an ethical decision, we rely on the precepts of our Torah. For some Jews, these precepts have the force of immutable law; for others, they are guideposts for ethical behavior. All Jewish ethics come from the Torah and its interpretation.

Torah Must Be Interpreted to Be Fully Revealed

Jews of all movements approach the Torah with great humility. The text of the Torah, whether human or divine, is multifaceted. It contains many meanings, and no one is a master of them all. We are always in dialogue with the text, looking for readings that are not obvious on the surface. Every sentence, phrase, word, and even letter can yield multiple meanings.

This kind of interpretation can add to our understanding of morality in the world. Here are two ethical precepts from the book of Leviticus: "When you reap the harvest of your land, you shall not reap all the way to the edges of your field, or gather the gleanings of your harvest. . . . You shall leave them for the poor and the stranger: I the Lord am your God. You shall not steal" (Lev. 19:9–11). On the surface this looks like two separate imperatives. Leave the gleanings of your fields for those in need, and do not steal.

Reading between the lines yields a richer understanding. Why do these two precepts stand next to each other? Are they simply two items in a list of ethical behaviors, or is it possible to see in this juxtaposition an argument that suggests harvesting your own field to its very corners is theft? Those who have much also have a responsibility to share with those who have little. Not to share our bounty with others is an act of thievery.

It is appropriate for commentators on the text to connect one idea to another in this way. In fact, the format of the text encourages it. Think of the Torah in its original Hebrew form. To this day, these words are written on parchment scrolls by the hand of a scribe. The text predates vowels and punctuation. Ideas are not divided, as are the ideas in this chapter, by commas, periods, and other identifying marks.

When Jews encounter the text of the Torah, the meaning does not begin and end with the simple syntax of words. There are many ways to analyze the text, and from it, to tease out a meaning, sometimes even a meaning that appears to contradict the text itself.

Jewish Ethics Evolve

This is the most controversial of our three statements about Jewish ethics. Orthodox Judaism teaches that the Torah is immutable law, and Orthodox Jews might object to the idea of evolution in ethics. From a traditional point of view, if ethical behavior among Jews changes over time, it is not because the text was wrong to begin with. It is not because we are reading something new into the text. Rather, the meaning was always there, and God intended it. We just did not understand until now.

More liberal Jews, on the other hand, are willing to depart from the Torah text. They see the text as being written by humans and, therefore, as flawed. While still looking to the text for guidance, they also reach a point where they break from a text and say that our ancestors spoke for the ideology of their times and we speak for the ideology of our time. Nevertheless, Jewish ethics comes from Torah text, and even when Jews depart from the letter of the text, they never leave its spirit behind.

There is a familiar passage in Exodus that will be instructive for us: "The penalty shall be life for life, eye for eye, tooth for tooth" (Ex. 21:23–24). At its simplest, this text seems to be a law of direct and equal retaliation. Today, this may seem barbaric, but in its historical context it moderated the execution of wild justice. Before this law of retaliation, there was a law of vengeance. If someone put out your eye, you might respond by killing him. Disproportionate response was the law of the land. The Torah restrains unruly passions by insisting that the response be directly proportional: an eye for an eye, not a life for an eye. The new ethical principle sets a limit that prevents an escalation of violence.

The rabbis of the talmudic era extended the meaning of this text. Thus, "an eye for an eye, a tooth for a tooth" was reread as "the monetary value of an eye for an eye, the value of a tooth for a tooth." The logic of this reinterpretation was largely based on the following query: "What if a man with one eye puts out the eye of a man with two eyes?" A response that results in the blinding of a man is no longer proportional. Therefore, the rabbis concluded that the text must not have meant literally "an eye for an eye," but rather the *value* of an eye. In making this move, the rabbis were not negating the Torah. Instead, theirs was a creative response that ensured the ongoing relevance of Torah even as it yielded a new interpretation, which they claimed God had intended all along.

Can this argument be extended to the part of the text that says "a life for a life?" Should we oppose the death penalty because the text might be understood as the value of a life for a life? This question is a bit more complicated.

There are many misdeeds that the Torah claims are punishable by death. Disrespecting your parents is a capital crime, for instance. On the one hand, it is clear that these punishments were meant to have deterrent value, and we have no examples of a disrespectful child being put to death. On the other hand, the text preserves the right of a community to put to death those accused of capital crimes.

The rabbis of the Mishnah attempted to clarify the issue, but there was some disagreement in their arguments:

A Sanhedrin [rabbinic court of ancient days] that puts one man to death in seven years is called, "bloody." Rabbi Eliezer ben Azariah says, "Or one in even seventy years." Rabbi Tarfon and Rabbi Akiba say: "Had we been in the Sanhedrin none would ever have been put to death." Rabban Simeon ben Gamliel says, "They would have increased the level of bloodshed in Israel [by abolishing the death penalty]." (M. Mak. 1.10)

Rabbi Akiba would abolish the death penalty completely; Rabbi Simeon ben Gamliel would keep it as a deterrent and for use when necessary. Both of these rabbis, among the most illustrious of Jewish history, would argue that their interpretation is in the Bible.

The most fascinating text on capital punishment comes from the Talmud. In it, the rabbinic court moves out of the holy precinct of the Temple in Jerusalem so that they cannot enact any death penalties. They understood that the precincts of the Temple endowed them with power to pronounce judgment in capital punishment cases. By physically removing themselves, they rendered such a verdict impossible.

> Capital cases ceased. Why? Because when the Sanhedrin saw that murderers were so prevalent that they could not be properly dealt with judicially, they said: "Rather let us be exiled from place to place than pronounce them guilty." (B AZ 8b)

Their reasoning is quite remarkable. They do not take this action because the death penalty is outmoded, nor because they find it inhumane. They say that the capital cases are simply coming too quickly and too often for them to adjudicate them properly. It is better to move out of the Temple and take themselves out of the loop in capital crimes than to make mistakes in the administration of justice.

The Torah cannot be pinned down on this topic. There is good reason in the Torah to abolish the death penalty and replace it with the value of a life for a life. There is also an argument for retaining the death penalty for extraordinary circumstances. Perhaps the execution of Adolf Eichmann in Israel is the best example of extraordinary circumstances. One of the architects of Hitler's "Final Solution," Eichmann remains the only person to be executed by the State of Israel in its entire history.

The rabbis of the Sanhedrin could not make a definitive decision because they were so caught up in the times in which they lived, so they stepped out of time. They understood the Torah to mean they could only enact capital punishment when they ruled "in that place." So they left that place and by doing so effectively ended any possibility of capital punishment in the Jewish community. They thus forced an evolution of Jewish ethics that continues to this day, as many of the Jewish organizations in America today fight for the curtailing, if not outright abolition, of the death penalty in our legal system.

In this example we can see clearly how Jewish ethics develop over time, not in distinction from the Torah but in relationship with it.

There is no ethical principle today for which we cannot find a direct or indirect source in our texts. Even when the text is equivocal or contradictory it gives us the opportunity to look deeper and find the meaning that will spur us on to do good in the world. When a non-Jew approached the first-century Jewish sage Hillel and asked him to teach him the whole Torah while he stood on one foot, he replied, "Do not do to others what you would not want them to do to you. All the rest is commentary, go and learn it" (B. Shab. 31a). Hillel was right on two counts. His inversion of the Golden Rule is the skeleton of Jewish ethics, the impetus for doing good in the world, but if you don't learn the commentary, you are missing the flesh and muscle and heart of the matter.

The Christian View of Ethics

Christian Ethics Are
Grounded in the Life of Jesus

Christian ethics are grounded in Jesus' words and deeds. Since Christians believe that "God was in Christ" (2 Cor. 3:19), Christian ethical decision-making finds its touchstone in the life and teachings of Jesus. Although problematically simplistic, the currently popular question "What would Jesus do?" does indicate the starting point of Christian ethical reflection.

This does not mean Christians ignore Torah. On the contrary, Christian ethics are grounded in the life of Jesus, which in turn is grounded in the life of Torah. Jesus' teachings are anchored in the Torah, and both the content and character of his ethics are unintelligible apart from this heritage. The early church maintained continuity with Jesus' practice by claiming the Torah as its own and incorporating the "Old Testament" into its sacred Scriptures. In fact, many Christians take the Ten Commandments as a cornerstone of an ethical life and understand them as a gift of a gracious God to instruct people in the essentials of right behavior toward God and neighbor. Jesus' reliance on Torah is evident in the following text:

> One of the scribes came near and heard them disputing with one another, and seeing that [Jesus] answered them well, he asked him, "Which commandment is the first of all?" Jesus answered, "The first

is, 'Hear, O Israel, the Lord our God, the Lord is one; you shall love the Lord your God with all your heart, and with all your soul, and with all your mind, and with all your strength.' The second is this, 'You shall love your neighbor as yourself.' There is no other commandment greater than these." Then the scribe said to him, "You are right, Teacher; you have truly said that 'He is one and in Him there is no other;' and 'to love one's neighbor as oneself.'" (Mk. 12:28–33)

Jesus grounds his summation of the Ten Commandments by quoting here, as elsewhere, from Torah (Deut. 6:4 and Lev. 19:18). Although Christians affirm that "God is love" (1 Jn. 4:8), they do not understand such love in sentimental terms, nor as separated from God's longing for justice and for a holy people shaped and guided by Torah.

Consider Jesus' relationship to Torah expressed in the Sermon on the Mount (Matthew 5–7):

Do not think that I have come to abolish the law or the prophets. I have not come to abolish but to fulfill. For truly I tell you, until heaven and earth pass away, not one letter, not one stroke of a letter, will pass from the law until all is accomplished. Therefore, whoever breaks one of the least of these commandments, and teaches others to do the same, will be called least in the kingdom of heaven; but whoever does them and teaches them will be called great in the kingdom of heaven. (Mt. 5:17–19)

Following this proclamation, Jesus proceeds to intensify and, in some cases, radicalize, the precepts of Torah. A case in point, which bears on Christian responses to capital punishment:

You have heard that it was said, "An eye for an eye and a tooth for a tooth." But I say to you, Do not resist an evildoer. But if anyone strikes you on the right cheek, turn the other also; and if anyone wants to sue you and take your coat, give your cloak as well; and if anyone forces you to go one mile, go also the second mile. Give to everyone who begs from you, and do not refuse anyone who wants to borrow from you. You have heard that it was said, "You shall love your neighbor and hate your enemy." But I say to you, Love your enemies and pray for those who persecute you, so that you may be children of your Father in heaven; for he makes his sun rise on the evil and on the good, and sends rain on the righteous and on the unrighteous. For if you love those who love you, what reward do you have? Do not even the tax collectors do the same? And if you greet only your brothers and sisters, what more are you doing than others? Do not even the Gentiles do the same? Be perfect, therefore, as your heavenly Father is perfect. (Mt. 5:38–48)

Christian interpreters have often misread this text by setting the teachings of Jesus over against the ethical standards of his Jewish contemporaries. But such a judgment knows little of Jewish interpretation. What Jesus is doing here is not "fulfilling" the law, in the sense of abrogating it, but rather radicalizing or intensifying the Torah teaching. The effect of "You have heard it said . . . but I say to you . . ." is to affirm the law and then extend its application in a more radical direction. By redefining the boundary of who is a neighbor to include the enemy, Jesus' imperative exceeds, and perhaps even breaks with, the logic of proportional justice. Indeed, Jesus may have reinterpreted the Torah so that his teachings no longer fit within a Jewish ethical framework.

On the face of it, this ethical stance may register as utopian or naïve, potentially undermining all notions of accountability before God and neighbor. Yet, the command to love one's enemy may well disarm and defuse evil precisely because it breaks the cycle of violence that the concept of retributive justice unwittingly perpetuates. For Christians, the motivation for such a radical ethic finds its justification in the experience of God's love for us, a love that knows no limit, that embraces the just and the unjust alike, and that will ultimately restore the entire creation.

As regards the issue of capital punishment, Christians, like Jews, hold a variety of stances. Although the life and teachings of Jesus are a common starting point for all Christians, the paths taken from that point are many and varied. Because of the size of the Christian community (approximately 2 billion adherents), and because of its great cultural and denominational diversity, Christians hold different, and sometimes even opposing, ethical positions. This diversity is born in large part from the variety of ways in which Christians read Scripture, as well as from the different weight given to different biblical teachings. There are Christians who read the biblical text from a literalistic-nonhistorical perspective, and others who read it in a historical-redactive way. There are Christian communities hierarchically organized, wherein clergy delineate the ethical positions incumbent on members of their tradition, and there are Christian communities more democratically organized, wherein each believer is guided by his or her own conscience. As a consequence, Christians are among the most outspoken supporters of the death penalty, and they are among the most vociferous protesters against it.

Clearly, the text from Matthew places a heavy burden on those who sanction the death penalty. Yet, Jesus' teaching challenges the standards and expectations of *all* Christians regarding how they are to live in the world precisely because he overturns the logic of self-preservation. Rather than providing ready-made solutions that his followers can universalize, the teachings of Jesus rattle Christians out of their ethical complacency. They introduce disorienting demands that overthrow moral certainties and contest ethical practices. As a result, Christians are constantly driven to reexamine their assumptions and reimagine the boundaries of their responsibilities. The difficulties of determining the identity of the neighbor and the obligations of nonviolent engagement impel Christians to recognize their own limitations and to seek God's guidance. Ethical decisionmaking in the Christian tradition therefore requires prayerful reflection, which in turn may lead to practices that defy "common sense" and go against the grain of the dominant culture.

The Place of Prayer in Christian Ethical Decisionmaking

With confidence in Jesus' promise that "where two or three are gathered in my name, I am there among them" (Mt. 18:20), Christians often seek guidance through prayer when confronted with an ethical decision, particularly at the personal level. The following example of a family seeking what is good and right for an aging parent illustrates this aspect of Christian decisionmaking.

An elderly Christian woman was diagnosed with terminal cancer. Her children, in consultation with a physician, had to decide whether to prolong her life with chemotherapy. Further compounding the problem was the fact that the woman had suffered a stroke that severely limited her ability to communicate. She had been an active and devout member of her church, and her children knew she did not fear death but saw it as the doorway to new life with God. Their mother had often stated she desired never to become a burden to any of her children. But how best to provide for her care? Should she receive chemotherapy or not? Should she be placed in a nursing home or taken into the home of one of her children?

Faced with a dilemma that defied neat answers, the children decided to take time to pray, to seek God's guidance in discerning the best path to take. They acknowledged their need to break the grip of their own self-concern, taking into account the best interest of the larger family. They prayed individually, and then together, seeking wisdom and guidance beyond their own. During this time, Jesus' words "If any one would come after me, let him deny himself and take up his cross and follow me" (Mk. 8:34) came to the son. Hearing these words, he came to realize that to follow Jesus in this instance would entail embarking upon a path of self-sacrifice. As a consequence, he offered to take a leave of absence from his work, move his mother into his home, and care for her with the help of a hospice agency. His sisters agreed that no further treatment should be undertaken and offered to extend visits with the mother so that their brother and his family might have respite. All felt they had come to the decision that best honored their and their mother's beliefs, that was in accord with Jesus' teaching, and that was just and good in terms of all of them participating in their mother's care.

In this example, prayer enabled a resolution that brought the family together. That, of course, is not always the case. Yet, the acknowledgment of prayer as an essential aspect of Christian ethical decisionmaking is grounded not in the optimism of "happy endings" but in the sure knowledge that God belongs in all our deliberations.

A Shared Concern: Compassion
Toward the Stranger

Having looked at a social ethical issue from a Jewish perspective and a personal ethical issue from a Christian perspective, we turn now to a shared ethical concern. The most often cited mitsvah, as we mentioned earlier, is "Do not oppress the stranger, remember you were strangers in the land of Egypt."

Many Christian texts also speak to this concern. For example, in Matthew 25, Jesus tells this parable, "Then the ruler shall say to those on the right: 'Come you blessed of God my Maker, inherit the realm prepared for you from the foundation of the world. For I was hungry and you gave me food, I was thirsty and you gave me drink, I was a stranger and you took me in" (Mt. 25:34–35). Christians understand this text as teaching that the resurrected Christ (*Christ* is the Greek word for messiah, and Greek is the language of the Christian Bible) dwells among people in need. Seeking to serve Jesus, they are to act ethically toward such as these.

Or again, in the famous parable of the Good Samaritan, Jesus speaks of the crucial role of our attitude toward the stranger:

> Jesus said, "A man was going down from Jerusalem to Jericho, and he fell among robbers, who stripped him and beat him, and departed, leaving him half dead. Now by chance a priest was going down that road; and when he saw him he passed by on the other side. So likewise a Levite, when he came to the place and saw him, passed by on the other side. But a Samaritan, as he journeyed, came to where he was; and when he saw him, he had compassion, and went to him and bound up his wounds, pouring on oil and wine. Then he set him on his own beast and brought him to an inn, and took care of him. And the next day he took out two denarii and gave them to the innkeeper, saying, 'Take care of him; and whatever more you spend, I will repay you when I come back.' Which of these three, do you think, proved neighbor to the man who fell among the robbers?" [The man] answered, "The one who showed him mercy." And Jesus said to him, "Go and do likewise." (Lk. 10:30–37)

Since the two men who passed by this poor, unfortunate stranger were Jews, both Christians and Jews have often read this parable as an anti-Jewish polemic. In its historical context, however, this parable was more likely understood as an *anti-priest* polemic, excoriating a priestly class corrupted by Rome. Jesus asks his hearers to extend compassion beyond the boundaries of ethnicity, religion, and class—and to take risks in doing so. One's ethical response is not to be determined by the status of the one in need. As such, Christians are part of the messianic hope for the world and are to embody, both individually and corporately, the way of Christ among all people, particularly among strangers.

Deepening this ethical claim is the Christian community's understanding of itself as the body of Christ in the world.

> For just as the body is one and has many members, and all the members of the body, though many, are one body, so it is with Christ. . . . If one member suffers, all suffer together; if one member is honored, all rejoice together. Now you are the body of Christ and individually members of it. (1 Cor. 12:12, 26–27)

Through the sacrament of baptism, Christians believe they are initiated into the body of Christ; through the sacrament of Holy Communion, they believe they are nourished as that body for its work in the world. The metaphor of the body is intended to make clear that all the variety of gifts—teaching, healing, helping, advocating, organizing—are needed by the body to do its work of justice and compassion, just as the human body requires its various parts. As Christ's body in the world, Christians are to be about the work of Jesus, their messiah.

This double understanding—of Christ as dwelling among the strangers of the world, and of Christians as being the body of Christ in the world—is intended to move Christians past the social inequities perpetrated by patronizing attitudes toward those who are being helped. Christ's presence in the stranger means that Christian compassion cannot be seen as flowing from the "have" to the "have not." Rather, Christian compassion is a welcoming of the stranger who embodies Christ as surely as Christians believe themselves to be embodied in Christ. Christ intends the Christian community to seek justice with, not only for, the stranger, and this can be done only if the stranger is welcomed both as a member of Christ's body and as an embodiment of Christ in the world.

In addition to the words of Torah, Judaism has a rich folkloric tradition related to the stranger. At the Passover Seder, Jews open the door for Elijah. This is an act of faith, signifying belief that the Messianic Age will one day dawn, and that Elijah, the prophet, will be its harbinger. But it is also an affirmation of the stranger. In folk tales, Elijah is often portrayed as a beggar, a victim of the world. We open the door at Passover to all who are hungry. One of the hungry people in the world is surely Elijah.

Similarly, the story is told of a homeless person making his way into a crowded church one Sunday morning. Unkempt, unwashed, and with ragged clothes, he would have stood out among the congregation even if he had been able to slip into a back pew. But the service had already begun, and the church was packed; no seats were to be had. So the visitor made his way up the center aisle and sat down on the floor right in front of the altar. The head usher, well dressed and always proper, saw all this happen, as did most of the congregation, and was perplexed as to how to respond. In but a moment, he knew what action to take. He walked down the aisle, sat himself down on the floor next to the visitor, and there they worshiped together.

In the Torah God makes an impassioned plea for the treatment of the stranger:

> You shall not wrong a stranger or oppress him, for you were strangers in the land of Egypt. You shall not ill-treat any widow or orphan. If you do mistreat them, I will heed their outcry as soon as they cry out to Me, and My anger shall blaze forth and I will put you to the sword, and your own wives shall become widows and your children orphans. (Ex. 22:20–23)

This text teaches us that our mistreatment of the stranger has an impact on us. In fact, we become the stranger. At some time, in some place, we have all been the one who did not know, did not fit, the one who stood out and apart from the crowd. The Torah teaches us to welcome that person, just as we would like to be welcomed. Christianity teaches us to imitate a great teacher, Jesus, who lived the words he spoke.

A Jewish mystical legend teaches us that there are thirty-six wholly righteous souls in the world, and because of them the world continues to exist. When one dies, another is born. Always there are thirty-six *tsaddikim,* righteous ones. The trick is that we never know if we are talking to one, we never know if we might even be one. So we must live our lives as if every human being we meet is one of the thirty-six, and we must act each day as if we ourselves are one of the thirty-six. If we lived in that way, then indeed the world would be well on its way to ethical wholeness. When we welcome the stranger we are no longer strangers. This is the path for all who study Jewish and Christian ethics. There are differences, and there are overlaps, but when we seek to understand each other, we need not be strangers.

Discussion Questions

1. What, if anything, does God have to do with the making of your ethical decisions? Is there a place for God?

2. What makes an ethical decision Christian? Jewish? Is it framing the question in the context of one's religious tradition? Does it have to do with the religious authorities one consults?

3. A "case study" from the Talmud. [If you know the Talmud's solution to this story, please do not give it away.] Two men are in the desert. They have one skin of water, just enough for one of them to survive and reach safety. If they share the water, they will both die. What should they do? Is there a solution that you would derive from the ethical teachings of Christian tradition? Jewish tradition?

4. In Leviticus 19:19 it reads, "You shall love your neighbor as yourself." What does "love" mean in this context?

5. Having studied the ethical obligations to the stranger, do you think the Bible essentially commands us to love the stranger? Is there a difference between loving one's neighbor and loving the stranger? Based on your religious tradition, is it reasonable and fitting to be commanded to love your enemy?

6. To what degree do our own ethical actions contribute to the repair, redemption of the world? How?

7. If there is a conflict between what your tradition teaches and what your conscious dictates, how do you resolve it?

6

What Is the Meaning of "Israel" for Jews and Christians?

CHRISTOPHER M. LEIGHTON,

DONALD G. DAWE, AND

AVI WEINSTEIN

Few words stir the emotions or challenge our thoughts as deeply as *Israel*. The term is loaded with meanings central to the identity of both Jews and Christians. *Israel* evokes ancient memories of land, people, covenant, and God that shape our understanding of belonging, of connection, and of home.[1] These multiple associations are grounded in Scriptures sacred to both communities. The founding of the State of Israel in 1948 further challenges Jews and Christians to reconcile the biblical conceptions of Israel with the realities of a modern state. Christians and Jews have yet to resolve the theological significance of Israel as land, people, and covenant in light of the rebirth of the Jewish nation. Differences over Israel's identity and purpose in history often divide Jews and Christians, sometimes splintering them into irreconcilable camps. This polarization happens not only between these two faith communities but also within them.

We will explore how Christians and Jews use the term *Israel* in different ways so that we can better understand the religious significance Israel holds for each tradition. We will pursue our inquiry through an examination of biblical texts, rabbinic commentaries, theological reflections, and church confessions that wrestle with Israel.

The Meanings of *Israel*

Both Jews and Christians consider themselves heirs to the ancient nation of Israel that God called into existence through the Jewish patriarchs and matriarchs: Abraham, Isaac, and Jacob; Sarah, Rebekah, Rachel, and Leah. God promised this nation the land. The people suffered slavery, experienced the Exodus, wandered for forty years, took possession of their homeland, and endured centuries of foreign domination as well as internal political disunity. Following the destruction of the First Temple in 586 B.C.E., the Jewish people were exiled in Babylon. In 536 B.C.E. they returned to the land to rebuild their temple and their national life. In 70 C.E., Rome destroyed Jerusalem and the Second Temple, which ended Jewish political sovereignty.

The multiple meanings of Israel that grew out of this history are embedded in the Tanach.

1. Israel is the biblical name of the Jewish people. The Tanach seldom uses the word *Jew*. The people are called Israel, the Children of Israel, or Israelites.
2. Israel refers to the people with whom God has formed a covenant and to whom God has given Torah. They are the chosen people through whom God's revelation is given to the world. This covenant was initially made with Abraham and continues through the particular line of Jacob's offspring.
3. Israel is the land given by God to this people. It is not just any piece of land but a particular geographical location to which the people are called by God.

To understand how Jews and Christians use the term *Israel*, we start with the accounts in Genesis that record how Jacob's name was changed to Israel, and how Jacob and his descendants were called to a new destiny.

Jacob was left alone; and a man wrestled with him until daybreak. When the man saw that he did not prevail against Jacob, he struck him on the hip socket; and Jacob's hip was put out of joint as he wrestled with him. Then he said, "Let me go, for the day is breaking." But Jacob said, "I will not let you go, unless you bless me." So

he said to him, "What is your name?" And he said, "Jacob." Then
the man said, "You shall no longer be called Jacob, but Israel, for
you have striven with God and with humans, and have prevailed."
(Gen. 32:24–28)

God appeared to Jacob again when he came from Paddan-aram, and
he blessed him. God said to him, "Your name is Jacob; no longer
shall you be called Jacob, but Israel shall be your name." So he was
called Israel. God said to him, "I am God Almighty: be fruitful and
multiply; a nation and a company of nations shall come from you,
and kings shall spring from you. The land that I gave to Abraham
and Isaac I will give to you, and I will give the land to your offspring
after you." (Gen. 35:9–12)

The Hebrew word for Jacob, *Yaakov,* means "the one who followed." The Hebrew word for Israel, *Yisrael,* means "He who
wrestled with God." In Genesis 32, God's messenger bestowed the
name *Yisrael* upon Jacob. In Genesis 35, God appeared directly to
Jacob and reiterated this change.

The name change is followed by a promise that has two parts.
First, progeny, "a nation and a company of nations" shall spring
from the newly named Israel. Second, Jacob is declared worthy of
the land already promised to Abraham and Isaac. Abraham and
Isaac spawn other nations, but Jacob-Israel is the father of the
twelve tribes of the nation Israel. The land and the people become
inextricably bound to the name Israel. Later, at Sinai, God establishes or, better, reestablishes the covenant with the Children of Israel and reaffirms the promise to give them the land. The covenant
included the expectation that the Children of Israel would follow
God's commandments and be a holy people. The story connects a
holy land to a divinely covenanted people who come to be called
the Children of Israel.

The People, the Land, and God

What is the relationship between the people of Israel, the land of Israel, and the God of Israel? The beginnings of an answer may be
found in Deuteronomy 11:13–15:

So you are to keep all the commandments that I command you today, in order that you may have the strength to enter and to take possession of the land that you are crossing into to possess, now it shall be if you hearken, yes, hearken to my commandments that I command you today, to love YHWH your God and to serve Him with all your heart and with all your being: I will give forth the rain of your land in its due-time, shooting-rain and later-rain; you shall gather in your grain, your new-wine and your shining-oil. I will also provide grass in the fields for your cattle, and thus you shall eat your fill.

The land is rough and arid and on its own cannot sustain the people. If Israel is to flourish in the land, then it must maintain its covenant with God. If God's commandments are followed, God's favor rests upon both the land and people.

It is clear that through the land, Jews concretize their relationship with God. Indeed, many rabbinic passages declare that the way of life to which the people Israel are called can be fully realized only within this land. Heeding God's commandments will bring forth the dew and the rain; without these, the land will bear no fruit. When the Jews are in exile, these verses become a metaphor for the Jewish concept of reward and punishment and the land becomes an object of messianic yearning, a symbol of what the world will be when all is as it should be.

The relationship between the land, the people, and God is explicit in the central unit of Jewish liturgy, which is built around the recitation of Deuteronomy 6:4 ("Hear, O Israel, YHWH is our God, YHWH alone") and which includes the verses from Deuteronomy 11 cited above. The declaration of Israel's acknowledgment of God's oneness and its acceptance and fulfillment of God's law is inexorably connected to the people's survival on the land.

Christians and the Meaning of Israel

Israel is a term applied to a people, a covenant, and a land within the Jewish tradition. Each of these meanings also resonates powerfully within the Christian tradition. The historical tensions between Christians and Jews are more comprehensible when we understand the Christian claim to have inherited the blessings promised to Israel.

Israel the People

Jesus, his disciples, and his earliest followers were all Jews. They lived within the Jewish community, gathered in synagogues, worshiped in the Jerusalem Temple, treasured the Torah, and shared in the hopes for the imminent coming of the kingdom of God. Although this messianic movement grew out of Jewish soil, it failed to attract many followers among Jews. Instead, the movement increasingly found its adherents among the Gentiles, and this shift in ethnic composition profoundly altered the character of the Christian community. Nonetheless, the early church found itself confronted by two inescapable questions: (1) If Jesus and his earliest followers observed Jewish law, are not his followers also obligated to become Jewish and obey that same law? (2) If Jesus directed his ministry to "the lost sheep of Israel" (Mt. 10:6), why did Israel fail to recognize his prophetic proclamations or his messianic calling?

The New Testament and the writings of the church fathers signal a diversity of responses to these challenges. Matthew and Paul framed two predominant responses to this dilemma, and these responses subsequently developed in ways that proved troublesome for Jewish–Christian relations.

Matthew offers a portrait of Jesus that maintains deep connections with a Torah-observant life. In his most famous of teachings, known as the Sermon on the Mount, Jesus declared:

> Do not think that I have come to abolish the law or the prophets; I have come not to abolish but to fulfill. For truly I tell you, until heaven and earth pass away, not one letter, not one stroke of a letter, will pass from the law until all is accomplished. Therefore, whoever breaks one of the least of these commandments, and teaches others to do the same, will be called least in the kingdom of heaven; but whoever does them and teaches them will be called great in the kingdom of heaven. (Mt. 5:17–19)

To be sure, Matthew presents Jesus as a teacher whose interpretations of Torah depart from those of the Pharisees. Yet, Jesus and the Pharisees share a commitment to the authority of Jewish law. The attempt to underscore the solidarity of Jesus and his followers with the Torah remained a central concern for many within the early church. There were significant voices within the church insisting that dietary regulations and circumcision are requisite boundary markers for followers of Jesus no less than for other Jews. Indeed, significant efforts to reconnect the church with Torah observance continued to surface among Christians through the fourth century.

As Judaism and Christianity became distinct communities, church leaders branded advocates of Torah observance "Judaizers," and "Judaizing" became a heresy. Within the Jewish community, faith in Jesus was deemed unacceptable. Both emerging Christianity and rabbinic Judaism rejected followers of Jesus who continued to observe Jewish law.

Matthew's emphasis on the continuity between Israel and the church led subsequent Christians to maintain that they carried forward the covenantal legacy, that Jesus brought to fulfillment what was only foreshadowed in Israel's Scriptures, and that the church therefore can confidently claim the title of "the New Israel."

Paul's thinking moves the church in a radically different direction and eventually leads to an emphasis on the discontinuity of Christian faith and Jewish practice. Paul's outreach to the Gentiles provides an alternative response to the question concerning how followers of the Torah-observant Jesus cannot live in accordance with the law themselves? In his mission to the Gentiles, Paul insisted that faith in Christ eclipses trust in the saving power of Torah:

> For all who rely on the works of the law are under a curse; for it is written, "Cursed is everyone who does not observe and obey all the things written in the book of the law." Now it is evident that no one is justified before God by the law; for "The one who is righteous will live by faith." But the law does not rest on faith; on the contrary, "Whoever does the works of the law will live by them." Christ redeemed us from the curse of the law by becoming a curse for us—for it is written, "Cursed is everyone who hangs on a tree"—in order that in Christ Jesus the blessing of Abraham might come to the Gentiles, so that we might receive the promise of the Spirit through faith. (Gal. 3:10–14)

Scholars will continue to debate the content and character of Paul's convoluted argument. Some argue that Paul does not impugn

Torah observance per se, but limits his attack to those who maintain that Gentiles must first become Jews in order to become followers of Jesus. Yet, there is no doubt that later generations of Christians regarded Paul as a convert to Christianity who not only abrogated Torah observance, but insisted that salvation comes only through faith in Jesus Christ. This understanding of Paul's theology is emphasized in the Gospel of Luke and the book of Acts and yielded a Christian self-understanding that is disconnected from Judaism.[2] The people Israel are no longer defined by descent from Jacob/Israel but by those who respond to the call of God made through Jesus Christ. In the words ascribed to John the Baptist, "Bear fruits worthy of repentance. Do not begin to say to yourselves, 'We have Abraham as our ancestor'; For I tell you, God is able from these stones to raise up children to Abraham" (Lk. 3:8).

This understanding of Paul coalesced in an ideology that increasingly captured the Christian imagination. "The new covenant in Christ has made the first one obsolete. And what is obsolete and growing old will soon disappear" (Heb. 8:13–14). The appeal of this position, which we have referred to elsewhere as supersessionism, resides in its power to resolve the inescapable question: "Why did not the Jews place their faith in Jesus Christ?" The response takes the following form: Jesus comes to the Jews; the Jews reject Jesus; so God rejects the Jews and turns to the Gentiles. These Gentile followers of Jesus are reconstituted as "the New Israel."

Whether relying on Matthew or Paul, the claims to the title *Israel* are difficult to sustain in the midst of a vibrant Jewish community that reads "the Old Testament" in its original Hebrew and therefore can claim a more authentic interpretation. The task of substantiating the church's covenantal legitimacy is inseparable from the establishment of its interpretation of the Old Testament. To validate the truth of their scriptural reading, the church fathers adapted the methods of interpretation largely developed by the Alexandrian Jew, Philo. They maintained that the Bible has layers of meaning, most notably a literal and a spiritual dimension. Jews, it is said, dwell on the surface of the text. They float on the "fleshly" or "carnal" exterior of the Scriptures, in contrast to Christians, whose faith in Christ enables them to dig into the "spiritual" depths of the Scriptures where the real truth resides. In other words, Jews may claim large biblical holdings, but they do not possess the Scriptures because they do not understand them. This polemic was then buttressed with appeals to history. If God holds the Jews dear, if they are indeed the Chosen People, then why would God destroy their Temple and disperse them? The fact that Christianity emerged as the official religion of the Holy Roman Empire was used to support Christians' own status as God's Chosen People.

Christian supersessionism captured the imagination of Christians by the fourth century, and the notion has continued to grip Christians ever since. This formulation promised reassurance in the face of polemical battles that challenged the self-definition of the church as Israel. Although the historical pressures help us explain how these ideas took hold, they in no way justify their continuation. The Shoah makes the underlying pathology of Christian supersessionism inescapably clear. Whenever the church's own affirmations depend upon the negation of Judaism and the Jewish people, the church not only undermines its own ethical integrity but also advances an incoherent theological position, namely, that God cannot be trusted to remain faithful to God's promises. And, if God can dispense with the Jews because of their so-called faithlessness, then Christians have even greater cause for panic. So, one of the key tasks to demand the attention of Christians, whether Roman Catholic, Protestant, or Eastern Orthodox, is to neutralize the ideological alignments that have produced the rotten fruit of theological arrogance.

Israel the Land

Christian attitudes toward the land of Israel are no less varied or problematic than their perceptions of Israel the people. One view of the land can be traced back to the book of Acts, where Stephen delivers an impassioned speech leading up to his martyrdom. After rehearsing the history of the Israelites in positive terms, Stephen enters into a tirade with the following words:

> Our ancestors had the tent of testimony in the wilderness, as God directed when he spoke to Moses, ordering him to make it according to the pattern he had seen. Our ancestors in turn brought it in with Joshua when they dispossessed the nations that God drove out before our ancestors. And it was there until the time of David, who found fa-

vor with God and asked that he might find a dwelling place for the house of Jacob. But it was Solomon who built a house for him. Yet the Most High does not dwell in houses made with human hands; as the prophet says, "Heaven is my throne, and the earth is my footstool. What kind of house will you build for me, says the Lord, or what is the place of my rest? Did not my hand make all these things?" (Acts 7:44–50)

According to Stephen, the faithfulness of the Israelites extended from the patriarchs through Moses up through David. The rupture in their relationship with God occurred as a result of Solomon and the construction of the Jerusalem Temple. The Greek word translated here as "made with hands" *(cheiropoietos)* is used elsewhere to describe the fabrication of idols and signals an indictment of the sacrificial system integral to Temple worship. In other words, Stephen condemns the attempt to confine God to a particular place.

The process of unhinging the connections between land, Temple, and holiness is also evident in John's Gospel. In addressing the Samaritan woman, Jesus proclaims:

Woman, believe me, the hour is coming when you will worship the Father neither on this mountain nor in Jerusalem. You worship what you do not know; we worship what we know, for salvation is from the Jews. But the hour is coming, and is now here, when the true worshipers will worship the Father in spirit and truth, for the Father seeks such as these to worship him. God is spirit, and those who worship him must worship in spirit and truth. (Jn. 4:21–23)

In all likelihood, the attitudes of Jesus' followers were profoundly reoriented by the destruction of the Temple in 70 C.E. Both Jews and Christians were compelled to redefine their religious practices without reliance on the sacrificial rites of the Temple. Many Christians adapted to this new situation by spiritualizing the idea of Temple and land. The sanctity once concentrated in the land of Israel is extended to all creation. Since God is the Creator, all lands bear the imprint of the divine. Furthermore, the entire earth points beyond itself to the spiritual reality that provides the essential undergirdings of all physical existence. This distinction between the earthly, physical realm and the true, eternal domain of the spiritual animates the Epistle to the Hebrews, which redirected the community away from the Jerusalem that laid in ruins to the heavenly Jerusalem that is the true home of the faithful (Heb. 12).

The denial of earthly attachments to the land of Israel, to Jerusalem, and to the Temple is intensified in the writings of some of the preeminent church fathers, particularly Origen. In reflecting upon the prophetic promises of Israel's restoration, these writings point beyond the reestablishment of the Jewish nation to a spiritual vision of eternal bliss in a "heavenly country." As Robert Wilken has noted, the only time Origen used the phrase "the holy land" was in reference to a spiritual home situated above and beyond this earth.[3] Jews as well as Christians dared to dream of a "heavenly Jerusalem." Yet, the refusal both to pair the earth-bound place with the heavenly one and to insist that the two are inseparably bound together set Origen apart from the Jewish tradition.

The views of the land of Israel developed by Origen have continued to shape large segments of the Christian community, and the position still holds fast among liberal Protestants today. As a result, any attempt to attribute theological significance to the land of Israel is greeted with skepticism or criticism. The belief that the land of Israel holds a sanctity that does not exist elsewhere is all too frequently dismissed as an anachronistic and tribal attachment bordering on idolatry.

Although many early Christians rejected the sacred significance of the land of Israel, others found in this land an irreplaceable connection to their foundational stories. No other place invited Christians to occupy the same ground as their Lord and Savior. No other place enabled Christians to walk in the footprints of their ancestors in the faith as pilgrims on a sacred journey. The witness of the New as well as the Old Testaments strengthened an irresistible gravitational force, which not even the lofty rhetoric of " a heavenly land and a new Jerusalem" could overcome. One of the beatitudes in Matthew's Gospel is usually translated "Blessed are the meek, for they shall inherit the earth." Yet, New Testament commentators note that the more accurate rendering of the Greek term *gayn* is *land*, and the land that kept Christians as well as Jews in its thrall was not just any spot on the globe, but the placed called Israel. It is this particular land to which the hopes of Christians and Jews have been bound historically.

The intensity of the desire "to possess the land" is reflected in the writings of various church fathers, especially Justin Martyr and Irenaeus. In their insistence on the physical import of Israel, they stood in radical contrast to Origen. This difference is illustrated in Justin's *Dialogue with Trypho,* when he first alludes to the Holy Land:

> Jesus the Christ will cause the dispersed people to return and distribute the good land to each though not in the same way. For the former (Joshua) who was neither Christ nor the son of God gave them temporary possession; but the latter after the holy Resurrection will give us an eternal possession. In Christ, God will renew both the heaven, and the earth, and will cause an eternal light to shine in Jerusalem. (113.3–5; adapted from the translation quoted in Wilken, *The Land Called Holy,* 57–58)

Irenaeus maintained that the inhabitants of the land now include Gentiles as well as Jews, for the promises of inheritance extend to all who believe in God. In response to those who understood Israel and Jerusalem as nothing more than symbols of a spiritual reality, Irenaeus underscored the earthbound character of the prophetic witness. Irenaeus shared a vision of the future kingdom of God that recapitulated a familiar pattern within the Jewish tradition, namely, a restoration of the original creation where people will live in harmony with God's purposes.

When the emperor Constantine (324 C.E.) converted to Christianity, he expressed his devotion by becoming the first great builder of churches in the Holy Land. This bond was deepened by Constantine's mother, Helena, who was celebrated in the later tradition as the first pilgrim and is associated with construction not only in Jerusalem but at Bethlehem and the Mount of Olives. In the fourth, fifth, and sixth centuries the construction continued unabated and heightened Israel's appeal as the key pilgrimage site. The roots of the church in Israel run far deeper than most western Christians or Jews recognize, and the presence of Christians in the land provides eloquent testimony to the enduring attachment. To many Christians, especially the Eastern Orthodox, the land of Israel has acquired characteristics that are normally associated with a sacrament. In other words, the encounter with the physical landmarks of a sacred past make possible a kind of mystical participation in the life, death, and resurrection of Jesus.

Despite the importance of this connection, the indigenous Christian community has become anxious about its long-term prospects in the Holy Land. In recent history, Christian families who have lived in the land for many generations now find themselves squeezed by the growing ranks of Muslims and Jews. The demographic decline of its own community intimates a future when the Christian presence becomes little more than a token minority whose principal work is to preserve the relics of a distant past and to prop up their beleaguered holy sites.

Rabbinic Understandings of Israel

The rabbinic tradition emerged in the aftermath of the revolt against Rome that culminated in the destruction of the Second Temple. Since the Jews regarded the Bible's promise that they would be a "kingdom of Priests and a Holy Nation" as an eternal one, the tragedy of the Destruction and the eventual exile of Jews from Jerusalem in 135 C.E. required a response from the rabbinic leadership. The rabbinic sages understood exile and dispossession as a temporary condition caused by the sins of Israel. In the Babylonian Talmud, for instance, we read: "Rabbi Abba bar Zavda said, 'even though Israel has sinned, they are still called Israel'" (B. Sanh. 44a). In fact, according to Rabbi Bar Zavda, even transgressing the entire covenant would not cause the name *Israel* to be removed from the people. This declaration was certainly meant to lift the spirits of those Jews living in the land of their ancestors in the third century C.E.; it may also have been a response to Christian claims to be the new Israel. Throughout the ages, Jews turned to the statement of Rabbi Bar Zavda to support their belief that God had not abandoned them in spite of all evidence to the contrary.

Just as God remains faithful to Israel, the ancient Jewish sages insist that Israel remain faithful to God by scrupulously observing the mitsvot. This teaching is derived from a reading of Exodus 32:16,

"And the tablets were the work of God, and the writing of God was inscribed *(charut)* on the tablets." Rabbi Acha Bar Ya'akov said, "No nation or tongue will conquer them, for do not read the word as 'inscribe' *(charut)*, but as 'free' *(cherut)*" (B. Er. 54a).[4] When the Jews obey the law written on the tablets, they are free. Rabbi Acha Bar Ya'akov is teaching that the freedom of the Jewish people is intrinsically tied to their obedience to the law. Adherence to the commandments ensures that even though the Jews may live in foreign lands under foreign rulers, their souls are not subject to the oppression of others. He also expresses the belief that no nation would ultimately prevail against this people or control its land.

The hope that the kingdom of Israel will be restored and that all Jews who are in exile will return finds expression in daily liturgy, along with prayers for the rebuilding of the Temple and Jerusalem and for the coming of the Messiah. *How* and *when* these events will occur is a contested matter within the Jewish tradition, but *that* they are going to happen is an essential tenet of traditional Judaism.

Jewish Theological Views of the Modern State of Israel

Zionism, the modern movement to reestablish an independent Jewish homeland in the land of Israel, was founded primarily by secular Jews as a response to the more than a thousand years of exile and anti-Semitism (whose evils peaked with the Holocaust). They were seeking a political solution to an age-old problem, and by focusing on history, culture, and language, rather than religion, they defined Jewish nationhood in terms of the secular nationalism of the nineteenth and early twentieth centuries. Orthodox Jews were divided about Zionism. Some were opposed to it because they believed that only God could bring about the promised redemption. In their view, any action by humans to hasten the messianic time demonstrated lack of faith. Others agreed with the secularists that only Jewish political self-determination could end the oppression and degradation of the Jews. In addition, they hoped that a Jewish state would promote traditional Jewish belief and observance. Some believed that building the land and working for its independence were holy acts.

Reform Judaism emerged in Germany in the early 1800s at a time when Jews were beginning to win their rights as citizens in European nations. Responding to the charge that Jews believed themselves a separate nation and could never be loyal citizens, the early Reformers redefined Jewish identity in terms of religion alone, and they rejected the national aspects of being Israel. Therefore, most Reform Jews did not embrace Zionism, which was based on a decidedly national self-definition.

The religious opposition to Zionism that came from both Orthodox and Reform Jews virtually disappeared with the growth of Nazism and, subsequently, with the Shoah. The horror of the Holocaust convinced most Jews that a national homeland that could serve as a safe haven was a practical necessity, regardless of its theological implications.

For some religious Jews, the founding of the State of Israel has theological significance. Rabbi Abraham Isaac Ha-Cohen Kook, who was the chief rabbi of Palestine during the British Mandate, was the most outstanding advocate to this perspective. He understood the secular state to be the beginning of a process that would end once the entire Jewish nation committed itself to observing Torah. Secular Zionists were unwittingly doing the Lord's work and preparing for the ultimate redemption. For Kook, the founding of the State of Israel in 1948 was part of the divine plan. He wrote:

> Deep in the heart of every Jew, in its purest and holiest recesses, there blazes the fire of Israel. There can be no mistaking its demands for an organic and indivisible bond between life and all of God's commandments; for the pouring of the spirit of the Lord, the spirit of Israel which completely permeates the soul of the Jew, into all the vessels which were created for this particular purpose; and for expressing the word of Israel fully and precisely in the realms of action and ideas.
>
> In the hearts of our saints, this fire is constantly blazing up with tongues of holy flame. Like the fire on the altar of the Temple, it is burning unceasingly, with a steady flame, in the collective heart of our people. Hidden away in the deepest recesses of their souls, it exists even among the backsliders and sinners of Israel. Within the Jewish people as a whole, this is the living source of its desire for freedom, of its longing for a life worthy of the name for man and community, of

its hope for redemption of the striving toward a full, uncontradictory, and unbounded Jewish life.[5]

The victory in the 1967 Six Day War, and especially the return of the Old City of Jerusalem, including the site of the ancient Temple, reawakened and intensified traditional messianic expectations among religious Zionists. This theme finds expression in the prayer, authorized by Israel's chief rabbinate, for the well-being of the State of Israel: "Our father in heaven, Rock of Israel and its redeemer, bless the state of Israel, the first sprouting of our redemption."

Some religious Zionists think the redemption is already underway. They insist that all the land of Israel whose borders are defined by the Bible, including Judea and Samaria (the West Bank, also captured during the Six Day War), must remain under Israeli dominion so that the process of redemption can proceed. A more moderate camp sees spiritual significance in Israel's rebirth but is not prepared to see Jewish sovereignty over land outside of the 1949 UN-negotiated partition of Palestine as necessary for the Messiah's coming.

Each of these camps recites the prayer for the well-being of the State of Israel but disagrees about the meaning of the phrase "Israel, the first sprouting of our redemption." Some Jews see the founding of the State of Israel as a confirmation that God redeems in history and as a sign that God will ultimately redeem Israel and the rest of the world. Others assert that the rebirth of Israel and, especially, the recapture of Jerusalem signal that the final redemption is at hand and that Jews are obliged to do all in their power to push this process to its conclusion. For these Jews, an exchange of land for peace violates the terms of the covenant and impedes the coming of the Messiah.

Also living in Israel are religious non-Zionists who refuse to recite this prayer because the state was founded by secular Jews who, they say, have no fidelity to the Torah and its precepts. By definition, therefore, the political entity known as the State of Israel has absolutely no spiritual significance. Most of these religious non-Zionists acknowledge the political necessity for a Jewish homeland, and most prefer to live in a Jewish polity. But since a state outside the Torah's statutes can, by definition, have no intrinsic spiritual significance, they offer no formal blessings to Israel's political leadership.

There is even a small group of religious anti-Zionists who view the founding of the state as heresy against God. They share much in common with the non-Zionist camp but believe that Zionists are committing heresies against the following statement from the Babylonian Talmud (B. Ket. 110b): "There were three oaths that the Holy One exacted from Israel: One, that the people would not go to Israel en masse. Another, that Israel was made to promise that they would not rebel against the nations of the world and that He made the gentile nations promise not to enslave Israel too harshly." (B. Ket. 111a)

The preceding discussion of religious Zionists, religious non-Zionists, and religious anti-Zionists provides an overview of the responses to the State of Israel from within the traditional or Orthodox Jewish community, both in Israel and in the Diaspora. However, the majority of Jews both in Israel and abroad are not Orthodox. So, for example, in Israel the number of Jews who identify themselves as Orthodox is around 20 percent. In North America, the importance and influence of the Orthodox are growing, but demographically they remain less than 10 percent. Conservative, Reform, Reconstructionist, and secular Jews hold a variety of views of the theological significance of the State of Israel. These views may reflect aspects of Orthodox positions but are also determined by their unique theological perspectives, especially concerning the concepts of redemption and the messianic age.

In order to understand fully the attachment of contemporary Jews to the State of Israel, the personal impact of anti-Semitism, and especially the Shoah, must be taken into account. Most North American Jews and a significant number of Israeli Jews (especially those who founded the state) trace their roots to eastern Europe. For these Jews, the experiences of prejudice and persecution that typified life there are integral not to some detached history but to family lore. Jews from Mediterranean and Arab countries also have a heritage of oppression. But it is the destruction of European Jewry that has caused some people to refer to the Jewish community as a "wounded community." Living among the Jews today are those who suffered unspeakable horrors, who lost parents, siblings, entire families at the hands of the Nazis. And many Jews (and others) wonder how the world allowed the Shoah to occur, and whether there was something they personally could have done, if not to prevent the Shoah, at least to save more Jews from the gas chambers.

Among the tragic chapters of the Shoah was the unwillingness of countries around the world (including the United States and Canada) to take in Jewish refugees. This unwillingness is dramatically represented in the book and movie *Voyage of the Damned.* Many Jews believe that had there been an independent Jewish state in the years leading up to and during World War II, thousands, perhaps hundreds of thousands, of Jews could have been saved. It is not surprising, therefore, that Jewish support for the State of Israel became a way to respond to the Shoah. What Jews could not do to save other Jews from the Nazis, they could do by building a state so that a holocaust could never happen again. Rising like a phoenix from the ashes of concentration camps, Israel symbolizes rebirth, renewal, and hope in the face of desolation.

Threats to Israel were (and, for some, still are) seen through the prism of the Shoah. For several generations of Jews, their relationship with Israel became a primary component of Jewish identity and activity, especially when Israel was young and its survival precarious. The Israeli government reinforced these passions by placing Yad Vashem, the Holocaust memorial, next door to Mount Herzl, the most prominent military cemetery in Israel.

More recently, the relationship between Diaspora Jews and the State of Israel has begun to change. Many younger Jews do not have the same emotional relationship to either the Shoah or Israel as their parents; they did not live through the Shoah, and they cannot remember a time when there was no Israel. Israel is now firmly established and is much less dependent on financial support from Jews abroad. At the same time, the relationship between Israel and the Palestinians, as well as the relationship between Israel and its own Arab citizens, challenges values that many American Jews hold dear. And tensions between religious and secular Jews in Israel alienate those who are committed to religious pluralism.

For many in the past generation, the impact of the Shoah and support of Israel formed the foundation of their Jewish identity. Jewish leaders now recognize that as time passes, these factors are losing their primacy, as can be seen in the results of opinion polls and in the amount of money raised for Israel. The rise of interest in Jewish ritual and spirituality and the resurgence of Jewish education are evidence that Jews are seeking other ways to express their identity, and that the community is attempting to respond to these needs. The changing relationship of Jews to the State of Israel is one of the most important dynamics in the evolving nature of Jewish identity.

The Modern Challenge to Religious Particularity

For many contemporary Jews and Christians, traditional biblical sensibilities are incompatible with modern ideas of an "enlightened" society. In a modern democracy that claims all people are equal, the declaration that only some are God's chosen (whether Jews or Christians) evokes discomfort in our religious communities and is greeted by suspicion, if not contempt, by our secular neighbors. Both traditions are grounded in religious claims that are scandalous because their core affirmation is that God is made manifest in a particular people, in a particular land, and at particular historical moments. In other words, the God of the Bible does not work through all peoples in the same way. Furthermore, the assertion that God is manifest in some places more than others is thought to contradict the rational standards that need to obtain if we are to avoid the territorial struggles that have stained the earth with so much unnecessary blood. When judged by the standards of modernity, Christianity and Judaism are both dismissed as advocates of a narrow deity who plays favorites. In terms of Christianity, God is not equally manifest in everyone but is only disclosed fully in the person of Jesus Christ. In terms of Judaism, only the Torah reveals the requirements of living in accord with God's covenant. There are no abstract substitutes, no set of ethical standards or theological doctrines that can replace the particular allegiances that define either Christians or Jews.

Christians and Jews cannot and should not avoid the challenges posed by modern secular thinkers: How can religious communities maintain their distinctive affirmations without lapsing into irrationalism and the arrogant privileging of their own group over and against the other? There is something unruly about the passionate attachments developed within Judaism and Christianity. Both traditions make particular truth claims that are mutually exclusive.

Both insist that they have a special divine mandate to serve as a light to the nations. Both have questioned the authenticity of the other's claims. Jews and Christians have at different times and places either ignored, avoided, or competed with each other. Indeed, Christians have done worse, much worse, in their negation of the Jewish people. This is the legacy that we have been handed: Jews and Christians believe that they have little or nothing of religious significance to learn from the other. Christians are given a tradition that makes them wonder why the Jews are still around. Jews are bequeathed a heritage that makes them wonder why God needs so many Christians. These are the unresolved questions with which we are left: Can Christians and Jews learn to listen and live in a creative partnership with the other? Can they recognize or honor the particular blessings that belong to the other alone, and in so doing demonstrate how God's kingdom always holds room for the unexpected stranger?

If Christians and Jews cannot offer new answers to these very ancient questions, then the criticisms of the modern secular world may prove warranted. In the meantime, Christians and Jews are challenged to demonstrate that their particular covenantal claims are an invaluable source of wisdom that can advance the causes of justice here and now. Both Christians and Jews belong to traditions that refuse to opt out of the detailed entanglements of living this particular life. They are forbidden to inhabit a land of abstractions. They must build from the ground up, learning how to live and to love in a particular family, in a particular community, in a particular land, at particular times. Judaism and Christianity have an enormous amount to say about how to make a home in this world. These two traditions have much to teach about how to move beyond the confines of the familiar and sanctify the world. Yet, the wisdom of each tradition comes from the recognition that the work of repair must be completed one stitch at a time, with attention to the messy details not just the grand design.

There is of course more to the challenge, which brings us back to questions of Israel—as people, land, and covenant. Can the term *Israel* encompass both Jews and Christians? Or does the category collapse when it is enlarged to include both Jews and Christians, with their respective claims of a covenantal connection with the God of Israel? Are the religious claims of Christians and Jews on the land of

Israel comparable? Are they compatible, or mutually exclusive? To what degree does the future viability of Judaism depend on the State of Israel? In what sense does the future of Christianity also require a stable Christian presence in the Holy Land? Perhaps Christians and Jews will have to recognize that God has bestowed blessings on the other that they cannot claim for themselves. Perhaps, there is divine wisdom that we can learn only from the other. If we are going to sort out what we Christians and Jews mean when we each speak the name *Israel*, we will need to enter one another's houses and learn from one another how and when to be a respectful visitor and how and when to be a welcoming host.

Discussion Questions

1. Both Christians and Jews see themselves as Israel, God's covenantal partner. Who is Israel? Does your notion of Israel include both Jews and Christians, or is it limited to Jews alone, Christians alone?
2. From your point of view as a Jew or Christian, is the land of Israel holy? Why/why not?
3. Today, many hold that the claim that God chooses a particular people (and particular land) leads to rivalries between Christians and Jews. How can Christians and Jews maintain their particularistic claims while affirming the integrity of the other? Does affirming the integrity of the other require any revision of your tradition?
4. What, if any, is the religious significance of the State of Israel for you as a Christian?

Notes

1. The religious significance of this land also holds for the Muslim community, and this fact requires careful consideration. It is beyond the scope of this chapter, however, to address the issue here.

2. The Gospel of Luke and Acts are generally dated around the year 85 C.E., whereas Paul's Epistles were written between 48–58 C.E.

3. Robert L. Wilken, *The Land Called Holy* (New Haven: Yale University Press, 1992), 75.

4. This sort of pun is typical of rabbinic exegesis.

5. Rabbi Abraham Isaac Ha-Cohen Kook, "Eretz Israel" (The Land of Israel), in *Orot*, 2d ed. (Jerusalem: 1950), par. 5. Paragraphs 1, 3, 4, 5, and 8 of this essay appear in *The Zionist Reader: A Historical Analysis and Reader,* edited and translated, with an introduction and bibliographic notes, by Arthur Hertzberg, with a foreword by Emanuel Neumann (1959; reprint, New York: Atheneum, 1969); paragraph 5 is on page 419.

7

Is Suffering Redemptive? Jewish and Christian Responses

SHARON COHEN ANISFELD

AND CYNTHIA TERRY

There is much at stake in any religious conversation about suffering. What hangs in the balance is nothing less than our capacity—as Jews, as Christians, as human beings—to make sense out of our lives and the world we live in. For many people, the experience of suffering seems to contradict the notion of an all-powerful benevolent God. To ask "Is suffering redemptive?" is also to ask: Why do we suffer? Does God cause our suffering? Is suffering somehow a punishment for sin? How are we to come to terms with the terrible suffering that people inflict upon one another? Is suffering meaningless, or is there a purpose to our pain?

These questions are not new. They are timeless, and in this sense, we believe that they can never be fully or finally answered. Yet, this makes the questions no less urgent for the individual whose world has been shaken by suffering or sorrow. Indeed, all religious traditions, in one way or another, give expression to the human search for meaning in the face of unpredictable tragedy and loss.

We stand humbly before the mystery of human suffering. We acknowledge that no single universal answer could possibly explain all of the brokenness in the world, or give meaning to all human pain. No single answer could suffice because not all suffering is the same. There is the suffering that comes with death or loss, suffering that we understand to be part of the way of the world. There is the suffering that a person causes through his or her own actions, either consciously or unconsciously. There is the suffering that comes from societal injustice or the cruelty of one human being toward another.

People also respond to the experience of suffering in profoundly different ways. As Rabbi David Hartman has observed:

> Human relationships and human relationships with God are so individual, so closely tied to the unique sensibility of a particular person, that it is hard to be sure why some people are sustained for years by memories of joy, whereas others have a low threshold for tolerating pain. Some abandon the covenant after the death of a single loved one, but others retain belief in God's love for and commitment to themselves despite having lost whole families in the Holocaust. One human being leaves Auschwitz as an atheist and another as a person whose belief has grown stronger. For some, suffering is bearable if it results from the limitations of finite human beings, but it becomes terrifying and demonic if it is seen as part of the scheme of their all-powerful creator. Others would find life unbearably chaotic if they could not believe that suffering, tragedy, and death were part of God's plan for the world. Feeling that there is meaning and order in the world and that God in his wisdom decided to terminate the life of a loved one makes their tragedy bearable.[1]

It should be stated at the outset that Judaism and Christianity both place great emphasis on preventing or alleviating the suffering of others whenever possible. We begin with this fundamental and shared commitment that is so powerfully articulated by both traditions—the responsibility to love the stranger, to give assistance to those in need, to offer comfort to those in pain. To the extent that we can redeem others from suffering, we are unequivocally obligated to do so.

But, even as we affirm our shared responsibility to alleviate suffering whenever possible, we are nonetheless forced to confront the reality of its presence in the world. Even as we acknowledge the limits of any single response to the questions that arise out of the experience of suffering, we look to the accumulated wisdom of our religious traditions for insight about how to respond when tragedy occurs. It has been argued that the attitude toward suffering constitutes a major distinguishing factor between Judaism and

Christianity.[2] Is this true? How do our traditions respond to this essential human problem? Can there be redemption not only from suffering but also through suffering? Does suffering itself serve a redemptive purpose?[3]

The Conversation Begins

Jewish Response

"Is suffering redemptive?" The question itself has a Christian ring to it. It is not a question that most contemporary Jews would even be inclined to ask. It is certainly not a question that most contemporary Jews would be inclined to answer affirmatively. As Robert Gibbs has noted:

> In the Jewish community today, there is little patience with a theology of suffering. Our communal suffering, particularly the Shoah, makes us intolerant of any description or theological justification of suffering. . . . An elevation of suffering, even a reflection on suffering, seems un-Jewish. It would be, we Jews often think, something that Christian thinkers do. They praise suffering; they imagine expiation. We have had enough of it.[4]

And yet, our question is an instructive and important one for several reasons. First, it brings into relief some of the basic differences—and similarities—between Jewish and Christian views of suffering. Second, it illuminates some of the areas of ambiguity or dispute within our own religious traditions. And finally, for Jews in particular, it opens up a conversation about the meaning of suffering that we perhaps too readily dismiss as un-Jewish. Surely, if Jewish tradition is to speak to our deepest and most urgent questions about life, it must have something to say about our individual and collective experiences of suffering.

There is a well-known passage from Elie Wiesel's Holocaust memoir, *Night*, that stands out as one of the most stark and powerful protests against any attempt—theological or otherwise—to attribute meaning to the suffering endured by Jews at the hands of the Nazis. In it, Wiesel describes a public hanging that he witnessed while he was a prisoner in the concentration camp at Auschwitz. As Wiesel recounts the scene, we are brought face-to-face with the impossibility of affirming such horror as an expression of God's will, or as part of any redemptive scheme:

One day when we came back from work, we saw three gallows rearing up in the assembly place, three black crows. Roll call. SS all round us, machine guns trained: the traditional ceremony. Three victims in chains—and one of them, the little servant, the sad-eyed angel.

The SS seemed more preoccupied, more disturbed than usual. To hang a young boy in front of thousands of spectators was no light matter. The head of the camp read the verdict. All eyes were on the child. He was lividly pale, almost calm, biting his lips. The gallows threw its shadow over him.

This time the Lagerkapo refused to act as executioner. Three SS replaced him.

The three victims mounted together onto the chairs.

The three necks were placed at the same moment within the nooses.

"Long live liberty!" cried the two adults.

But the child was silent.

"Where is God? Where is He?" someone behind me asked.

At a sign from the head of the camp, the three chairs tipped over.

Total silence throughout the camp. On the horizon, the sun was setting.

"Bare your heads!" yelled the head of the camp. His voice was raucous. We were weeping. "Cover your heads!"

Then the march past began. The two adults were no longer alive. Their tongues hung swollen, blue-tinged. But the third rope was still moving; being so light, the child was still alive. . . .

For more than an hour he stayed there, struggling between life and death, dying in slow agony under our eyes. And we had to look him full in the face. He was still alive when I passed in front of him. His tongue was still red, his eyes not yet glazed.

Behind me, I heard the same man asking: "Where is God now?"

And I heard a voice within me answer him: "Where is He? Here He is—

He is hanging here on this gallows. . . ."

That night the soup tasted of corpses.[5]

This passage virtually screams out the answer to our question: "No! Suffering is not redemptive!" To see anything redemptive, even remotely meaningful, in the agony of that little boy hanging on the gallows, or those forced to watch him die, would be nothing short of scandalous to Wiesel and to most contemporary Jews. "Where is God? He is hanging here on this gallows." With these words, Wiesel absolutely rejects the notion that such suffering can be seen as an expression of the will of the living God.

Yet, in rejecting this notion, Wiesel raises more questions than he answers. In fact, his account of this scene is filled with images and phrases that are deliberately troubling and confusing from a religious perspective. Is Wiesel saying that God is dead? What does that mean to him? What is God's role here? Was this act of horrible violence a betrayal of God, or a betrayal by God, or both?

For contemporary Jews, the question "Is suffering redemptive?" must be asked against this backdrop. As Rabbi Irving Greenberg has written: "No statement, theological or otherwise, should be made that would not be credible in the presence of the burning children."[6]

Christian Response

The horror of this scene in *Night* is unavoidable, for all readers. For Christians, however, the end of the story sounds familiar; echoes of the crucifixion of Christ are easy to hear: three people executed while others stand by; the question, "Where is God?"; the answer, "On the gallows." For Christians, the image of God hanging on the gallows introduces an element of hope into this unbearable scene, for Christian faith teaches that Jesus Christ, the Son of God, did in fact die, but he was also raised from the dead. So to imagine the death of God is not unfathomable; to the contrary, for Christians, it has already happened, and death was not the ultimate winner.

In the scriptural stories of the crucifixion of Jesus, two of the four Gospel writers include a cry by Jesus, "My God, my God, why have you forsaken me?" (Mt. 27:46, Mk. 15:34, quoting Ps. 22:1) Implicit in this cry is Jesus' sense of abandonment by God. Yet the other two Gospels do not include this statement. In these two accounts, Jesus is portrayed as more knowing, more accepting. Biblical tradition is not altogether clear as to whether or not the death of Jesus is abandonment and betrayal by God. If the story ended at the cross, the ambiguity would be crucial, but because the story continues with the resurrection of Jesus from the dead, there is a resounding answer that God has not abandoned Jesus. To the contrary, God raises him from the dead, thus conquering death.

Wiesel's image of God hanging on the gallows, the very image that for Jews represents a tragic and unredeemable loss of innocence and faith, evokes for Christians echoes of the crucifixion and raises the possibility—even the promise—of a redemption that will yet come out of all this suffering.

It seems unlikely, in fact, that Wiesel was unaware of the Christian symbolism in this passage. Indeed, the foreword to *Night* is written by a French Christian novelist, François Mauriac, who comments on the same passage and underscores the painful discrepancy between Jewish and Christian responses to the image of God on the gallows. He describes meeting Wiesel for the first time and struggling with what to say to him:

> What did I say to him? Did I speak of that other Israelite, his brother, who may have resembled him—the Crucified, whose Cross has conquered the world? Did I affirm that the stumbling block to his faith was the cornerstone of mine, and that the conformity between the Cross and the suffering of men was in my eyes the key to that impenetrable mystery whereon the faith of his childhood had perished? Zion, however, has risen up again from the crematories and the charnel houses. The Jewish nation has been resurrected from among its thousands of dead. It is through them that it lives again. We do not know the worth of one single drop of blood, one single tear. All is grace. If the Eternal is Eternal, the last word for each one of us belongs to Him. This is what I should have told this Jewish child. But I could only embrace him, weeping.[7]

The conclusion of Mauriac's foreword is understated, but enormously important. In spite of his sense of all that he "should have told this Jewish child," ultimately, his own encounter with Wiesel began in speechlessness. "I could only embrace him, weeping." One is left wondering whether, without this initial act of embracing and weeping together, any further conversation would have been possible.

How Should We Respond When Tragedy Occurs?

Jewish Response

The Jewish reluctance to view suffering itself as redemptive, although intensified by the experience of the Holocaust, is not simply a twentieth-century phenomenon.[8] The story of the Exodus is one of the oldest and most central narratives of communal suffering and communal redemption for the Jewish people. If one examines the biblical account of the Exodus, it is quite apparent that the suffering of the Israelites was not understood as redemptive. We were not redeemed *by* slavery in Egypt; we were redeemed *from* slavery in Egypt:

> A long time after that, the king of Egypt died. The Israelites were groaning under the bondage and cried out; and their cry for help from the bondage rose up to God. God heard their moaning, and God remembered His covenant with Abraham and Isaac and Jacob. God looked upon the Israelites, and God took notice of them. (Ex. 2:23–25)[9]

In this context, suffering does not appear to have any inherent value or meaning. It is *from* our suffering that we need to be rescued and redeemed by God.

How then are we to find meaning or maintain faith in the covenantal relationship in the midst of such great suffering? There are three elements in the biblical treatment of this episode in Israel's history that become important sources of religious meaning. First, though our suffering as slaves is not viewed as intrinsically valuable or redemptive, it is certainly understood to be part of a divinely ordained redemptive scheme. God, in fact, tells Abraham much earlier, in the book of Genesis, that his descendants will serve as slaves in a foreign land for four hundred years. This prediction comes as part of God's covenantal promise to Abraham.[10] Thus, assurance is offered that God has a plan for the Jewish people, and that our suffering is not a sign of the end of the covenant, but a sign that the covenantal relationship will endure and will ultimately lead to redemption.

Second, although human history is understood as the unfolding of a divine plan, enormous emphasis is placed on our response in each specific moment. Thus, in the verses quoted above, God intervenes to end our suffering in Egypt only after hearing our moaning and groaning. Subtly, the Torah teaches, redemption will come if we are willing and able to cry out. Crying out for help then becomes an important religious act. It is, after all, an act that affirms at least the possibility of a response, the possibility of a continuing relationship with God.

Finally, the Torah teaches that our *memory* of slavery, our *memory* of suffering, has the potential to become an important source of moral pathos and action. Memory, in fact, becomes a defining feature of Torah law and retroactively offers a way of making meaning out of our suffering in Egypt. We are obligated to translate our own experience of suffering into empathy for others: "You shall not oppress a stranger, for you know the feelings of the stranger, having yourselves been strangers in the land of Egypt."[11] Thus, we become God's partners in the ongoing process of redemption. Having been redeemed from slavery in Egypt, we assume the responsibility to redeem others from suffering through our own moral behavior.

It is not suffering itself, therefore, but our response to suffering that is religiously significant from a Jewish perspective. This is true not only in the Hebrew Bible, where the focus is primarily on communal suffering and redemption, but in rabbinic literature, where greater attention is given to the suffering of the individual. The question that preoccupied the rabbis of the Talmud with regard to suffering was not "Is suffering redemptive?" but, when tragedy occurs, "What might we learn from it?"[12]

The following passage from the Talmud outlines the response that is expected of an individual who is confronted by suffering:

Rava (some say Rav Hisda) said: If a man sees that suffering comes upon him, first he should examine his deeds, as it is written, "Let us search and examine our ways, and turn back to the Lord" (Lam. 3:40).

If he examines his deeds and finds no [justification for his suffering], let him consider the neglect of Torah [as the possible cause his suffering]. As it is written, "Happy is the man whom You discipline, O Lord, the man You instruct in Your teaching" (Ps. 94:12).

If he considers this and does not find [justification], he can be certain that these are sufferings of love, as it is written, "For whom the Lord loves, He rebukes, as a father the son whom He favors."[13]

Note that the primary concern of the Talmud in this discussion is anthropological rather than theological. This emphasis is characteristic of the general rabbinic approach to the problem of suffering. The stress is not on the philosophical problem of theodicy but on the human problem of enduring pain and finding a response that will encourage the individual to "sustain and give meaning to the covenantal relationship despite the mystery of suffering."[14]

How then, according to Rava, should the individual respond when confronted with tragedy? One should respond first through a process of personal reflection and repentance. According to both biblical and rabbinic tradition, some instances of suffering should be understood as punishment for, or consequence of, sin. The individual is urged to consider this possibility first. What have I done—either through misdeeds or through neglect of Torah—that might be causing or contributing to my current suffering? For many modern Jews, this idea is highly problematic, at least in its most literal formulation. The suggestion that our suffering may be a punishment from God seems both psychologically cruel and theologically untenable. But the idea of responding to tragedy by looking inward, by reflecting on changes that we might need to make in our lives, is one that still has enormous relevance and credibility and can be understood in a way that is more compatible with modern sensibilities. Thus, the above text can be interpreted as suggesting that we respond to tragedy by seeing it as a wake-up call, by engaging in serious soul-searching, and, specifically, by utilizing our suffering as "a catalyst for moral renewal."[15]

Rava's teaching, even literally understood, makes it clear that there is no simple equation of suffering and sin. In fact, the progression of the text is quite remarkable in this regard. The first response of the individual in pain should be one of self-reflection and, if necessary, *teshuvah* or repentance. But Rava places clear limits on the process of self-critical introspection. Having seriously considered one's failings, both in the realm of moral behavior and in the realm of Torah study, *the individual may reach the conclusion that his or her suffering is simply not justified.* In this case, self-blame must stop. "The individual may be *certain* that these are sufferings of love" (my italics). Thus, while implicitly acknowledging the uncertainty of all human interpretations of suffering, Rava concludes with an astounding declaration of certain consolation.

Rava's teaching reflects a strong tendency within the rabbinic tradition to recognize the "ethical or theological value of suffering, without assigning intrinsic value to suffering."[16] The following description of the martyrdom of Rabbi Akiva is one of the most radical expressions of the view that we can, through our response, give meaning to the experience of suffering. But even here, the Talmud stops short of seeing intrinsic value in the suffering of Rabbi Akiva:

> When they took Rabbi Akiva out to kill him, it was time for the recitation of the morning *shema*. As they were tearing his flesh from his body with metal combs, he began to intone the words of the *shema*. (Literally: "He accepted upon himself the yoke of the kingdom of heaven.") *Hear, O Israel, the Lord is our God, the Lord is One. And you shall love the Lord your God with all your heart, and with all your soul, and with all your might.*
>
> His students said to him, "Our rabbi, even now?"
>
> He said to them, "All my life I have been troubled by the phrase 'with all your soul'—meaning that you must offer your very soul [to God]. I said to myself, when will an opportunity come, that I might fulfill this commandment? Now it has come; should I not fulfill it? And he extended the word "one"—so that his soul departed while still saying the word "one."
>
> A heavenly voice came down and said, "Happy is Rabbi Akiva, for his soul departed with the word 'one.'"[17]

The tradition of *kiddush hashem*, Jewish martyrdom, is classically expressed in this passage about Rabbi Akiva's death at the hands of a Roman executioner. Rabbi Akiva gives ultimate meaning to his own suffering by suggesting that the mitsvah of *"b'chol naf-shecha"*—accepting the yoke of the kingdom of heaven "with all your soul"—can be fulfilled only in death. Yet, even here, it is Akiva's fulfillment of the mitsvah that is redemptive, and not the suffering that he is forced to endure.[18] This fact is particularly important because it denies any implication that the Roman executioner is somehow in cahoots with God, enacting, however perversely, a divine plan that necessitates Rabbi Akiva's death by torture.

The point becomes even more striking when we compare the ancient Talmudic account of Rabbi Akiva's death at the hands of the Romans with Wiesel's modern account of the murder of Jewish prisoners in Auschwitz at the hands of the Nazis. On the one hand, the two texts stand on opposite sides of a profound divide, for Rabbi Akiva affirms the possibility of a faith that Wiesel ultimately denies. On the other hand, there is a deep, and perhaps characteristically Jewish, commonality between the two texts, for neither asserts that such suffering is required or desired by God. The underlying view of suffering in both cases, then, is not one of intrinsic redemptive value. The executioner thus remains fully culpable for the suffering that he has inflicted, even as the victim struggles—either successfully or unsuccessfully—to find meaning in his own experience.

Christian Response

For Christians, the question of human suffering is primarily a theological question. The story of the crucifixion of Jesus Christ is central to our faith tradition. Clearly, we cannot begin to address the question of suffering without looking at the death and resurrection of Christ. What, then, does the crucifixion really mean for Christians?

Jesus Christ embodies redemption for Christians, but our understandings of this redemption are multifaceted. There is an understanding that Jesus assumed the role of the scapegoat (Lev. 16) and the Passover lamb (Ex. 12:21–23). In both cases, the image of the sacrificial animal is interpreted to support the notion that Jesus bore the sins of the community and died in our place. "The next day John the Baptist saw Jesus coming toward him and declared, 'Here is the Lamb of God who takes away the sin of the world!'" (Jn. 1:29)

Redemption through Jesus Christ includes an understanding that it is God's love that sent Jesus to be human, to take on our sins once and for all. "For God so loved the world that He gave His only begotten son, so that everyone who believes in him may not perish but may have eternal life" (Jn. 3:16). Christian redemption also relies on the resurrection of Jesus—by God—from the dead, asserting that through his resurrection, Jesus conquered death, thus breaking the hold that it has over us:

> Death has been swallowed up in victory. Where O Death, is your victory? Where, O death, is your sting? The sting of death is sin, and the power of sin is the law. But thanks be to God, who gives us the victory through our Lord Jesus Christ. (1 Cor. 15:54b–57)

Any individual Christian or Christian community may emphasize different aspects of the redemptive nature of the Christ event, but there is a clear consensus among Christians that Jesus Christ redeems us.

For Christians, Isaiah 53, one of the "Suffering Servant" passages in Isaiah, is the clearest scriptural text pointing to the suffering of Jesus as redemptive. This long, poetic passage about one who suffered for others is understood by Christians, reading retrospectively, to refer to Jesus Christ:

> *He was despised and rejected by others;*
> *a man of suffering and acquainted with infirmity;*
> *and as one from whom others hid their faces*
> *he was despised, and we held him of no account.*
> *Surely he has borne our infirmities*
> *and carried our diseases;*
> *yet we accounted him stricken,*
> *struck down by God, and afflicted.*
> *But he was wounded for our transgressions,*
> *crushed for our iniquities;*
> *upon him was the punishment that made us whole,*
> *and by his bruises we are healed.*
> *All we like sheep have gone astray;*
> *we have all turned to our own way,*
> *and the LORD has laid on him*

the iniquity of us all.
Yet it was the will of the LORD to crush him with pain.
When you make his life an offering for sin,
he shall see his offspring, and shall prolong his days;
through him the will of the LORD shall prosper
Out of his anguish he shall see light;
he shall find satisfaction through his knowledge.
The righteous one, my servant, shall make many
  righteous,
and he shall bear their iniquities.
Therefore I will allot him a portion with the great,
and he shall divide the spoil with the strong;
because he poured out himself to death,
and was numbered with the transgressors;
yet he bore the sin of many,
and made intercession for the transgressors. (Is. 53:3–6,
  10–12)

The suffering servant is innocent, yet he bears "the sins of many"; he is "wounded for our transgressions, crushed for our iniquities"; upon him rests "the punishment that made us whole"; "by his bruises we are healed." The suffering of this one, understood by Christians to be Jesus Christ, is clearly redemptive.

Jesus himself points to the necessity of his own suffering, first in predicting his death: "Then he began to teach them that the Son of Man must undergo great suffering, and be rejected by the elders, the chief priests, and the scribes, and be killed, and after three days rise again" (Mk. 8:31). Later, at the Last Supper with his disciples, Jesus emphasizes the redemptive significance of his own suffering. "For this is my blood of the covenant, which is poured out for many for the forgiveness of sins" (Mt. 26:28). Jesus also tells his disciples that they must suffer: "If any want to become my followers, let them take up their cross and follow me. For those who want to save their life will lose it, and those who lose their life for my sake, and for the sake of the gospel, will save it" (Mk. 8:34–35).

Dietrich Bonhoeffer, a German Christian theologian and pastor executed by the Nazis in World War II, addressed the question of human suffering by further elaborating and affirming the idea that Christian discipleship requires suffering.[19] For Bonhoeffer (following the theology of Martin Luther), suffering is a mark of the true Christian—not suffering per se, but suffering for the sake of Christ. Christians are not to seek suffering; rather, a cross awaits each of us, as part of our lives. Christians must "take up" their cross. This notion points to the importance of our response to suffering. To "take up" one's cross is to accept it, to carry it, not to avoid it. Bonhoeffer is clear that Christ's is the only suffering that leads to atonement, but he argues that Christians share in bearing the sins and burdens of the world.

Because to follow Jesus is to suffer, suffering "is a joy and a token of [Christ's] grace."[20] From here, Bonhoeffer goes on to suggest that in some way those who are in communion with God cannot really suffer, because to suffer is to be cut off from God. Jesus has taken this separation on himself through his suffering; therefore, we no longer must endure the separation. "As it follows him beneath the cross, the Church stands before God as the representative of the world."[21] Bonhoeffer subtly points to the suffering of both individual Christians and the church, the community of Christians.

For Bonhoeffer, there is a clear sense that the truest mark of discipleship is suffering; in other words, suffering is a sign of faithfulness. This is a somewhat dangerous path to embark upon, one that potentially leads to self-martyrdom, to the seeking out of suffering. It is important to remember that in Mark 8, Jesus tells his followers that they must "take up *their* cross," the one that belongs to them, not that they must seek out a cross. The clear implication is that everyone has a cross, that some suffering will be part of our lives. Instead of seeking suffering, we must "take up" the suffering that comes to us. This idea resonates with what we know to be true: We cannot live a life without suffering. By extension, our response to suffering (how it is that we take it up) is crucial.

An additional New Testament text offers significant insight into the role of suffering for Christians. Paul writes in Romans 5:3–5:

> And not only that, but we also boast in our sufferings, knowing that suffering produces endurance, and endurance produces character, and character produces hope, and hope does not disappoint us, because God's love has been poured into our hearts through the Holy Spirit that has been given to us.

Paul maintains that there is a progression that begins with suffering and leads to hope, not just any hope, but a hope that will not disappoint, because God's love has been given to us through the Holy Spirit. Taken together with the admonishment that one must "take up one's cross" in order to follow Jesus, there is a clear call here for Christians to endure suffering, knowing that it will lead to character and hope.

In a letter to another early Christian community, Paul writes: "No testing has overtaken you that is not common to everyone. God is faithful, and [God] will not let you be tested beyond your strength, but with the testing [God] will also provide the way out so that you may be able to endure it" (1 Cor. 10:13). "Testing" is sometimes translated as "temptation," but it is not translated as "suffering." Yet this is a common interpretation and understanding of this text. Paul clearly is writing to provide encouragement to communities of new Christians who are suffering; he casts their suffering into the realm of "testing." He wants them to know that suffering is part of the Christian life, that God will use the suffering to produce endurance, character, and hope, and that God will not allow them to suffer beyond what they can bear.

It is clear in Christian theology that suffering is not simply a punishment for sin. Not only has Jesus taken our sins upon him, offering us redemption and forgiveness, but there is also a sense that suffering is part of the life of a Christian.

Offering Comfort and Consolation

Jewish Response

The problem of justifying suffering becomes even more acute when we are confronted not with our own suffering but with the suffering of another. The following text from the Talmud complicates the teaching by Rava cited earlier in this chapter. In fact, it is most likely a self-conscious reflection on that teaching, for it appears just a few lines later on the same page of the Talmud:

> R. Eleazar ben Pedat fell ill, and R. Yohanan came to visit him. When
> R. Yohanan saw that R. Eleazar was lying in a dark room, he bared

his arm and light radiated from it. Then he noticed that R. Eleazar was weeping. So he asked, "Why are you weeping? Is it because you did not study enough Torah? Surely we have learned: 'The one who does much and the one who does little have the same merit, and provided that their hearts are directed to Heaven.' Is it perhaps because of your meager livelihood? Not everybody has the privilege of enjoying two tables: one of Torah and one of wealth. Is it perhaps because of [your lack of] children? Here is the bone of my tenth son!"[22]

R. Eleazar replied, "I am weeping on account of this beauty of yours,[23] which will in the end waste away in the earth." R. Yohanan: "On that account, you surely have good reason to weep." And they both wept.

Presently, R. Yohanan asked him, "Are your sufferings cherished by you?" R. Eleazar replied, "Neither they nor the reward for them." R. Yohanan: "Give me your hand." R. Eleazar gave him his hand, and R. Yohanan raised him up [out of bed]. (B. Ber. 5b)

This poignant story of two friends, both leading rabbis of their generation, further humanizes the rabbinic discussion about suffering. It subtly turns our attention to the question of consolation. We become concerned not simply with the response of the individual confronted by tragedy, but with the role of the friend coming to offer comfort. Here a strong distinction is made. Whereas an individual may ask whether his or her own suffering is the result of sin, this is emphatically not the role of the comforter. The person seeking to offer consolation must be willing to be in the presence of another's pain, without attempting to justify it or explain it away. *"And they both wept."* Nothing more or less is asked of the friend offering comfort.

The act of justifying another's suffering is not only emotionally unhelpful; it is ethically and theologically dangerous. This point is made most strongly perhaps in the Book of Job, a sustained reflection on the mystery of human suffering. As the subject of a wager between God and Satan, Job is forced to endure what most of us would consider unendurable suffering. He loses everything: first his possessions, next his children, and finally his own health, when he is afflicted with a horrible and painful skin disease. In the midst of these trials, Job is visited by several friends, each of whom tries, in one way or another, to convince him that he must have done something to deserve the suffering that has befallen him. It is, in part, their simple equation of sin and suffering, their assertion of divine justice in the face of Job's painful experience of apparent injustice, that finally breaks Job's spirit and causes him to cry out against God. The climax of the book is God's response to Job out of the whirlwind, in which Job is rebuked for having bitterly questioned God's justice. Yet, significantly, just a few verses later, it is Job's friends who are rebuked: "After the Lord had spoken these words to Job, the Lord said to Eliphaz the Temanite, 'I am incensed at you and your two friends, for you have not spoken the truth about Me as did My servant Job'" (Job 42:7).

Commenting on this verse, Solomon Freehof, a contemporary theologian writes:

> Now the friends are rebuked for being unjust to Job in declaring him to be sinful when they had no evidence of any wrong he had committed. God says to the friends, "You have not spoken of Me the thing that is right." That is to say: It is well that men should try to demonstrate My righteousness, but to defend My righteousness on the basis of what is untrue is an injustice to Me. You defended Me with falsehood. But Job spoke what is right, though he spoke bitterly. The friends had accused Job of what they did not know is true, namely, his supposed sin. Job insisted upon what he knew was true, namely, his innocence.[24]

Another rabbinic text cites Job's friends as an example of precisely what one should not do when speaking to a person who is afflicted by illness or other personal tragedy:

> Just as there is overreaching in trade, so too is there oppression in words, and moreover, oppression by words is [a] greater [wrong] than oppression with money. . . . If illness and sufferings were coming upon him, or if he buries his children [who have died prematurely], one should not speak to him as Job's colleagues spoke to him.[25]

The message is clear. Although we can and should seek to find meaning in our own suffering, we are forbidden to justify the suffering of another. Not only does our obligation to offer comfort to the person in pain override our obligation to defend God's justice, but also we, in fact, can never know the reason for human suffering. In the face of this uncertainty, asking what we might have done to bring suffering upon ourselves is an act of profound humility. Asking what another might have done to bring suffering upon him/herself is an act of supreme arrogance.

Christian Response

Although Christian theology has attempted to make meaning out of suffering, the fundamental questions raised by the reality of suffering still remain. There is too much evidence that people do suffer more than they can bear; there is too much evidence of suffering that does not eventually lead to a hope that will not disappoint. How do we find comfort, even while accepting that some of our questions can never be fully answered?

The Reverend William Sloan Coffin struggled with many of these unanswered questions in the days following the death of his son, Alex; his struggle was shared publicly in a sermon preached the Sunday after Alex's death.[26] Coffin is clear that this death was not the will of God: "Never do we know enough to say that. My own consolation lies in knowing that it was not the will of God that Alex die; that when the wave closed over the sinking car, God's heart was the first of all our hearts to break."[27]

There is no seeking out of suffering here. This is a heartbroken man, struggling to make sense of a senseless tragedy. There is acceptance that he must now live with the death of his twenty-four-year-old son; there is also a poignant movement toward consolation through the presence of others: "people who only want to hold your hand, not to quote anybody or even say anything, people who simply bring food and flowers—the basics of beauty and life—people who sign letters simply, 'Your broken-hearted sister.'"[28] There will also be consolation, Coffin knows, in the learning, although the learning, and therefore the consolation, will not come yet. Such learning, such consolation, can come only with time. And he says that the learning "better be good, given the price."[29] So, too, is there consolation in words of Scripture, not always the ones shared easily by his colleagues but those that speak of the reality of grief and pain.[30] Finally, Coffin concludes his sermon affirming that he—and we—shall "seek consolation in that love which never dies, and find peace in the dazzling grace that always is."

Discussion Questions

1. How do you respond to the image of "God hanging on the gallows" in the passage from Elie Wiesel's Holocaust memoir, *Night*?
2. Has the Holocaust had a strong influence on your own thinking about the problem of suffering?
3. Can you think of a time in your life when you felt betrayed or abandoned by God? What was going on in your life to cause those feelings? How did that feeling of abandonment or betrayal change over time?
4. Knowing that many people have suffered more than they can bear, how do you understand Paul's words in 1 Corinthians 10:13?
5. When, if ever, have you seen "good" to come from suffering in your life?
6. How has suffering or tragedy in your experience changed you?
7. What have you learned from suffering in your life?
8. What types of responses from other people have you found most helpful or comforting during times of crisis?
9. Is making or finding some meaning in suffering the same thing as redemption?

Notes

1. David Hartman, "Suffering," in *Contemporary Jewish Religious Thought*, ed. Arthur A. Cohen and Paul Mendes-Flohr (New York: The Free Press, A Division of Macmillan, Inc., 1988), 945.

2. See reference to M. Brod's two-volume work entitled *Heidentum, Christentum, Judentum* (1921) in "Suffering," *Encyclopedia Judaica*, vol. 15 (Jerusalem: Keter Publishing House, 1971–1972), 485–486.

3. Redemption itself is a complex and multifaceted concept in both Jewish and Christian thought. For a fuller discussion of the idea of redemption, see Chapter 9.

4. Robert Gibbs, "Suffering," in *Christianity in Jewish Terms*, ed. Tikva Frymer-Kensky, David Novak, Peter Ochs, David Fox Sandmel, and Michael A. Signer (Boulder, Colo.: Westview Press, 2000), 221.

5. Elie Wiesel, *Night* (New York: Avon Books, 1960), 75–76.

6. Rabbi Irving Greenberg, "Cloud of Smoke, Pillar of Fire: Judaism, Christianity, and Modernity After the Holocaust," in *Auschwitz, Beginning of a New Era?* ed. Eva Fleischner (New York: KTAV, 1977), 25.

7. François Mauriac, Forward to Wiesel, *Night*, 10–11.

8. See Gibbs, "Suffering," 221, for his discussion of contemporary and traditional Jewish attitudes toward suffering.

9. All biblical references in the Jewish responses are from the Jewish Publication Society translation. All biblical references in the Christian responses are from the New Revised Standard Version.

10. See Genesis 15:13.

11. See Exodus 22:20. There are numerous references to this principle in the Hebrew Bible.

12. Hartman, "Suffering" 944.

13. B. Ber. 5b, translation by Sharon Cohen Anisfeld.

14. See discussion of this issue in Hartman, "Suffering," 944.

15. Ibid.

16. Leora Batnitsky, "Suffering," in Frymer-Kensky et al., *Christianity in Jewish Terms*, 205.

17. B. Ber. 61b, translation by Sharon Cohen Anisfeld. Akiva lived from approximately 50–135 C.E. and was one of the foremost scholars of his age. He supported the Bar Kochba revolt against Rome in 132 C.E. and was first imprisoned and later tortured to death by the Romans for openly teaching the Torah in defiance of their edict.

18. *Mitsvah* literally means commandment and refers to the religious obligations of a Jew as defined by the Torah and rabbinic law.

19. Dietrich Bonhoeffer, "Discipleship and the Cross," in *The Cost of Discipleship*, 2d ed. (New York: The Macmillan Company, 1959), 76–83.

20. Bonhoeffer, "Discipleship and the Cross," 81. A simple yet significant definition of grace stands with the definition of mercy. Mercy is when God does not give us what we deserve; grace is when God gives us what we do not deserve.

21. Ibid., 82.

22. According to the Talmud, Rabbi Yohanan had ten sons, all of whom died.

23. According to the Talmud, Rabbi Yohanan was a man of legendary beauty.

24. Solomon Freehof, *Book of Job: A Commentary* (New York: Union of American Hebrew Congregations, 1958), 261.

25. *The Tosefta*, as cited in Batnitsky, "Suffering," 219.

26. William Sloane Coffin, "Alex's Death," in *A Chorus of Witnesses: Model Sermons for Today's Preacher*, ed. Thomas G. Long and Cornelius Plantinga Jr. (Grand Rapids, Mich.: William B. Eerdman's Publishing Company, 1994), 262–266. William Sloane Coffin is a contemporary preacher and theologian; he served as chaplain of Yale University and pastor of Riverside Church in New York City.

27. Ibid., 264.
28. Ibid.
29. Ibid., 265.
30. On page 266, Coffin cites several specific verses of Scripture that spoke to him of consolation. He quotes the King James Version. "Cast thy burden upon the Lord and He shall strengthen thee" (Ps. 55:22); "Weeping may endure for a night, but joy cometh in the morning" (Ps. 30:5); "Lord, by thy favor thou hast made my mountain to stand strong" (Ps. 30:7); "For thou has delivered my soul from death, mine eyes from tears, and my feet from falling" (Ps 116:8); "In this world ye shall have tribulation, but be of good cheer; I have overcome the world" (Jn. 16:33); "The light shines in the darkness, and the darkness has not overcome it" (Jn. 1:5).

8

How Do Jews and Christians Understand Sin and Repentance?

JANE WEST WALSH,

MARY KATHERINE ALLMAN,

CHRISTOPHER M. LEIGHTON,

ROSANN M. CATALANO, AND

DAVID FOX SANDMEL

This chapter is a collaborative endeavor that has evolved through an attempt to answer three questions: (1) What is unique in each of our tradition's understandings of sin and repentance? (2) Where did these ideas come from? (3) How are these teachings embodied in the liturgies of each tradition?

A Jewish Understanding of Sin and Repentance

For thousands of years, the Jewish people have confronted sin and repentance most tangibly, both individually and communally, on Yom Kippur, the Day of Atonement.[1] Yom Kippur is considered the most awe-inspiring day of the Jewish calendar year. In ancient Israel, the well-being of the nation was dependent upon its fulfillment of the covenant. When the Second Temple still stood in Jerusalem, and the *kohanim* (priests) conducted regular routines of sacrifice, atonement for the various sins of the Jewish people was achieved through an elaborate ritual of cleansing and sacrifice. The *kohen gadol* (high priest) confessed the sins on behalf of the entire Jewish community. He symbolically placed these sins upon the head of a goat that was then sent into the wilderness, understood to be an inaccessible region.[2]

In 70 C.E., when the Romans destroyed the Second Temple, the priestly rituals of sacrifice and the traditions that had been carried out by the kohanim and the kohen gadol on behalf of the people ended. Since that time, animals have not been sacrificed nor sent into the wilderness on behalf of the Jewish people. The role of communal leadership exercised by the kohanim eventually died out. By the second century C.E., what is now called rabbinic Judaism was emerging as the authoritative interpretation of Jewish life and tradition. Under the leadership of generations of rabbis, what was once an ancient sacrificial tradition developed into a rich tradition of individual and communal prayer. According to this tradition, Jews pray three times each day: once in the morning, once in the afternoon, and once in the evening. Except on the Sabbath,[3] a prayer for forgiveness of sins is included in the *amidah*, a fundamental section recited during each of these daily services.

With the Torah, written and oral, as a guide, rabbinic Judaism has taught that atonement for transgressions or sins, once carried out by priests, is now the responsibility of the Jewish people themselves. Today, Jews understand atonement as an obligation that is carried out by each individual, and just as importantly, by each individual as a member of the Jewish community. *Tefilah* or prayer, *tsedakah*, the giving of one's personal wealth on behalf of others, and *teshuvah* (repentance) are responses to sin that, when done with the appropriate intention, demonstrate sincere repentance and can lead to God's forgiveness.

One Jewish tradition records three categories of wrongdoing. Commenting on the phrase "forgiving iniquity, transgression and sin" (Lev. 16:21), the Talmud assigns each term a different value. "Iniquity" *(avon)* is a deliberate wrong or misdeed; "transgression *(peshah)* is a rebellious deed; and "sin" *(chet)* is an inadvertent omission or "missing the mark."[4] These distinctions help convey the idea that transgressions have different levels of seriousness and consequence.[5]

A famous text in Mishnah Yoma states: "For transgressions *(averot)* between an individual and the Omnipresent, the Day of Atonement atones. For transgressions between one individual and another, the Day of Atonement atones only if the transgressor will regain the good will of his fellow."[6] The phrase "transgressions between an individual and the Omnipresent" is usually understood to refer to the violation of a ritual law (such as the dietary regulations or Sabbath regulations) that does not involve harming another person. Since there are only two parties involved, the sinner and God, sincere repentance before God (using the appropriate liturgy and ritual) for this kind of transgression is sufficient. However, when another person has been harmed, the sinner must seek forgiveness and make amends to the other person. Then, and only then, can God's forgiveness be sought.

Teshuvah literally means "returning." It is the way Jews respond to an awareness that they have done wrong. It is a process of turning away from wrong action, transgression, or sin and at the same time turning toward a right relationship with God and fellow human beings. It is also the recognition that one's behavior both toward God and toward other people (indeed, toward all of creation) can imperil the covenantal relationship that binds both the Jew as an individual and the Jews as a people to God. Over and over again, the master story of the Jewish people, recorded in the Torah and in rabbinic and other sacred literature, teaches the Jewish people that their actions and choices cause them to come closer to God. Likewise, people's actions and choices can also cause them to become more distant from God, and in need of repentance. It is the awareness of the distance and separation between God and people, between one person and another, and between who we are and who we are supposed to be that calls Jews to begin the process of teshuvah.

The great Jewish scholar Maimonides (1135–1204 C.E.) focused on teshuvah in one volume of his monumental work, the *Mishneh Torah*. In this volume, referred to by its Hebrew name, *Hilchot Teshuvah* (Laws of Repentance), Maimonides records the collective wisdom of the generations that preceded him. He discusses repentance and how one is to achieve it in great detail. Here is an example:

> 2:1 Who has reached complete *teshuvah*? A person who confronts the same situation in which he sinned when he has the potential to commit the sin again, and nevertheless, abstains and does not commit it because of his *teshuvah* alone and not because of fear or a lack of strength. For example, a person engaged in illicit relations with a woman. Afterwards, they met in privacy, in the same country, while his love for her and physical power still persisted, and nevertheless, he abstained and did not transgress. . . .
>
> 2:2 What constitutes *teshuvah*? That a sinner should abandon his sins and remove them from his thoughts, resolving in his heart never to commit them again as Isaiah 55:7 states: "May the wicked abandon his ways. . . ." Similarly, he must regret the past as Jeremiah 31:18 states: "After I returned, I regretted." . . . One must verbally confess and state these matters which he has resolved in his heart.

Teshuvah is a lifelong process, and one can repent at any time. Indeed, the rabbis teach that the "gates of repentance" are always open. However, there is one special forty-day season within the Jewish calendar year when the central theme is teshuvah. The thirty days of the month of Elul, the last month of the Jewish calendar year, is a month of personal and communal reflection. This month is followed by a period called the Ten Days of Repentance *(aseret yemei teshuvah)*, also known as the Days of Awe *(yamim nora'im)*. The first of the ten days is Rosh Hashanah, the New Year;[7] the tenth day is Yom Kippur, the Day of Atonement itself. Rosh Hashanah also commemorates the creation of the world. At the end of the creation narrative in Genesis 1, God judges the world to be very good. But the sinful actions of humans threaten to return the world to chaos. Repentance is the effort to return the world to its ordered, peaceful, holy state.

Confessional Prayers Within the Jewish Tradition

Reading the *Vidui,* the section of confessional prayers from the Yom Kippur service that includes the *Ashamnu* and *Al Chet* prayers, illuminates key aspects of the Jewish response to sin, characterized by the process of teshuvah.[8] Reciting these prayers in unison in the synagogue on Yom Kippur is a communal and public process, in which Jews, both as individuals and as a community, ask God for forgiveness. The actual recitation is one step in the process of teshuvah. Studying these prayers is also one way to gain insight into what Judaism considers to be wrong behaviors and actions.

Our God and God of our ancestors, hear our prayer; do not ignore our plea. We are neither so brazen nor so arrogant to claim that we are righteous, without sin, for indeed we have sinned.

The Ashamnu prayer (short form of the Vidui)

We abuse, we betray, we are cruel. We destroy, we embitter, we falsify. We gossip, we hate, we insult. We jeer, we kill, we lie. We mock, we neglect, we oppress. We pervert, we quarrel, we rebel. We steal, we transgress, we are unkind. We are violent, we are wicked, we are xenophobic. We yield to evil, we are zealots for bad causes.

We have ignored your commandments and statutes, but it has not profited us. You are just, we have stumbled. You have acted faithfully, we have been unrighteous. What can we say to You; what can we tell You? You know everything secret and revealed. You know the mysteries of the universe, the secrets of everyone alive. You probe our innermost depths, You examine our thoughts and desires. Nothing escapes You, nothing is hidden from You. May it be therefore Your will, Lord our God and God of our ancestors, to forgive us all our sins, to pardon all our iniquities, to grant us atonement for all our transgressions.

The Al Chet prayer (long form of the Vidui)

We have sinned against You unwillingly and willingly. And we have sinned against You by misusing our minds. We have sinned against You through sexual immorality. And we have sinned against You knowingly and deceitfully. We have sinned against You by wronging others. And we have sinned against You through prostitution. We have sinned against you by deriding parents and teachers. And we have sinned against you by using violence. We have sinned against

You through foul speech. And we have sinned against You by not re-sisting the impulse to evil.

For all these sins, forgiving God, forgive us, pardon us, grant us atonement. We have sinned against You by fraud and falsehood. And we have sinned against You by scoffing. We have sinned against You by dishonesty in business. And we have sinned against You by usuri-ous interest. We have sinned against You by idle chatter. And we have sinned against You by haughtiness. We have sinned against You by re-jecting responsibility. And we have sinned against You by plotting against others. We have sinned against You by irreverence. And we have sinned against You by rushing to do evil. We have sinned against You by false oaths. And we have sinned against You by breach of trust.

For all these sins, forgiving God, forgive us, pardon us, grant us atonement.[9]

Note that the Vidui is a series of verbs and verb phrases, each written in the first-person plural—("we have . . . "), an expression of the idea that we are a community of Jews, responsible to each other, standing together before God in a repentant posture, asking for forgiveness. These prayers are written as acrostics; each word or phrase begins with the subsequent letter of the Hebrew alphabet so that in each prayer the entire alphabet is spelled out in order.[10] Al-though this practice demonstrates the liturgist's poetic skills, it also implies that these confessional prayers cover any sins that people could possibly think of, as in the English expression "from A to Z." Reading the list gives shape and form to the difficult idea of how we miss the mark. However, we are not to assume that every Jew has committed every one of these particular sins. Reciting these prayers aloud, repeatedly, together as a community of penitent individuals, is a way to help Jews understand that the nature of sin and trans-gression is both personal and communal. The impact of sin and repentance, then, touches us all.

For some Jews, reciting the Yom Kippur confessional prayers also has a physical dimension. The Ashamnu is traditionally recited while beating one's chest over the heart (lightly) with the right hand at the recitation of each sin. Such a public confession of sin along with one stroke of the hand to the chest is a reminder that goes to one's very bones. It is not meant to be physically painful. However, the repetition of this action and the symbolism of "beating one's breast" as a sign of contrition can heighten the process of reflection and teshuvah, especially since it is done in the midst of the Yom Kippur daylong fast. This fast begins at sundown, when Yom Kippur begins, and lasts until the following sunset. Fasting on Yom Kippur can be understood in several ways. Like beating one's breast, it is symbolized contrition. Some suggest that it is also a demonstration to oneself and to God that it is possible to control the appetites. It is also a way of helping those at prayer to focus their intention on the work of teshuvah.

The process of teshuvah, of fasting, confession, prayer, and reconciliation, underscores the Jewish idea that we have the free will to make choices. When we make the wrong choices, we have the opportunity and the obligation to reach out to those we have wronged and to (re)turn to God as a source of forgiveness, renewal, and strength.

Sin and Repentance in Christian Thought and Practice

Christian conceptions of sin emerge against the backdrop of two fundamental claims. On the one hand, Christians maintain that God created the world and that the results of this divine initiative are good through and through. As a consequence, this world is not an accident, nor is it the flawed handiwork of an inept deity. Christians further believe that the grandeur and beauty of the creation continues to carry traces of the divine. On the other hand, even as Christians insist that God did a wondrous good when God created the universe and all that dwells therein, they also note that something has gone dreadfully awry. The world around us is filled with injustice and poverty, suffering and death. Creation is not a mirror image of God's goodness, nor is the world in complete accord with God's purposes.

Sin is the central concept that Christians use to name the gap between God's good creation and the fact that the world is a mess. Christians claim that sin is not an evil that can be attributed to God or any other supernatural agency. Sin comes into the world as a consequence of human freedom that has run amok. Sin is sometimes linked with an act of disobedience, and sometimes traced to a failure to assume responsibility for one's deeds. Sin is sometimes said to emerge from the human bid for power and control, and sometimes from humanity's refusal to acknowledge its relationship, and especially its indebtedness, to the transcendent. All attempts to understand sin and to account for its origins entail imaginative leaps. Christian speculation moves between biblical stories like Genesis and the more abstract and elaborate formulations of theologians. In the final analysis, Christians concede that they cannot explain sin or account for its intrusion into God's creation. Sin is real, and it is a given. It is a reality that Christians believe they must face. Finally and decisively, sin must be overcome.

Why can't people simply accept sin and learn to live with its imperfections? The reason goes to the heart of the Christian faith. Christians maintain that we were created to be in relationship with one another, with the world, and with God. Sin separates and divides us, making genuine respect and mutuality impossible. Sin is the concept that Christians use to describe a condition of brokenness, alienation, despair, unbridled desire, and absolute self-absorption. Sin is described as stemming from the misguided exercise of human freedom, and the consequences of one person's choices reverberate far and wide. In the words of Exodus 34.7, "the iniquity of parents is visited upon the children and children's children." Indeed, in the Christian imagination, the impact of our transgressions is more extreme than the view in Exodus, for sin is not necessarily brought to an end after three or four generations. The wrongs that we commit often become etched into the structures of family and society. Violations against the environment, for example, can leave an enduring stain on the creation. The habits of exploitation become the way business is done, and the legacy of sexism and racism lives on in both societal and church structures. For better and for worse, we inherit a world that has come to us already shaped by the good, the bad, and the ugly. This awareness undergirds the Christian notion of "original sin."

So understood, sin is not simply a problem that we can solve by therapy, technology, or better social engineering. People are incapable of fixing what is broken, and for two reasons. First, they are unable to change the mistakes of the past. What is done cannot be undone, and people do not have the power to erase the past and start all over again with a clean slate. Second, sin is sustained by self-deception. We are ensnared by a failure to comprehend the depth and breadth of the human plight because sin makes us captives of our own self-regard. In the words of John Calvin, sin curves us in upon ourselves and distorts our vision. Self-absorbed, we cannot take an accurate measure of what is wrong. Sin clouds our perceptions of ourselves, of others, and, most fundamentally, of our relationship with God.

What then do Christians think is necessary to overcome the predicament? Christians believe that sin is so pervasive, its power so grave, that, on their own, people cannot clean up the mess they have both inherited and contributed to. The magnitude and depth of the problem requires nothing less than a God who would step into the fray.

Christians have traditionally understood that God has saved the world from sin through Jesus Christ, and therefore to be saved one must believe in Jesus Christ. An increasing number of contemporary Christians find this view problematic and so are developing new ways of thinking about God, sin, and repentance. They acknowledge that God has confronted the problem of sin in different ways with different peoples. The covenant between God and the people Israel holds redemptive power over sin because God has given Jews a way of life (Torah) that enables them to right relationships with God and others when they go awry. The Christian path follows a different, albeit related, pattern of living. Christians believe that God has invited them into a covenantal partnership through the person of Jesus Christ. Whereas Jews traditionally believe that God concentrated his presence in a book (Torah), a land (Zion), and a people (the Jews), Christians maintain that God limited God's self in a radically new way by manifesting his presence in the person of Jesus. By means of the Incarnation, God experienced the entire spectrum of what it means to be human and participated fully in this reality. On the cross, Jesus encountered the pain and desolation that people endure in the midst of affliction. Suffering overwhelms one's awareness of everything, leaving one in complete isolation—alienated from self, from others, and from God. Christians believe that this is what Jesus experienced on the cross, and through Jesus, God also experienced the depths of pain. Knowing the absolute and utter desolation of human suffering as never before, God responds to Jesus' death by raising him to new life. In so doing, God establishes the hope that nothing—neither sin nor death—can separate us from God. This is the fundamental affirmation of the Christian doctrine of the Resurrection.

Why do Christians need Jesus Christ to save them? To Christians, this question registers as analogous to the query "Why do Jews need to be liberated from Egypt?" Christians believe that Jesus Christ freed them from the bondage of sin and defined a new way to embody a covenantal life that resists despair and oppression. Every Passover, Jews experience liberation from bondage through the reenactment of the Exodus in the Seder. Every Easter, Christians experience liberation by entering into the life, death, and resurrection of Jesus. The Christian move from enslavement to freedom is perhaps most decisively expressed in baptism, the liturgical practice that makes and defines the Christian.

Baptism takes place within the context of public worship and is one of the most formative moments in the life of a Christian. It is an ancient ritual that from earliest times shaped both Christian practice and the Christian imagination. Although baptism has undergone adaptations over time, two basic emphases have endured: It is the ritual by which (1) an individual becomes a member of the Christian community and (2) is freed from "original sin."

For an understanding of baptism, we begin with a text written by the apostle Paul to the church at Rome about 55–57 C.E.[11] Romans 6:3–11 occupies a central place in the formation of the Christian identity. It is one of the scriptural texts read at the Easter Vigil, and it is a key text for understanding the relationship between baptism and sin:

> Do you not know that we who have been baptized into Christ Jesus were baptized into his death? Therefore, through our baptism into his death we have been buried with him, so that, just as Christ was raised from the dead by the glory of God, so we too might live a new life. For if we have been united with Christ in his death, we certainly have been united with him in his resurrection. This we know: our old self was crucified with Christ so that we might no longer be enslaved to sin. And if we have died with Christ, we believe that we also live with Christ. We know that Christ, being raised from the dead, will never die again; death no longer has dominion over him. His death was death to sin, once for all; and his life is life in God. In the same way,

consider yourselves dead to sin and alive in God in Christ Jesus. (Rom. 6:3–11)

Paul's logic goes something like this.

1. To be baptized is first and foremost to be baptized *into* Christ. For Paul, the church is the body of Christ, that is, the living presence of the risen Christ in the world. Thus, to be baptized *into* Christ is to become a member of that body, which is the church. Baptism joins Christians to generations past and yet to come in the life of a single community that itself is bound to the risen Lord. This identification is absolutely essential for Christian self-understanding.

2. The consequence of being baptized *into* Christ Jesus is that one thereby participates in all that happened to Christ Jesus. To be baptized *into* Christ is thus to die with him, to be buried with him, and, so too, to be raised up with him by the power of the living God.

3. To participate in all that happened to Jesus Christ is to die with him. What does Paul mean when he says that we have "died" with Christ? What of us has "died"? For Paul, it is the "old self," the self born into a sinful world. Christians believe that every human being is born into a history that already carries the consequences of human freedom run amok. It is this sinful self that is crucified with Christ and dies.

4. The "new" self that is raised up with Christ is a self "no longer enslaved to sin." Because God raised the dead Jesus to *new and eternal* life, the Risen One can die no more. By this act, God has broken for all time the grip death holds over life—Christ's life, our life, and, indeed, *all* life. *Nothing*, Paul tells us further in Romans, can separate us from the love of God: "Neither death, nor life, nor angels, nor rulers, nor things present, nor things to come, nor powers, nor height, nor depth, nor anything else in all creation, will be able to separate us from the love of God in Christ Jesus our Lord" (Rom. 8:37–39).

5. Because sin separates us from God, sin and death are synonymous for Paul. But because God in Jesus Christ has con-

quered death, sin, too, has been conquered. So, for Paul, to be baptized *into* Christ is to be raised up with him and to live a *resurrected* life.

The Ritual: Baptism, the Rite of Christian Initiation

The ideas embedded in Romans find expression in the rite of baptism in most Christian denominations. Here we will examine the ritual as practiced in the Roman Catholic Church, assuming, for the sake of the example, that the person being baptized is a young girl. After a word of welcome, Romans 6:3–11 is read. Just prior to the act of baptizing, the priest blesses the baptismal water. Here is a portion of that prayer:

> Father, . . . at the very dawn of creation your Spirit breathed on the waters, making them the wellspring of all holiness.
>
> The waters of the great flood you made a sign of the waters of baptism, that make an end of sin and a new beginning of goodness.
>
> Through the waters of the Red Sea you led Israel out of slavery, to be an image of God's holy people, set free from sin by baptism.
>
> In the waters of the Jordan your Son was baptized by John and anointed with the Spirit.
>
> . . . You created us in your own likeness: cleanse this child from sin in a new birth to innocence by water and the Spirit.
>
> We ask you, Father, with your Son to send the Holy Spirit upon the water of this font. May all who are buried with Christ in the death of baptism rise also with him to newness of life. We ask this through Christ our Lord.

At the conclusion of this prayer, the priest baptizes the child, saying: "I baptize you in the name of the Father, and of the Son, and of the Holy Spirit." Each time he invokes one of the divine names, he places the child in the water, so that baptism in fact entails a triple immersion. After the third immersion, the priest then offers another prayer.

> God the Father of our Lord Jesus Christ has freed you from sin, given you a new birth by water and the Holy Spirit, and welcomed you into his holy people.

> You have become a new creation, and have clothed yourself in Christ.
> You have put on Christ,
> in him you have been baptized.
> Alleluia, Alleluia.

> Dearly beloved, this child has been reborn in baptism. She is now called the child of God, for so indeed she is.

> By God's gift, through water and the Holy Spirit, we are reborn to everlasting life. In his goodness, may he continue to pour out his blessings upon this daughter of his. May he make her always, wherever she may be, a faithful member of his holy people. May he send his peace upon all who are gathered here, in Christ Jesus our Lord.

Repentance

Baptism opens the door to a new condition of freedom. Yet, the world in which Christians find themselves is a work in progress. The structures of injustice and suffering continue to pull Christians away from their new life, and invariably Christians squander the opportunity to live in solidarity with others and God. To resist the despair and disillusionment that come from their failings, Christians depend on God's forgiveness. Once again Christians come to their understanding of the dynamics of repentance and forgiveness by directing attention to both the person of Jesus and the teachings of their Scriptures. A pattern that we encountered in Mishnah Yoma is also expressed in Jesus' Sermon on the Mount.

> So when you are offering your gift at the altar, if you remember that your brother or sister has something against you, leave your gift there

before the altar and go; first be reconciled to your brother or sister, and then come and offer your gift. (Mt. 5:22–23)

Repentance cannot occur without the encounter between the offender and the offended, and this face-to-face exchange comes prior to ritual worship. In this text we find a familiar order of repentance: There can be no appeal to God that sidesteps the obligation to set things right with one's neighbor. Although this process of repentance is deeply etched into Christian life and practice, the Gospels preserve a second model for the restoration of damaged relations that also has its roots in the life and teachings of Jesus. The following story captures a contrasting model, one that places forgiveness prior to repentance. This second approach helps illuminate an enduring tension within the Christian tradition between two different understandings of repentance and forgiveness.

Early in the morning he came again to the temple. All the people came to him and he sat down and began to teach them. The scribes and the Pharisees brought a woman who had been caught in adultery; and making her stand before all of them, they said to him, "Teacher, this woman was caught in the very act of committing adultery. Now in the law Moses commanded us to stone such women. Now what do you say?" . . . When they kept on questioning him, he straightened up and said to them, "Let anyone among you who is without sin be the first to throw a stone at her." . . . When they heard it, they went away, one by one, beginning with the elders; and Jesus was left alone with the woman standing before him. Jesus straightened up and said to her, "Woman, where are they? Has no one condemned you?" She said, "No one, sir." And Jesus said, "Neither do I condemn you. Go your way, and from now on do not sin again." (Jn. 8:1–11)

This incident presented Jesus with a violation that undermines the honor of the family and imperils the covenantal bonds with God. The seriousness of this sin stemmed from the connection the Hebrew Scriptures make between adultery and idolatry (e.g., Jer. 3:1–5). Both entail behaviors that damage a fundamental trust and threaten the prospects of ongoing fidelity. For this reason, the sin of adultery was met with decisive and public punishment (e.g., Lev. 20:10).

By protecting her from the prescribed punishment, what was Jesus doing? Was he failing to hold her accountable? Was he dispensing forgiveness without the demands or even expectations of repentance? This reading is hard to square with the conclusion of the story. Jesus reasserted the communal standard of fidelity when he instructed the woman to sin no more. At the same time, Jesus advanced an argument that everyone in the community is a sinner. No one can point a self-righteous finger at others as though either the individual or the community is blameless.

Jesus' action toward this sinner suggests that his primary interest centered on her reinstatement back into the community. Rather than concede that the sinner should be removed from the community's midst, Jesus exhorted the men to examine themselves and to confront their own hypocrisies. This teaching implies that human sins cannot separate people from God's love, nor should sins distance the sinner from the community's care and healing attention.

Another noteworthy feature of this story emerges when we direct our attention to the process of teshuvah within the Jewish tradition then and now. Teshuvah is inseparably connected to the acknowledgment of wrongdoing, the commitment to avoid repetition, and the work of making restitution. In this story and others (Lk. 19:1–10), Jesus does not make repentance a precondition for forgiveness. The sinner is received and solidarity reestablished without any strings attached. Jesus' welcoming embrace of the sinner may then lead the person to repent, but Jesus' unconditional acceptance comes first.

This teaching may well mark a fundamental difference in the ways in which Jews and Christians understand the relationship between sin and repentance. The reordering of the process of repentance in this story indicates an approach that departs from Jewish practice. The basis of this new teaching is grounded in the assumption that sinners are often immobilized by their sin and therefore lack the power and awareness to initiate any transformation. What sinners need is an affirmation that empowers them to confront themselves, others, and God. This impetus comes from without and is known in the awareness, sometimes acute and sometimes dim, that there is no escape from God's love. This new sequence of repentance offers a different understanding of how God engages people and of what makes human response possible. The reordering of repentance also helps explain why Christians frequently understand forgiveness as a starting point rather than the culmination of the work of repentance.

These two models of repentance are given different emphases at different times and different places within the liturgical and pastoral life of the church. The challenge is to preserve the enduring tension created by these two traditions. Perhaps the best place to see how these two perspectives are embodied in the life of the Christian is to turn to the liturgical rhythms practiced every Sunday in nearly every Christian church. The "Confession of Sin" is prominently placed at the beginning of Christian worship, for we cannot respond to God until and unless we own up to our individual and communal shortcomings and turn to God for help. To exemplify these tensions, consider the "Confession of Sin" and "Assurance of Pardon" found in the *Book of Common Worship* (1993) of the Presbyterian Church (U.S.A.).

Confession of Sin: *(Words spoken by the minister)* The proof of God's amazing love is this: while we were sinners Christ died for us. Because we have faith in him, we dare to approach God with confidence. In faith and penitence, let us confess our sin before God and one another.

(The following prayer is recited by the entire congregation.) Merciful God, you pardon all who truly repent and turn to you. We humbly confess our sins and ask your mercy. We have not loved you with a pure heart, nor have we loved our neighbor as ourselves. We have not done justice, loved kindness, or walked humbly with you, our God. Have mercy on us, O God, in your loving-kindness. In your great compassion, cleanse us from our sin. Create in us a clean heart, O God, and renew a right spirit within us. Do not cast us from your presence, or take your Holy Spirit from us. Restore to us the joy of your salvation and sustain us with your bountiful Spirit. Lord, have mercy. Christ, have mercy. Lord, have mercy.

Declaration of Pardon: *(Words delivered by the minister)* Hear the good news! Who is in a position to condemn? Only Christ, and Christ died for us, Christ rose for us, Christ reigns in power for us, Christ prays for us. Anyone who is in Christ is a new creation. The old life has gone; a new life has begun. Know that you are forgiven and be at peace. Amen.

Since God has forgiven us in Christ, let us forgive one another. The peace of our Lord Jesus Christ be with you all.

(The entire congregation replies.) And also with you. *(The people then exchange with one another, by words and gesture, signs of peace and reconciliation.)*

At the outset of their worship, Christians make a decisive move. They confess their sin, they own up to their failings, and they admit their complicity in a sinful world. This act of confession follows a pattern of repentance that is part of the Jewish tradition and repeated in Christian teachings (Mt. 5:23) consistent with the first model. What follows this prayer of confession is a radical leap into the second model. Before Christians even begin to undertake the work of repairing what they have broken, the minister assures them of God's forgiveness. How are we to understand this unconditional affirmation of forgiveness? How can pardon be given prior to and apart from the work of repentance?

The answer to these questions is inseparably bound to the activity of worship. In the acknowledgment of our sin, we are brought face-to-face with ourselves and God. The Christian confession indicates that every sin against people is a sin against God, and every sin against God has an impact on the community. However, what Christians discover in this act of confessional worship is that nothing we can do or say can separate us from the love of God. It is therefore the recognition of God's faithfulness that emboldens Christians to undertake the work of repentance. Apart from this faith, Christians are disposed to despair. The acknowledgment of God's forgiveness therefore empowers Christians to pursue justice confident that together we can advance God's purposes. Christians leave worship under the divine mandate to take the necessary steps of repentance and to repair the fractures of this world.

Discussion Questions

1. How do you, as a Christian or Jew, understand the concept of sin?

2. The "Confession of Sin" and the "Assurance of Pardon" from the Presbyterian *Book of Common Worship* and the Jewish Yom Kippur Vidui liturgy are examples of how Jews and Christians might respond to sin and repentance. Following a group reading of these texts, consider: What patterns or themes emerge as you read the list of sins? Which are surprising to find there? Which might be the most difficult to stop doing? Which are the most troubling? Are there any on the list that seem more relevant as a person ages? Invite dialogue participants to talk about their experiences reciting these prayers.

3. What is the process of repentance described in the Jewish tradition? How does that compare to what happens in the Christian tradition?

4. Do people have the capacity to overcome sin? Some will claim that this cannot be done without God. Do you agree?

5. The authors write, "Sin clouds our perceptions of ourselves, of others, and, most fundamentally, of our relationship with God." Do you agree? Why, why not?

Notes

1. This is not to say that Jews think about sin and repentance *only* on Yom Kippur; the daily liturgy contains confessionals, and there is a famous rabbinic dictum that states, "Repent the day before your death" (B. Shab. 153a). The implication is that since we do not know when we will die, we should repent every day.

2. These rituals are described in Leviticus 16.

3. Also referred to as Shabbat (Hebrew) or Shabbos (Yiddish), the Sabbath begins at sundown Friday and ends with the appearance of three stars at sundown on Saturday. On the Jewish calendar, every day begins at sundown.

4. *Chet* as an idea was originally linked to the inadvertent omissions of the priests when performing their rituals in the ancient Temple. In attempting to fulfill their obligations in the performance of Temple rituals, understood then to be a fulfillment of God's will, the priests sometimes made unintentional errors. Over the generations, *chet* has taken on a more moral dimension. Like the unintentional errors of the priests in fulfilling God's directions, *chet* came to be understood as the unintended negative outcomes that result from our daily lives. It is often explained this way: Like an archer, aiming for a bull's-eye yet missing the mark, we also miss the mark when we attempt to behave in right ways, and unintentionally, miss the mark in our interactions.

5. B. Yom. 36b.

6. M. Yom. 8:9.

7. Rosh Hashanah is generally celebrated for two days.

8. The Ashamnu is understood to be a short form of the Vidui prayer, whereas the Al Chet is a longer version. Over the course of Yom Kippur, the congregation repeats them up to ten times, in unison.

9. This version of the Vidui is a gender sensitive adaptation of the translation published in the *Mahzor for Rosh Hashanah and Yom Kippur: A Prayerbook for the Days of Awe,* ed. Jules Harlow (New York: Rabbinical Assembly, 1972).

10. Any attempt to translate the Vidui into English presents one with a dilemma: Does one retain the original author's Hebrew acrostic with its sense of all the sins from "A to Z," or does one literally translate each word? In the above translation, the Ashamnu translation retains the acrostic in English, as an effort to maintain the Hebrew author's desire to express the totality of corporate sinfulness. The Al Chet translation abandons the acrostic, becoming a more literal translation.

11. The Letter to the Romans, the most comprehensive description of Paul's thought, has had a profound and lasting impact Christian faith.

9

What Do Jews and Christians Believe About Redemption, Salvation, and Life After Death?

CHRISTINE EATON BLAIR,

JEFFREY A. MARX,

CHRISTOPHER M. LEIGHTON,

ROSANN M. CATALANO, AND

DAVID FOX SANDMEL

In days to come the mountain of the Lord's house shall be established as the highest of the mountains, and shall be raised above the hills; and the nations shall stream to it. Many peoples shall come and say, "Come, let us go up to the mountain of the Lord, to the house of Jacob; that He may teach us His ways and that we may walk in His paths." For out of Zion shall go forth instruction and the word of the Lord from Jerusalem. He shall judge between the nations, and shall arbitrate for many peoples; they shall beat their swords into plowshares, and their spears into pruning hooks; nation shall not lift up sword against nation, neither shall they learn war any more. (Is. 2:2–4)[1]

Isaiah's vision of the end of days is one that both Jews and Christians value. Yet, how this future will come about, who will share in it, and what its exact nature will be have evoked different responses both within and between Judaism and Christianity. In this chapter, we will explore the questions of redemption, salvation, and the afterlife. Although redemption and salvation are highly technical terms in the Jewish and Christian traditions, we will use them as they are more popularly understood, referring to key concepts in our traditions, such as God's kingdom, Messiah, the first and second coming, resurrection, and the afterlife. Within our respective traditions, the understanding of these concepts has changed over time and continues to change. We will present traditional understandings of these ideas as well as contemporary beliefs.

Summary Statements

In this chapter, we will unpack the following two statements and tease out key differences and similarities between our two religious traditions. Our understanding of salvation and redemption grows out of the trust in both our traditions that the Holy One cares for us human beings, desires us to live lives of goodness, and goes to great lengths to be in relationship with us.

For Jews

Through adherence to God's commandments as revealed in the Torah, we work to bring the coming of the Messiah, who, as God's servant, will redeem the Jewish people by bringing us back from the four corners of the world to the land of Israel, where national sovereignty will be established and God's presence will shine forth from Jerusalem to all the world.

For Christians

Redemption and salvation are grounded in God, who saved us through the life, death, and resurrection of Jesus of Nazareth. Raised up to new life by God, Jesus Christ still lives and works with us to redeem the world in this age and will come again for the final redemption in the age to come.

Salvation and Redemption

For Jews

When used as a term for human activity, "redemption" (*ge'ulah* in Hebrew) in the Tanach means to buy back a kinsman from slavery or to repurchase a family plot of land so it does not become lost to an outsider (e.g., Lev. 25:25). When used as a term for God's actions, "redemption" refers to our national liberation from Egyptian slavery or from foreign oppression: "Therefore say to the Israelites: 'I am YHVH, and I will bring you out from under the burdens of the Egyptians, and I will deliver you from their bondage, and I will redeem you with an outstretched arm, and with great judgments'" (Ex. 6:6).[2]

Throughout the prophetic writings, God's redemption is understood to involve the ingathering of Jewish exiles and the restoration of our people to our former sovereignty and national glory. Often, this time is pictured as an era of universal harmony (e.g., Is. 2, above). During Roman rule and throughout our ages of oppression in foreign lands, Jews have understood redemption to be national in character:

> But now, assuredly, thus said YHVH, the God of Israel, concerning this city of which you say, "It is being delivered into the hands of the king of Babylon through the sword, through famine, and through pestilence": See, I will gather them from all the lands to which I have banished them in My anger and wrath, and in great rage; and I will bring them back to this place and let them dwell secure. (Jer. 32:36–37)

> Look upon our affliction and champion our cause; redeem us speedily for Your name's sake, for You are a mighty Redeemer. Blessed are You, YHVH, Redeemer of Israel. . . . Sound the great Shofar for our freedom; lift up the banner to bring our exiles together, and assemble us from the four corners of the earth. Blessed Are You, YHVH, who gathers the dispersed of Your people Israel. (Daily Prayerbook)

For Christians

Although human beings are made in God's image and likeness (Gen. 1:27–28), Christians interpret Genesis 3 as a fundamental break in our relationship with God, expressed in the reality of sin and death. The condition of estrangement from God and other people, often called "original sin," makes possible humanity's wars, social injustice, and suffering. Salvation means first and foremost being restored to wholeness with oneself, one's neighbor, and God, and being empowered to work in accord with God's ultimate purpose for creation. Salvation also holds the promise of eternal life with God after death. Christians believe that salvation is God's work, through Jesus Christ, and not the work of humans. In other words, God's love reaches out to humanity through Jesus Christ and puts us back into right relationship with God.

The sacrament of baptism (a ritual through which a person becomes a Christian by being sprinkled by or immersed in water) symbolizes the Christian's death to sin and restoration to a new and holy life made possible by God's love. Through baptism, a person becomes a member of the body of Christ, which is the church.

American Protestant Christianity has emphasized the individual: the individual's repentance, faith, piety, and life after death. God's action of saving love, called "grace," takes precedence over human repentance. Many texts and hymns describe the experience of being converted by God's grace. One such hymn is "Amazing Grace," written by the former slave trader Captain John Newton in 1779:

> *Amazing grace, how sweet the sound*
> *That saved a wretch like me;*
> *I once was lost, but now am found,*
> *Was blind, but now I see.*
>
> *'Twas grace that taught my heart to fear*
> *And grace my fears relieved;*
> *How precious did that grace appear*
> *The hour I first believed.*

The stress on the individual, emphasized in "Amazing Grace," should, however, be understood in the context of a more fundamental Christian affirmation, namely, that the individual Christian is saved through participation in the covenantal reality of the church.

The church is Christ's continued presence on earth, serving, healing, reconciling, and teaching of God's love in the name of Christ. ("Now you are the body of Christ and individually members of it" (1 Cor. 12:27). To be Christian, by definition, is to be a part of this body and requires participation with others in worship, service, and mission.

For Jews

Although we, too, trust in God's love and compassion for each individual, the phrase "original sin" is foreign to Judaism. We believe that we are born as "clean slates," neither good nor bad, and yet, we all have within us impulses to do good and drives to do evil. Our *yetzer hara* (the impulse to do evil) can be brought under control through adherence to God's commandments found in Torah. For Jews, sin is the failure to follow these commandments. *Talmud torah* (study), *teshuvah* (repentance), and *ma'asim tovim* (deeds of goodness) bring us back to God's path. These three activities are life-long endeavors, for our yetzer hara causes us to slip from the paths of righteousness. God, who desires our teshuvah, commands us to engage daily in study, self-examination, deeds of goodness, and reconciliation with those we've wronged. Teshuvah enables us to return to God's way.

> Rabbi Yohanan said in the name of Rabbi Bana-ah: "The Jewish people are to be congratulated—when they occupy themselves with the study of Torah and with deeds of loving-kindness, their impulse to evil is mastered by them, and not they by their impulse. (B. AZ 5b)

> On the first day of the week he (Adam) went into the waters of upper Gihon until the waters reached up to his neck, and he fasted for seven weeks of days, until his body became like a species of seaweed. Adam said before the Holy One, Blessed Be He: "Sovereign of all worlds! Remove, I pray Thee, my sins from me and accept my repentance, and all generations will learn that repentance is a reality." What did the Holy One, Blessed Be He, do? He put forth His right hand, and accepted his repentance, and took away from him his sin.[3]

The Messiah

Few terms have given rise to greater misunderstanding and friction among Christians and Jews than the word "Messiah." More often than not Christians and Jews talk past one another whenever the idea of the "Messiah" comes into play, because each community places the term in a different religious framework and uses the idea to serve different purposes.

For Jews

"Messiah" (*mashi'ach*, in Hebrew) means "one who is anointed." According to the Tanach, Israel's kings and high priests were anointed with oil to signify their selection as God's appointed ruler. In some of the prophets and psalms such rulers are associated with a time when God will end the subjugation of Israel. In these visions, war is replaced by peace and prosperity. Israel and Judah, separated since the death of Solomon, are reunited and the people returned from exile. This salvation is not just for Israel but signals a permanent change for the whole world. In these prophecies, although the central figure is an ideal king descended from David, the role of kingship is not emphasized; it is God who brings all this about.

During the Second Temple period (which included the time of Jesus), belief in God's future salvation of Israel persisted, but references to an anointed human agent were rare. In rabbinic writings (second century C.E. and later), the person and the deeds of a Messiah gradually became more pronounced and defined. The rabbis (like the prophets) understood the Messiah to be a human (not divine) political ruler of the Jewish people, descended from King David. God will send the Messiah to throw off foreign rule and usher in God's kingdom. There are also traditions that the Messiah will judge all individuals in the afterlife (see below). Some modern, liberal Jewish movements have rejected belief in a single person who will usher in God's kingdom, instead stressing that it is through our collective efforts, in partnership with God, that the Messianic Age will be brought about. Other Jews see in the creation of the State of Israel messianic implications, an understanding that evokes a range of responses (see Chapter 6).

Then Samuel took the vial of oil and poured it upon his (Saul's) head, and kissed him, and said: "Is it not that YHVH has anointed you to be prince over His inheritance?" (1 Sam. 10:1–2)

(Rav) Samuel said: The only difference between this world and the days of the Messiah is that the subjection of the Jewish People will end. (B. Ber. 34b)

Rabbi Isaac taught: In the year when the king Messiah reveals himself, all the nations of the world will be agitated and frightened; they will fall upon their faces and be seized with pangs like the pangs of a woman in labor. And God (will say to the Jewish People): "My children, why are you afraid? Fear not. The time of your redemption is come. And this redemption will not be like your previous redemption (from Egypt), for after that redemption you again suffered anguish and enslavement by the kingdoms; but following this redemption, you will have no such anguish or enslavement."[4]

For Christians

The early followers of Jesus used a variety of titles to understand and establish the importance, indeed the divine status, of their resurrected Lord. One of these titles was the term "Messiah," and the concept when applied to Jesus is somewhat surprising for at least two reasons. First, the question whether Jesus himself laid claim to the title "Messiah" is hotly debated. On this point the Gospels are ambiguous. Mark's Gospel in particular presents a portrait of Jesus resisting messianic claims made by his followers. The other Gospels also express ambivalence regarding testimony that links Jesus to the idea of a royal messiah. Second, the title proved problematic whenever applied to Jesus by his followers. Because the concept was so closely associated with the exercise of political power and the rebuilding of the nation Israel, proclaiming Jesus as "the Messiah" ran the risk of misleading his followers to expect a political resolution and, thereby, of provoking suspicion among the Roman authorities.

Nonetheless, the sign the Romans posted over the crucified Jesus read "The King of the Jews." While his executioners used this inscription to mock Jesus, his followers came to believe that the epitaph conveyed a deep and abiding truth. In ways that could not have been anticipated, the postresurrection community believed that Jesus was indeed a "king." Thus one of the principal tasks of the early church was to define the nature of Jesus' kingship and of the kingdom that his death and resurrection inaugurated. Although it is highly unlikely that Jesus identified himself as "the Messiah," the title nevertheless helped his followers to explain an important dimension of both his identity and his enduring achievement, precisely because the term was vague enough to be stretched and ultimately redefined. The idea that the Messiah would be crucified and raised from the dead was foreign to traditional Jewish teaching. Jesus' ignoble death was evidence enough that he had not met the expected job requirements. Why? Because after his death, Roman oppression persisted, and the vast majority of the Jewish population continued to live beyond the boundaries of the Promised Land.

The Christian conception of the Messiah developed as early followers turned to the Hebrew Scriptures, brought together a diverse assortment of key passages, and applied them to Jesus. In describing a variety of central figures as "anointed," the scriptures underscore a common motif: God's "anointed" ones are divinely appointed and upon them rests the Spirit of God. In the New Testament, the special authority of each of these figures is applied to the person of Jesus. Thus, his royal standing, his charismatic leadership, his prophetic challenges and proclamations, his priestly intercessions, his wisdom as teacher and judge, and his miracle working identify him with figures that belong to an ancient past extending from David to Moses back to Adam. At the same time, the Christian conception of the Messiah pointed ahead to a future that God alone could establish. As Christians gradually came to believe that their risen Lord was the one who would usher in the reign of God at the end of days, judge the wicked, and redeem the oppressed, they reshaped the meaning of Messiah. In the Christian imagination, the concept of the Messiah is inseparably bound to the activities of God. In other words, Christians use the title "Messiah" to make claims about the unique ways in which the risen Jesus embodies God's presence for all of time.

Instead of realizing Israel's earthly messianic expectations, Jesus Christ was coronated in the heavens where he and God the Father are one. Over time, notions of divinity became attached to the Christian understanding of Messiah, and the kingdom where Jesus Christ reigns became spiritualized. This kingdom is made known, however imperfectly, in the church, and the church serves as a hopeful sign of God's ultimate commitment to redeem the world. What was inaugurated through the death and resurrection of Jesus thus awaits completion in the future. Because Christians await the restoration of the entire creation, they cannot settle for their own individual salvation. They anticipate a consummation of God's purposes for the whole world that will unfold when Jesus Christ returns.

In the formative centuries that followed their first uses of the title "Messiah" for Jesus, Christians transformed the content and character of the concept. As the church became increasingly composed of Gentiles, terms that were derived from Israelite kingship failed to illuminate the ultimate significance of Jesus. Furthermore, the Greek translation of the Hebrew word for Messiah is *christos,* a term that acquired new meanings within Gentile Christianity. *Christos* became so closely identified with Jesus that it ceased to function as a title and was used as his proper name.

As a consequence of the radical transformation that the title "Messiah" underwent in the centuries following the resurrection, Christians apply this title to Jesus in a way that does not correspond to Jewish conceptions of the Messiah. Historically, Christians have used this new understanding of "Messiah" to assert that Jesus is the "true Messiah" promised in the Hebrew Scriptures and that in their failure to recognize this, Jews have misunderstood their own Scriptures and rejected their Messiah sent by God. This logic has proven dangerous, even murderous, as our anguished history attests. For this reason, a growing number of Christians insist that the church must no longer use the term "Messiah" in speaking of Jesus. They urge their churches to limit themselves to the Greek term "Christ." However, others argue that the language of "Messiah" is too deeply embedded in the Christian imagination to excise. Yet, the task remains for Christians to learn how to recognize the divergent ways in which both Christians and Jews use the same term—and to discover how the church can validate its own hopes for the world's restoration without impugning the messianic hopes that sustain Jews.

The Messianic Age and Coming of the God's Reign

For Jews

We believe that the Messiah (or Messianic Age) has not yet come. We have only to compare our world to the prophetic visions of redemption for confirmation of this: injustice and hurt still abound; disease, war, and poverty are alive and thriving. The longing for final redemption has been reinforced by centuries of oppression. Throughout Jewish history, there have been many individuals who have claimed to be heralds of the Messiah or whom others have believed to be the Messiah but who failed to realize Jewish messianic expectations. Among them are Jesus of Nazareth (ca. 30 C.E.); Bar Kochba (who led a disastrous rebellion against Rome in 132 C.E.); David Reuveni (Italy, Portugal, sixth century); and Shabbetai Tzvi (Turkey, seventeenth century). Although historically the longing for the Messiah has been intense, the disappointment and disasters associated with false messiahs has led the rabbis to be wary of anyone who makes messianic claims. Jewish leaders discourage messianic speculation that tries to identify the Messiah, determine when the Messiah will come, or discover how to hasten his coming. God will bring redemption in God's time. Although Jews hope for the arrival of the messianic era, living in accordance with the mitsvot (commandments) here and now is the best way to prepare for the Messiah.

> If you are in the midst of planting a tree and someone comes to tell you that the Messiah has arrived, first finish planting the tree and then go to greet him. (ARN 3, chap. 21)

> Rabbi Samuel the son of Nahmani said in the name of Rabbi Jonathan: "Blasted be the bones of those who presume to calculate the time of redemption. For they are apt to say, 'since redemption has not come at the time expected, it will never come.' Rather, one must wait for it, as is said, 'Though it tarry, wait for it'" (Habbakuk 2:3). (B. Sanh. 97b)

> I believe with complete trust in the coming of the Messiah, and though he may tarry, still I trust. (Maimonides, *Commentary on M. Sanh.*, chap. 10)

Since the time of the prophets, the Jewish people have awaited the coming of God's kingdom, a time when Israel's independence will be combined with God's justice and peace. A good description of the kingdom of God is found in the daily liturgy:

> We therefore hope in you, YHVH our God, that we may speedily behold the glory of your might, when you will remove the abominations from the earth, and the idols will be utterly cut off, when the world will be perfected under the kingdom of the Almighty, and all the children of flesh will call upon thy name, when you will turn to yourself all the wicked of the earth. Let the inhabitants of the world recognize and know that every knee should bow to you, every tongue swear. Before you, YHVH our God let them bow and fall, and to your glorious name give honor, and let them all take upon themselves the yoke of your kingdom, so that you will soon reign over them for ever. For the kingdom is yours and you will reign in glory forever, as it is written in your Torah: "YHVH shall reign forever and ever." [Ex. 15:18] And it says, "On that day, YHVH shall be one and God's name shall be one." [Zech. 14:9]

The Messiah became a central figure in rabbinic Judaism and is closely associated with the coming of the kingdom of God. Yet, this prayer of rabbinic origin envisions the ultimate salvation of Israel and the world without reference to the Messiah. In Judaism, salvation depends on God, and the Messiah is merely God's human agent. At the same time, the Jewish tradition teaches that humanity plays an important role in bringing the Messiah and the kingdom of God. Jews use the phrase *tikkun olam* ("repair the world," as in the prayer above) to refer to acts that heal the world's wounds. By doing what is within our power to bring peace and justice to the world, we can bring the kingdom of God closer to being a reality.

> Rabbi Joshua the son of Levi met Elijah standing by the entrance of Rabbi Simeon ben Yohai's tomb. He asked him: "When will the Messiah come?"—"Go and ask him himself," was his reply. "Where is he sitting?"—"At the gate." So he went to him and greeted him saying, "Peace unto thee, Master and Teacher."—"Peace unto thee, O son of Levi," he replied. "When wilt thou come, Master?" asked Rabbi

Joshua. "To-day," was his answer. On his returning to Elijah, Rabbi Joshua said: "He spoke falsely to me, stating that he would come to-day, but has not!" Elijah answered him, "This is what he said to thee: Today, if you will but hearken to his voice." (B. Sanh. 98a)

Rabbi Jonathan said: Great is repentance, because it brings about re-demption, as it is said: "And a redeemer will come to Zion, and unto them that turn from transgression in Jacob." Why will a redeemer come to Zion? Because of those that turn from transgression in Jacob. (Yom. 86b)

For Christians

Christians see themselves living in a time between the "old" and the "new."[5] They believe that the kingdom of God has already dawned in Jesus Christ and that their participation in the covenantal reality known as the church affords them a glimpse of this kingdom. At the same time, the fullness of the messianic era lies ahead. The depth and breadth of poverty and injustice are constant reminders of the gap that separates the present world from its ultimate destiny. The world continues to fall short of its intended glory and therefore stands in constant need of repair. Christians therefore live in the ten-sion between the "seen" and the "unseen," the "already" and the "not yet," the "promise" and its "final fulfillment." On the one hand, God has made known in the person of Jesus Christ the promise of a redeemed world. On the other hand, the distance be-tween the promise and its fulfillment is the "in-between" time that Christians call their present reality.

Christians have often envisioned the kingdom of God as an other-worldly and eternal realm. Salvation is all too often conceived as an ethereal future that awaits believers on the other side of death, and the emphasis on this "otherworldly" reality has often led Christians to neglect the immediate demands to repair and redeem this world. A number of contemporary Christian thinkers have criticized this tendency to spiritualize the kingdom of God, and they reject any theology or spirituality that disconnects Christian hope from en-gagement with the injustices of the world. Although Christians in-sist that they cannot perfect the old nor create the new apart from

God, they nonetheless see themselves as co-partners in the work of redemption. The dream of salvation becomes real only when we are striving in the here and now to overcome the systems of oppression that keep people in a condition of economic and political powerlessness. This view of salvation does not provide a way out of this earthly mess but entails an active political vision that compels Christians to transform this world.

This vision is central to all theologies of liberation. The Latin American theologian Gustavo Gutierrez writes:

> A spirituality of liberation will center on a conversion to the neighbor, the oppressed person, the exploited social class, the despised race, the dominated country. . . . To be converted is to commit oneself to the process of the liberation of the poor and oppressed, to commit oneself lucidly, realistically and concretely.[6]

This more collaborative and earthly orientation also finds expression among Christians who insist that the scope of the Messianic Age must become less anthropocentric. As stewards of this world (Gen. 2:15), humanity has a responsibility to safeguard and protect our ecological resources. Our interdependence with the entire creation reminds us that our obligations include the air we breathe, the water we drink, and the ground on which we stand. Indeed, humanity is responsible to preserve all the mysterious facets of the universe, not just those upon which we depend. The kingdom for which Christians must work and pray extends well beyond humanity's grasp. The final consummation will entail nothing less than the restoration of the entire creation, all things great and small.

Judgment and the Afterlife

For Jews

Although there is little direct reference to the afterlife in the Tanach, a defining feature of rabbinic Judaism is its insistence on a world of reward and punishment after death, known as *olam haba* (the world to come). The rabbinic sources themselves, however, are not very specific and somewhat contradictory about the details. What follows is a general sketch of rabbinic notions of the afterlife. The world to come, although it will take place on this earth, brings an end to linear, human history. First, it involves the bodily resurrection of the dead:

> You are eternally mighty, Adonai, you resurrect the dead, great is your saving power. (Daily Prayerbook)

> Rabbi Alexandri said: Because You renew our spirits each and every morning (as we awaken), we are certain that in Your great faithfulness You will restore our spirits to us at the resurrection. (Gen. R. 78:1)

Judgment will follow the resurrection of the dead. The righteous will be rewarded and the wicked consigned to a place of punishment, known as *Gehenna* (hell). Some believe that the wicked will remain there forever; others believe that the wicked will remain in Gehenna no longer than one year's time. During that time, they will be cleansed through terrible punishments:

> Rabbi Phinehas, in the name of Rabbi Reuben, told this parable: A king made a banquet, and he invited guests to it, and he decreed that each guest should bring what he was to lie on. Some brought rugs, some brought mattresses, others chairs, and some brought logs and some brought stones. The king examined everything, and said, "Let every man lie on what he has brought." They that sat on logs and stones were angry with the king, and said, "Is it fitting for the king's honor that his guest should lie on logs and stones?" When the king heard what they had said, he said, "Not enough that you have polluted my palace, upon which I spent so much, but you are impudent and accuse me. I did not injure your honor; you injured it yourselves." So in the world to come, when the wicked are condemned to Gehenna (Hell), they will murmur against God, and say, "We hoped for Your salvation, and now this has come upon us." God will say, "In the other world were you not quarrelsome, slanderous, evil doers, men of strife and violence? Do you say that this is from My hand?! Nay, you did it to yourselves!"[7]

There are many different notions concerning the reward of the righteous. Some think the righteous will feast (in the lavish style of Greco-Roman banquet), and others speculate that the righteous will sit in bliss, basking in God's presence. Still others say that life will go on as usual, except that all bodily urges and drives will disappear:

> This was a favorite saying of Rab's: Not like this world is the world to come. In the world to come there is no eating or drinking, no procreation, no business and no envy, no hatred, and no competition. But the righteous sit with crowns on their heads, delighting in the radiance of the Divine Presence. (B. Ber. 17a)

> Rabbah said in the name of Rabbi Yohanan: (In the world to come) the Holy One will make a feast for the righteous out of the flesh of Leviathan (a mythical monster fish).[8]

> There are neither bodies nor bodily forms in the world to come but only the disembodied souls of the righteous. The good that is stored up for the righteous is the life of the world to come. This is life without death, and good without evil. The retribution of the wicked is that they do not merit this kind of life but are cut off from it and die. (Maimonides, Mishneh Torah Sefer Mada, Teshuvah 8)

Today, most Jews, although not believing in the detailed traditional descriptions of the afterlife, nonetheless affirm that the soul is eternal and will be united with God after death, in some fashion.

> Rabbi Hiyya the son of Abba said in the name of Rabbi Yohanan: All the prophets prophesied only about the days of the Messiah, but as for the world to come, "[No] eye has ... seen [it] beside Thee, O God" (Is. 64:3). (B. Shab. 63a)

For Christians

A common caricature suggests that one can live a wicked life but avoid God's just punishment by feeling remorse and proclaiming that Jesus Christ is Lord.[9] Yet, the Christian tradition holds that people are responsible for their choices. The decisions we have made, the habits we have developed, the attitudes we have adopted, and the actions we have performed are etched into the very core of our being. The last judgment entails a thorough reckoning with the mirror, a radical facing of ourselves, the world, and God. The shattering of our self-delusions and the confrontation with the truth about ourselves cannot be avoided and entails hard work. In the language of theology, the last judgment is associated with the purification that comes out of the refiner's fire.

Yet, to insist that there are some people beyond God's redemptive reach is also difficult to reconcile with Christian claims about God's mercy and God's power. To maintain that God's love cannot penetrate the depths of the human soul is to limit God's freedom. It is to substitute our own conception of justice for a mystery beyond our understanding. Little wonder that the last judgment often evokes such profound ambivalence among many Christians. On the one hand, the horrors depicted on the walls and ceilings of medieval churches have haunted Christians from their beginnings. This final reckoning still ignites both fear and dread. On the other hand, Christian conceptions of the End have also inspired confident hope. The Bible teaches that God can work wonders with flawed materials. Human failure is not an insurmountable obstacle to God, and so Christians make bold to hope that we are never beyond God's redemptive reach.

Over the centuries, an enormous variety of images about the afterlife, heaven, and hell have accumulated within the Christian tradition. Although it is well beyond the scope of this reflection to chart this vast conceptual terrain, most Christian notions of life after death are anchored in a few foundational affirmations. First, Christians maintain that God enters into a covenantal relationship with people, and the life they share together is defined by the power of love. Second, humans are finite. Whether death emerges as a consequence of "sin" or is simply an aspect of God's natural order, none of us can escape our mortality. Third, nothing can ultimately separate us from the love of God. God's desire for communion with his covenantal partners knows no bounds. In other words, Christians insist that God is stronger than death. We are not destined for oblivion but created to know, to love, "to glorify God, and enjoy him forever."[10] This transformation was given a classical Christian formulation by Paul in 1 Corinthians 15:

What is sown is perishable, what is raised is imperishable. It is sown in dishonor, it is raised in glory. It is sown in weakness, it is raised in power. It is sown a physical body, it is raised a spiritual body. If there is a physical body, there is also a spiritual body. . . . We will not all die, but we will all be changed, in a moment, in the twinkling of an eye, at the last trumpet. For the trumpet will sound, and the dead will be raised imperishable, and we shall be changed. For this perishable nature must put on the imperishable, and this mortal nature must put on immortality. When the perishable puts on the imperishable, and the mortal puts on immortality, then shall come to pass the saying that is written: "Death is swallowed up in victory. O death, where is thy victory? O death, where is thy sting?"

This description of the life after death may lack both the sublime and gory details added by subsequent generations of Christians, but one crucial feature of this vision is worth noting. Paul shares the Jewish assumption that the human being is an indissoluble unity of heart and mind, body and spirit. Therefore, life after death must entail physical resurrection. The life that God will restore involves embodied existence, although the nature of this imperishable and spiritual renewal is left vague.

This formulation stands in contrast to the dualistic conceptions within Hellenistic philosophy that posit a material body and an immortal soul. In Paul's formulation, death does not free the spirit from its material imprisonment, and heaven is not framed as an ethereal, disembodied existence with God. Although competing descriptions of the afterlife evolved in the Christian tradition (including scenarios that have a Platonic character), the affirmation of the physical reminds the Christian that God's original creation was good. God's redemption must therefore move beyond the purely human, and the final resurrection is increasingly claimed as a renewal that engages the entire creation.

Who is In? Who is Out?

For Jews

The question of who is in and who is out has not been as central a concern in Judaism as it has in Christianity, for both theological and historical reasons. From the theological perspective, God's covenant with the people Israel is unique but does not necessarily preclude God having relationships with other peoples, independent of Jews and Judaism. Thus, in the book of Jonah, the Ninevites are saved through their own repentance before God, not because they became Jews. This is not to say that Judaism does not have its share of exclusivist or elitist tendencies; indeed, the Tanach itself contains plenty of negative comments about "the nations." However, the specific national aspect of the Jewish understanding of covenant does not inevitably lead to exclusivity.

Historical circumstances are equally important to understanding this difference in emphasis. At no time in the past 2,000 years has Judaism been a dominant world power, as have both Christianity and Islam. For most of its history, Judaism has not been in the position to use the power of the state to force conversion or to oppress other traditions. Its experience as a persecuted religious minority and its concern not to appear triumphant have led Jews to stress those aspects of the tradition that, in contemporary terms, might be called more "pluralistic."

According to tradition, by virtue of belonging to the Jewish People, a "reserved place" is held for us in the afterlife. This "reservation," however, can be canceled through sinful deeds in our lifetime. Through study of Torah, we are led to prayer, repentance, and good deeds, which make us eligible for eternal life. Salvation is not solely for Jews. Non-Jews are also eligible to enter into eternal life in the world to come through their righteous conduct.

All Israelites have a share in the world to come, for it is written: "Your people shall all be righteous, they shall possess the land forever" (Isaiah 60:21).[11]

Rabbi Eliezer asked Rabbi Joshua, "What should a man do to escape the judgment of Gehenna?" He replied, "Let him occupy himself with good deeds. Everyone who walks in blamelessness before His Creator in this world will escape the judgment of Gehenna in the world to come."[12]

The Holy One declares no creature unfit, but receives all. The gates of mercy are open at all times, and he who wishes to enter may enter.

Scripture says: Open the gates, that the righteous Gentile may come in. (Is. 26:2)—not that "priests, Levites or Israelites may come in" but that "the righteous Gentile who keeps the faith may come in." (B. BK 38a)

The question "Who is in, and who is out?" highlights the tension created when traditional concepts of religious truth are challenged by contemporary notions of tolerance and pluralism. How can a Jew or a Christian maintain that his or her tradition is true without implying that other traditions are, by definition, lesser or even false? Indeed, the concepts of the anonymous Christian and the righteous Gentile assume that the "other" must meet a set criteria defined by the very tradition to which that "other" does not adhere!

David Novak considers the avoidance of relativism an essential component of interreligious dialogue: "The ultimate truth claims of Judaism and Christianity are not only different but mutually exclusive . . . [which] explains why Jews and Christians have so much to talk about and, also, why the stakes in the Jewish–Christian relationship are so high."[13] But Novak believes that Jewish and Christian anticipation of the end of days temper this mutual exclusivity and the danger of triumphalism inherent in it. Both Jews and Christians expect, says Novak, "a time when, unlike the present, 'the kingdom will be the Lord's' (Obad. 1:21)." To those Jews and Christians who claim that in the future their vision will triumph, Novak replies:

We must answer that the final judgment of all human history is not yet in. . . . Therefore Jews and Christians cannot see their past traditions or their present efforts and differences as the last words. The different claims of Judaism and Christianity are only tentative. Surely what God will do at the end of history will be radical enough to surprise everyone—Jews, Christians, and all others who wait for that time here and now.

For Christians

Christians have developed varied, often contradictory, conceptions of heaven and hell. The thinking of two great Christian teachers,

Augustine of Hippo (354–430 C.E.) and Origen of Alexandria (185–254 C.E.), is a case in point. According to Augustine, communion with God is essential for salvation, but because communion with God can be known only through Jesus Christ, the vast majority of human beings are beyond salvation, consigned to the realm of the damned. Hell is their final destiny, an eternal punishment from which there is no exit. Origen, on the other hand, envisioned a final restoration of all things, and therefore believed hell to be a drastic, but transitional, remedy for sinners. For Origen, God's benevolence and mercy will ultimately prevail, and so, at the end of time, God will restore the whole of creation, along with all human beings, to full communion with God.

In the history of classical Christian theology of salvation, Augustine and Origen clearly represent opposite ends of the spectrum. Yet, virtually every traditional Christian formulation concerning life after death shares a common belief—that outside the church, there is no salvation.[14] Over the centuries, this teaching has both magnified the Christian animus toward non-Christians and mobilized much of Christian missionary activity. Yet today, many Christians are growing increasingly uneasy with this exclusive formulation and the troubling behaviors resulting from it. Proponents for a more inclusive perspective argue that a careful reconsideration of this classic Christian teaching might retrieve a deeper understanding of this axiom's underlying affirmation. A brief sketch of this reformulation follows.

Christians maintain that in Jesus Christ the God of Israel acted on behalf of all humanity, and that through Jesus Christ God disclosed the consummate way of living and dying. Christians believe that all people will eventually recognize and acknowledge the truth of this affirmation, but does this mean that everyone must become a Christian and a member of the church in order to be saved?

For the better part of the last two thousand years, the standard answer to this question has been "Yes," a response that has blinded Christians to the ethical, religious, and spiritual integrity of anyone outside the church. Karl Rahner, the twentieth-century Jesuit theologian, is among many in the church who have sought to reinterpret this traditional teaching. Rahner begins his reformulation with the biblical insight that every human being is created in the image and likeness of God. By virtue of this insight, Rahner maintains that every person, Christian and non-Christian alike, is thus open to, and indeed predisposed to, living a life in accord with God's desire for us. It is at this most basic level that Rahner addresses the question of salvation. For Rahner, Jesus Christ is the example par excellence of how to live one's life in perfect accord with God, and Christians are those who are called to conform their way of living to the gospel of God made known in Jesus Christ. Nevertheless, Rahner maintains that one need not be Christian to be saved, that salvation is open to all who live righteously in the light of their conscience—Christian or non-Christian alike. To such non-Christians, Rahner gives the name "anonymous Christian."

Critics of Rahner maintain that the term "anonymous Christian" still carries with it the seeds of contempt for others because the distinct and particular character of other religious traditions is bleached out of the picture. To counter this problem, they offer an alternative proposal. Returning to the Bible and rereading their traditions, they begin with the biblical claim that God keeps God's promises. God's faithfulness thus implies that God's covenant with the Jewish people has never been revoked. Indeed, it is irrevocable. From this axiom, they argue that Christian supersessionism is irreconcilable with the God made known in the Bible. Christians are therefore obligated to recognize that Jews do not stand in need of Jesus to save them because they are already in right relationship with God.[15]

Discussion Questions

1. For Christians: How does the notion of Messiah as a political and national redeemer affect your understanding of Jesus? For Jews: How will we recognize the Messiah when he arrives? Given the fact that we believe he will be a political leader, what traits would we look for?
2. For Christians: What are signs in today's world of the kingdom of God at work? For Jews: What things in the world are helping to bring the coming of the Messiah one step

closer? (i.e., for both, what are the signs of goodness and redemption in today's world?)

3. If you knew for sure that the Messiah was coming (or coming back) next week, how would you spend the next seven
   days?

Notes

1. This quote, and all biblical quotes in the Christian sections, are taken from the NRSV.

2. This quote, and all biblical quotes in the Jewish sections, are taken from the JPS translation.

3. "The Repentance of Adam," in *Midrash Pirke De Rabbi Eliezer*, trans. and annotated Gerald Friedlander (1916; reprint, New York: Sepher-Hermon Press, 1981), chap. 20.

4. *Pesikta Rabbati*, trans. William Braude (New Haven: Yale University Press, 1968), Piska 35.

5. Note the tension within the Lord's Prayer, the most well-known of Christian prayers: "Our Father in heaven, hallowed be Your name, Your Kingdom Come, Your will be done, on earth as in heaven . . ." Here the emphasis is on the future, but in its conclusion, the prayer indicates that God's kingdom has already broken into the present: "For the kingdom, the power, and glory are Yours now and forever."

6. Gustavo Gutierrez, *A Theology of Liberation* (New York: Orbis, 1984), 204–205.

7. *Ecclesiastes Rabba*, trans. Rabbi Dr. H. Freedman and Maurice Simon (London: The Soncino Press, 1983), 9:1.

8. *Sifra de-be Rav*, ed. I. Weiss (New York: Om, 1947), 86b.

9. This view is often bound to Paul's assertion: " If you confess with your lips that Jesus is Lord and believe in your heart that God raised him from the dead, you will be saved" (Rom. 10:9).

10. Question #1, Westminster Larger Catechism, 1649.

11. *Mishnayoth, Tractate Sanhedrin*, trans. Philip Blackman (Gateshead: Judaica Press, Ltd., 1977), 10:1.

12. *The Midrash on Proverbs*, trans. Burton Visotzky (New Haven: Yale University Press, 1992), 17:1.

13. David Novak, "What to Seek and What to Avoid in Jewish–Christian Dialogue," introduction to *Christianity in Jewish Terms*, ed. Tikva Frymer-Kensky, David Novak, Peter Ochs, David Fox Sandmel, and Michael Signer (Boulder, Colo.: Westview Press, 2000), 5. The two quotations below come from page 6.

14. Although this axiom is frequently associated with St. Cyprian, the bishop of Carthage martyred in 258, others before and after him maintained a similar pos-

ture. See Francis A. Sullivan, *Salvation Outside the Church?* (Mahwah: Paulist Press, 1992).

15. Christian theologians are also rethinking the issue of the salvation of those who are neither Christian nor Jew, a question that is made more complex by the nonmonotheistic, noncovenantal nature of other world religions.

10

Living with the Other: Are the Irreconcilable Differences Between Christians and Jews a Blessing, a Curse, or Both?

NINA BETH CARDIN AND

FAYETTE BREAUX VEVERKA

Moral communities are necessarily particular because they have members and memories, members with memories not only of their own but also for their common life. Humanity, by contrast, has members but no memory, and so it has no history and no culture, no customary practice, no familiar lifeways, no festivals, no shared understanding of social goods. It is human to have such things, but there is no single human way of having them. At the same time, the members of all the different societies, because they are human, can acknowledge each other's different ways, respond to each other's cries for help, learn from each other, and march (sometimes) in each other's parades.[1]

As Diana Eck observes, we live in a world where religious pluralism is "an existential fact." Our inevitable encounters with religious "others" alert us to the possibility of beauty and spiritual depth in traditions other than our own. Although this encounter with another, especially the stranger, can expand, deepen, and enrich our lives, it can just as readily "challenge the very ground on which we stand."[2]

In America, for example, freedom of religion is not only a legal protection but also a personal privilege. Not only do religious groups have the right to the free expression of their beliefs, but individuals have the right to shed or adopt religious traditions as they desire. Where religious association is voluntary, choosing one set of beliefs means that we have not chosen others. Thus, to listen to another's religious views is not just to listen to someone else's stories; it is to be witness to a claim about the fundamental nature of the world that often differs from and challenges our own. To put it more bluntly, to hear another's religious story is to hear a rejection of our own.

The act of listening to another reflects a certain selflessness, and not a little bit of courage. Why, then, would the writers of this book, as well as anyone involved in other interfaith enterprises like it, want to hang out with people who have chosen to be different from them? What compelled us coauthors to leave our homes for a few days and spend time with people we had never met, people who not only believe and behave differently than we do but who in some way believe contrary to the way we do? And why, when our readers can be watching television, hanging out in coffee shops, or surfing the Internet, have they dedicated these precious hours of their lives to reading about different religious beliefs? What is it we hope to gain from this book? How does it advance the goodness of the world?

The answers to these questions depend in large part on how we understand the character of religious traditions and of the relationships among them. If we understand our own tradition as the sole bearer of truth, whereas all others are in error, there is little purpose in dialogue, other than to convert the other to one's own point of view. On the other hand, if all religious choices are merely subjective preferences, then nothing of consequence is actually at stake in the encounter with the other. But if one takes religious claims seriously and, at the same time, recognizes the existence of religious pluralism as a fact of life, then we need a way of understanding the relationship among religious traditions that affirms both religious particularity and pluralism.

On the Irreducible Particularity and
Pluralism of Religious Traditions

To assert that Jews and Christians have "humanly irreconcilable differences" is to evoke the image of a broken marriage that cannot be healed. Couples with "irreconcilable differences" acknowledge that they can no longer live together as partners in mutually enriching ways; differences have led to division, alienation, and, ultimately, separation and a parting of ways. Sadly, this oppositional, even adversarial view, has characterized much of the long, tragic history between Jews and Christians. Until recent times, most Christians believed, like the early Christian theologian John Chrysostom, that "the truth of one religion [is] dependent on the invalidity of the other."[3] For Christians who claim "ours is the only truth," engagement with non-Christians is primarily for the purpose of evangelization and conversion. Resistance to the truth—viewed as stubbornness or hardness of heart—must be worn down and overcome.

But are Jews and Christians fated to relate to one another as contentious litigants in a messy divorce trial or, even more tragically, as former spouses who want nothing to do with one another? Surely the Jewish and Christian authors of this volume understand their relationship with one another in quite different terms. It is not unreasonable to hope that by sharing our most treasured texts and deeply held beliefs, Christians and Jews will come to understand one another more deeply and even be transformed through the encounter. But clearly, these conversations are not intended to eliminate or resolve all differences between our two communities.

Although Jews and Christians affirm that God is infinite and one, we also acknowledge that our human apprehension of Holy Mystery is inevitably finite and plural. The differences dividing Jews and Christians are "humanly irreconcilable" not because we are incapable of careful listening, respectful dialogue, and discerning theological judgments. Rather, our communities cannot be "reconciled" in the sense that we enjoy distinct and different ongoing relationships with the One who is above every other name. What we can do, in dialogue, is to open windows into each other's worlds, illumining the rich, complex, and multifaceted character of religious traditions as distinctive ways of life that cannot be reduced solely to truth claims to be judged objectively "right" or "wrong."

As the opening quotation by Jewish social theorist Michael Walzer suggests, human beings are always religious in some particular way. There is no "generic" religion because our way to God is always mediated by some set of images and symbols, metaphors and stories, beliefs and practices. Judaism and Christianity emerged from a particular people's encounter with the divine over time. Each tradition is a unique and irreplaceable embodiment of the accumulated wisdom of a community bound together by common memories and hopes that shape the religious and moral imaginations of its members.

These memories and hopes are passed on from generation to generation. They are not only inscribed and encountered through text but also embodied and enacted in a whole range of cultural forms. Rituals of celebration and mourning mark the spiritual rhythms of our lives; the liturgical calendar demarcates a distinctive way of structuring space and time; holidays commemorate and reenact significant events in our history; practices and disciplines such as kneeling, bowing, wearing distinctive garb, or observing dietary laws establish habits that foster a kind of bodily knowing and remembering; architecture gives creative expression to a particular way of being in the world; religious objects and artifacts engage our senses; even games, music, and food contribute to our collective identity as a people. Thus, to encounter Judaism or Christianity is not simply to know in some abstract way what each tradition believes. It is to enter into a distinctive culture and way of life; to cultivate a feel for the distinctive "habits of the heart" that create a sense of solidarity and bind us together as a people.

When Jews and Christians come together to share our stories, we approach one another not as "blank slates" but as participants in living faith traditions. In our modern age, religious belief and commitment may be matters of choice, not destiny; but in practice, it is not surprising that most human beings end up embracing the spiritual traditions into which they were been born. Although it is always possible to choose differently, to be attracted to other spiritual paths for a variety of reasons, we come to these choices already "bent" to experience ourselves, the world, and the divine in particular ways. Although we can strive to recognize, even put aside, our biases and preconceptions, we cannot occupy some neutral, objective standpoint from which to view each other's worlds. We have a history. We carry with us certain habits of mind and heart that already orient our perceptions and values.

Of course, not all "Jews" and all "Christians" think or behave alike. Religious identity is not some static, unchanging essence. A "tradition" is not just a body of content to be handed on; it is also a dynamic process through which treasured religious meanings from the past are interpreted, reflected upon, refined, even reconstructed in light of new, ever changing historical and social circumstances. To participate in a living faith tradition is not only to identify with a historical people but also to participate in an ongoing communal conversation about how to live in a faithful, covenantal relationship with God in this time and this place. As a consequence, beliefs and practices that are defining characteristics in one age may become less salient in another. What some Jews or some Christians consider essential in one context, others may tolerate, ignore, or even reject in another. Both the developmental character of Judaism and Christianity as historical faiths and the internal pluralism characteristic of both traditions suggest that the "identity" of a religious tradition "can never be fixed or final because it is always in the making."[4]

The challenge of interfaith dialogue is to recognize the complexity of what we attempt when we speak to one another across religious boundaries. This challenge is especially present in the unique relationship between Christianity and Judaism. Our two traditions do not exist as isolated wholes but are deeply interrelated. Our traditions have been forged in relation to one another and to the larger cultures of which we are a part. Certain elements of one tradition have been appropriated and refashioned—or opposed and excluded—by the other. Thus, the history of each tradition has taken shape because of the impact of the other.

It must be acknowledged, however, that there is an asymmetry in the Jewish–Christian relationship. For Christians, "the encounter with Judaism is not only an external conversation with a religious other, but . . . an internal conversation between two parts of our own tradition—indeed, two parts of our written scriptures, what we have traditionally called the Old and New Testaments."[5] As

Christopher Leighton observes: "Christians walk a path that repeatedly crosses Jewish boundaries. There is no way around this stubborn fact. Christians cannot enter into relationship with the God of Israel without simultaneously becoming entangled with God's covenantal partner, Israel."[6]

To suggest that our identities as Jews and Christians are deeply intertwined is not to suggest that our differences are insignificant, nor is it to deny that for most of our history together, we have viewed each other, at best, as threats. But it is to argue that in a religiously pluralistic world, we cannot afford to ignore or merely tolerate one another. As Diana Eck argues, we need to find a way "to make a home for [our]selves and [our] neighbors." When we embrace religious pluralism as a value, interreligious dialogue can become, in Eck's terms, a "truth-seeking encounter" between religiously committed participants; a space where differences are actively engaged in order to find "ways to be distinctively ourselves and yet be in relation to one another."[7]

Jews and Christians as Blessings to Each Other

If, as we have argued, religious differences between Jews and Christians are intrinsically "irreconcilable," what can we expect to gain from dialogue as a "truth-seeking encounter"? Can Jews and Christians becomes "blessings" to one another, despite, or even because of, differences that have created historical enmity between our two communities? Let us suggest six important reasons for continued dialogue between our two communities.

1. In the words of Jewish scholar Jean Halperin, "We not only need to understand one another, we need one another to understand ourselves."[8] Because Judaism and Christianity, to differing degrees, evolved in response to one another, the more we know about the other, the better we understand our tradition and ourselves. Indeed, it is not just that knowledge of the other enriches my own self-understanding, but that the relationship with the other is in some sense constitutive of my identity as "Christian" or "Jew." Understanding how the historical relationship with the other has shaped and perhaps misshaped the historical development of our traditions

enables us to guide the development of our traditions in the future with far greater wisdom and insight.

2. We need a relationship with the other to know more of what it can mean to have a relationship with God. No matter how compelling and rich each of our traditions is, no matter how divinely given or divinely inspired, it is not complete, for traditions speak in human language, which is necessarily culture-bound and erring. Although we can see this incompleteness in others' traditions, it is difficult to see or acknowledge it in our own. Learning others' traditions, and seeing how our own tradition looks in their eyes, makes our own culture-bound expressions a bit more transparent. This transparency allows us to recognize the limits of our own expressions. In the encounter with other communities of faith, we are moved beyond the limits of our own particularity to recognize the Infinite Mystery beyond human understanding.

3. Dialogue enables us to understand the other on their own terms rather than through our own beliefs and convictions. Interfaith dialogue is an intensive course in empathic listening. Long-standing prejudices and stereotypes begin to lose their power as we learn to hear others in the way they want to be heard and not in the way we may choose to translate or interpret their story. Listening to others speak of their deepest beliefs, especially those that run counter to our own, requires enormous self-discipline. But the skills we learn here open us to hearing better all sorts of stories in our lives, especially the stories of our loved ones, which are often the most difficult to hear.

4. Interfaith dialogue also allows us to see ourselves through the eyes of the other. When the other recognizes the beauty and depth to be found in our tradition, our own appreciation grows for the gifts with which we have been blessed. When the other responds with suspicion, wariness, or fear, we are forced to acknowledge the tragic human failures that are also part of our history together. In dialogue, we become more aware of the selectivity of communal memories—the tendency to remember the best of who we are and to overlook ourselves at our worst. Dialogue with the other helps to keep us more honest.

5. The participants of interfaith dialogue often enjoy the gift of forming profound, intimate, and lasting relationships with their dia-

logue partners, a bond increasingly difficult to form in this atomized and virtual world. Along with our differences, we nonetheless discover shared hopes and common concerns for the human family. Together we learn about the challenges of maintaining the vitality of religious community in an individualistic age and of sustaining countercultural communities of memory as a bulwark against the moral vacuity of the modern consumerist society. We find partners who share a commitment to the work of social justice and to the building of the common good.

6. Finally, dialogue with the other is not simply a sociological necessity but a theological dynamic that issues forth from the intrinsic character of each tradition's internal religious life. It is tempting, given a diffuse sense of religious identity and the increasing fragility and permeability of communal boundaries in a postmodern world, to focus energy on strengthening the internal vitality of our faith communities. But religious traditions that insist on including the stranger cannot be content with communal forms based on the exclusion of difference. We honor both particularity and pluralism not by ignoring or obliterating differences but by exploring the various "borders" that inhabit our divided lives—the borders between various communities of discourse, between religious traditions, between faith communities and the public world, and even between the multiple commitments that structure our personal identities.

Engaging the Other

Once we understand our motivations and gather to dialogue, however, it is important that we learn how best to do it. Desiring to do something and knowing how to do it are two different steps. When one chooses to do something together in a group, it is helpful if everyone has clear expectations to serve as guidelines for conversation.

The first step in dialogue is to approach the other with openness and respect. We should speak the truth about our traditions, our beliefs, and our feelings honestly and respectfully, ever mindful about how our words will be received. We must receive what the other says openly and respectfully, even if we wish we did not have to hear it.

The second step is to craft a response to what you hear. Dialogue makes claims upon us. We cannot truly hear the other and then turn away unaffected. If we are out of range when someone calls to us, then we cannot know to respond. But if we hear the call and fail to respond, it is an act of cruelty or cowardice, or both. Likewise with dialogue, to hear and not respond denies the message and the speaker. Hearing lays a sacred claim upon the listener to respond.

Our responses can take one of three graduated forms: a change in attitude, a change in belief, or a change in behavior.

1. Attitude.   To hear what someone believes, in their own words and in their own terms, to experience the moment when someone takes the time and care to be there with us and speak quietly to us of their most precious beliefs, calls upon us to examine our attitude. Our response is most often not even a conscious response. Rather, over the course of the interfaith encounter, we often find our bodies loosening, our arms unfolding, our bodies leaning in to hear better. We find a joke slips out, an ease enters the room. We already are moving from seeing the other as stranger to seeing them as comrade, or neighbor, or cousin. Attitudinal changes are often reflexive, demonstrated through the body and fed back toward the soul. Such is the power of dialogue.

2. Belief.   To hear the passion of someone else's beliefs, to see how the system all fits together, to note how it lifts the believer and gives them purpose, challenges us to understand our historic and present responses to the other. Once it may have seemed easier, even desirable, to say "We are right and they are wrong"; but in today's global village, we see the variety of goodly truths spoken in God's name. (We are excluding from here the "truths" that contain as part of their essence a dogma that threatens and denigrates another's existence.) Even within our own traditions, we experience differences of belief and practice. Given the extraordinarily varied systems of belief around us, can we continue to deny all others their legitimacy? How can we assess their truth, and ours? Doesn't it make sense that God might choose to speak in many ways to many people? Or even if God spoke only once, does it make sense that the utterances were heard and translated differently? We know how teachers must craft the lesson to meet the learning style and ability of the student.

Would we expect less of God? If there are so many of us, why cannot there be so many different ways to God? Does it make sense that the infinite God would create a finite way to holiness?

To believe that the infinite God can call upon us in a multiplicity of ways challenges us to re-envision how we view the other. As with our attitudes, we might find that in the course of interfaith dialogue, our beliefs change in spite of us, unwittingly, unconsciously. Then when we turn to assess the other in light of dialogue, we find that we value the other, and we acknowledge their beliefs more deeply than we did at the start.

This potential for change in our belief regarding the other is both the blessing and the curse of interfaith dialogue. Some might choose to avoid dialogue, fearing that any changes will weaken the integrity of their beliefs or their attachment to their tradition. But most participants find that when they achieve a more sophisticated appreciation of the other's tradition, they deepen their appreciation of their own as well.

3. Behavior.   Once we feel that our attitudes and even our beliefs are changing, we then move to the one response to dialogue that does not happen without our effort. It is a change in behavior. Our inadvertent responses of attitude and belief move us to act. We begin to wonder: Do we have liturgies that delegitimize the other? Do our sacred texts and stories speak of others in ways that they would not speak about themselves? Have we acted toward the other, in law and life, in ways that renounce, threaten, and harm them? The last step of interfaith dialogue asks, "How shall we rid our traditions of these tendencies and transform our view of our neighbors?"

These three acts of change reveal how difficult, even subversive, dialogue is. It reveals why some religious leaders forbid dialogue, even among members of their own religion who belong to different movements. It reveals why some individuals may shun it. Often we define ourselves in opposition to the other. I am what they are not. To see "them" as not so different from "us" is to experience a potential loss of personal and communal boundaries. Indeed, sometimes religions and cultures craft rituals and beliefs that codify difference just so that boundaries can be kept neatly drawn. Boundaries, in and of themselves, are not dangerous. Each of us needs to know how to identify the family we belong to, and that we live in this house and not that one. And we want to know when we go home at night that we enter the house of the people who know what we did yesterday and what questions to ask us about the day, who know what medications we have to take and what time and what foods we like to eat for dinner. We want to know that our bed is reserved for us and that we can sleep in peace. And we want to know that our family is part of a greater grouping of like-minded families, for we want to be able to go out into the world and not be alone. We need to be able to identify others of our extended family by common acts, language, signs, holidays, or knowledge. That is the way humans create meaningful communities of belonging that are large enough to incorporate us and small enough to notice us. In my father's house, the saying goes, there are many rooms.

Dialogue shows us that in these ways we are not all that different. We are united by our questions and our quest. Where we differ is in our responses to common impulses: seeking the nature and purpose of creation, what we are called upon to do, responses to suffering, the nature of death, God's presence in the world.

Dialogue also shows us how real, deep differences do divide us. Some of us believe there is no such thing as grace; that Jesus was not the Messiah; or that Israel is no longer the covenanted nation of God. These beliefs fly in the face of fundamental tenets of the other. Even more, some of these tenets teach us that as good neighbors, we should work to change the other, save the other. Yet to this "other," such "kindness" is a violation, an intrusion.

Finally, dialogue reminds us that reconciliation is not always easy. What if we agree that we will speak about the other only in the terms they declare for themselves? What if we agree to declare mutual legitimacy and to move together on the path of reconciliation, but one partner desires more or moves more quickly than the other? What if one party makes changes in attitude, belief, and behavior while the other party does not change behavior? What if one party thinks it need not? What if one party atones and the other does not forgive in the way the atoning party sought? What will happen if one party feels rejected and the other feels coerced? Will dialogue make things worse?

Those committed to dialogue acknowledge and risk these feelings and consequences. Indeed, part of long-term dialogue is speaking of these dangers. Yet somehow, the dynamics of dialogue guide the participants past these rocky shoals. The power and holiness of looking into others' faces, hearing their voices, and responding when they create the silence for us to fill can guide us over these rough spots. We will not always achieve mutual satisfaction. We may not be able to agree. Yet, most who allow this enterprise to work over time, acknowledge that they achieve a clearer sense of self and community; a deepening of a commitment to their own tradition; a richer appreciation for other traditions; and a tool to help them through other hard parts of life with others.

Discussion Questions

1. Would you participate in another study session of this kind? Why? Why not?
2. The authors speak about three areas of possible change as a result of Jews and Christians encountering each other: attitude, belief, and behavior.
   - Have any your attitudes been challenged and, if so, in what way? Have any of your attitudes changed?
   - Have any your beliefs been challenged and, if so, in what way. Have any of your beliefs changed?
   - Have any of your behaviors been challenged and, if so, in what way? Do you think any of your behaviors will change?
3. For this kind of endeavor to be successful, is it necessary for there to be changes in attitude, belief, or behavior?
4. What is one thing that you learned, relearned, or were surprised by in this study session? Why?
5. Do you think that participation in this kind of study is good for Jews and good for Christians? Does it strengthen Jews and Christians in the particulars of their own traditions? Does it strengthen Jews and Christians as a community of religious people who come together?
6. Is this kind of study something you would work to encourage in your church or synagogue? Why?

7. Do you believe that there are irreconcilable differences between Judaism and Christianity? What are they? Are they a blessing, or a curse, or both?
8. What questions were raised for you during this process that were not answered or that you would like to explore in greater depth?

Notes

1. Michael Walzer, *Thick and Thin: Moral Argument at Home and Abroad* (Notre Dame: University of Notre Dame Press, 1994), 8.

2. Diana Eck, *Encountering God: A Spiritual Journey from Bozeman to Banaras* (Boston: Beacon, 1993), 167–198.

3. Robert. L. Wilken, *John Chrysostom and the Jews: Rhetoric and Reality in the Fourth Century* (Berkeley: University of California Press, 1983), 148.

4. The phrase is one historian Arthur Schlesinger applies to American identity, quoted in Ronald F. Thiemann, *Religion in Public Life: A Dilemma for Democracy* (Washington, D.C.: Georgetown University Press, 1996), 148.

5. Kendell Soulen, *The God of Israel and Christian Theology* (Minneapolis: Fortress, 1996), 21.

6. Christopher Leighton, "Christian Theology After the Shoah," in *Christianity in Jewish Terms* (Boulder, Colo.: Westview Press, 2000), 36.

7. See Eck's analysis of "pluralism" in *Encountering God*, 191–199.

8. Cited in Eck, *Encountering God*, 189.

Afterword

MARY C. BOYS AND

SARA S. LEE

Our fifteen-year collaboration in facilitating dialogue between Jews and Christians shapes our reading of *Irreconcilable Differences? A Learning Resource for Jews and Christians.* Our collaboration reinforces our belief in the importance of interreligious learning, increases our appreciation for the distinctive contributions of this study guide, and suggests subsequent directions for dialogue.

Interreligious Learning

Our era provides previously unimagined possibilities for learning about religions other than one's own. The phenomenon of globalization means that we encounter diverse cultures and traditions on an unprecedented scale. Fewer of us live and work in religious or ethnic enclaves than in any previous age. The "other" lives next door or works in the adjoining office. Technological advances in transportation enable us to travel to distant lands in a fraction of the time it would have taken our ancestors; and the computer erases borders of space and time altogether. The stranger now dwells in our midst, whether physically or virtually.

However valuable it is to meet a Sikh neighbor or visit a Buddhist monastery in Nepal or learn about Islam from a Website or CD-ROM, nothing substitutes for sustained and serious face-to-face encounter with the religiously other. Jews or Christians who read *Irreconcilable Differences?* will learn about the other's tradition, but using this study guide *together* will immeasurably enhance their learning. We have come to call this mode of dialogue built upon a foundation of mutual study "interreligious learning." It involves encountering a religious tradition *as the other embodies it.* Interreligious learning is energized by the desire to understand differences, by a willingness to take up difficult questions (especially about one's own tradition), and by the ability to enter empathetically into another's way of life without losing one's own boundaries.

Without question, history complicates interreligious learning between Jews and Christians. The anti-Judaism that has long infected church teaching—what the Catholic bishops of the Netherlands have called the "catechesis of vilification"—means that there are "still open wounds."[1] Christians, largely ignorant of the legacy and consequences of anti-Judaism in church teaching, may fail to acknowledge these wounds, whereas Jews may be preoccupied by them. It is thus all the more important that Jews and Christians study together in such a fashion that stereotypes and misconceptions are laid to rest and wounds begin to heal.

Our experience confirms what Rosann Catalano and David Fox Sandmel claim in their introductory essay: Jews and Christians who learn about each other *in each other's presence* come to a deeper self-understanding and an invigorated commitment to their own tradition. When dialogue moves beyond superficial exchange to the level of interreligious learning, participants see both the other and themselves in a new way. In many cases, interreligious learning helps us appreciate our own traditions in a new way, as was the case when a delegation of American Jews went to India at the invitation of the Dalai Lama. Writing of this encounter with Tibetan Buddhism, poet and professor of English Roger Kamenetz observed: "If only Jews could see themselves as sweetly as the Dalai Lama saw us. Then we would see Judaism renewed."[2]

The Distinctive Contributions of *Irreconcilable Differences?*

This study guide advances the dialogue between Jews and Christians by assigning importance to religious knowledge, elucidating key terms in each tradition, identifying commonalities without obscuring differences, and showing how interreligious dialogue deepens one's own religious heritage.

Religious Knowledge

Ignorance in the religious realm is costly. It results in a shallow self-identity incapable of sustaining commitment in our secular society. When combined with misunderstandings about the other, ignorance promotes misguided zeal that all too readily results in caricature, hate language, and even violence in the name of truth. If religions are to contribute to the health of society and the development of world peace, their adherents must be knowledgeable, about both themselves and others with whom they share this fragile planet. Jews and Christians must acquire a vocabulary and grammar that will enable them to converse about their practices and beliefs. Only then will they develop what Christopher Leighton and Daniel Lehmann term "a textured awareness of their distinctive religious identities that can flourish amid the pushes and pulls of a religiously diverse society."

We applaud the writers of *Irreconcilable Differences?* for this commentary on "Dabru Emet." Not only do they make the assertions of that bold statement more widely accessible, they provide readers with the requisite terms and concepts for intelligent discussion across the boundaries of Judaism and Christianity.

Key Terms

Dialogue between adherents of different religions is inherently complicated, if absolutely crucial. It is often difficult to find common terms and categories; concepts central to one tradition have no precise analogue in the other.

In contrast, it would appear that dialogue between Jews and Christians would be made easier by the vocabulary they share—such as redemption, salvation, sin, repentance, and judgment. Yet this shared vocabulary complicates their dialogue: The words carry different meanings. Those who study *Irreconcilable Differences?* will learn how Judaism and Christianity appropriate these words in distinctive fashion. Of note is the essay by Jane West Walsh, Mary Katherine Allman, Christopher Leighton, Rosann Catalano, and David Fox Sandmel on different understandings of sin and repentance—two terms so familiar to both communities that we may not appreciate the understandings characteristic of each. Readers will also get a glimpse of variant understandings of the terms within the same communities. Reform and Conservative Jews differ from Orthodox Jews (and from each other) in interpreting the force of revelation in providing norms for the community. Protestant, Orthodox, and Catholic Christians have different canons of the First ("Old") Testament and differ in the weight they assign to ecclesial commentary.

Irreconcilable Differences? is an ecumenical book for the interreligious encounter: Its authors are drawn from Judaism's denominations, as well as from mainline Christian churches, Protestant and Catholic. This ecumenical character adds an important dimension to the book, helping readers to appreciate the complex, diverse range of thought inherent in "Judaism" and "Christianity."

Commonalities and Differences

The statement "Dabru Emet" that inspired this study guide outlines some of the most important beliefs Jews and Christians hold in common. Christians and Jews worship the same God, seek authority from the same book, and accept the moral principles of Torah. The corresponding essays illumine how these shared beliefs assume distinctive contours in each tradition. For example, Philip Cunningham and Jan Katzew speak of Jews and Christians as "ethical monotheists" who share a foundation of "belief and action, a hope that differences derive from our limited, mortal perspectives of the Transcendent One." They assert that both Israel and the church know God as a personal God; Christians, however, image this personal God in Trinitarian language. Their essay shows how a commonality—belief in the One God—encompasses profound differences.

Irreconcilable Differences? gives insight into the different ways in which Christians and Jews seek authority from the Bible. Christian Bibles include all the books of the Jewish Bible (the Tanach), though in a different order. It is our distinctive interpretations that distinguish each of our traditions. Jews interpret the Tanach primarily through the lens of rabbinic commentary; contemporary Christians read the First Testament primarily through the lens of the Second or

New Testament. Both communities confront the new challenges that characterize interpretation today, as Amy Grossblat Pessah, Kenneth Myers, and Christopher Leighton point out in their essay on how Jews and Christians read the Bible. Can Jews find a biblical warrant to recognize the covenant Christians claim to have with the God of Israel? Can Christians replace supersessionist readings of the First Testament with interpretations that do justice to Judaism? Can both use modern scholarship as a tool for acknowledging the perspectives that shape biblical interpretation in each community, so as to enable Jews and Christians to appreciate differences in a new light? Can both draw upon this scholarship in ways that deepen their discernment of the Holy One's involvement in human history?

Christopher Leighton, Donald Dawe, and Avi Weinstein's essay on the Land of Israel also provides a resource for grappling with a complicated question. The centrality of the Land to Judaism has no precise correlate in Christianity, yet both the Land and the term "Israel" hold religious significance for Christians.

Interreligious Dialogue and Commitment to a Tradition of Faith

Dialogue between Jews and Christians is multidimensional. It includes an understanding of terms—Torah, Tanach, Mishnah, Talmud, tefilah, teshuvah, tsedakah, sacrament, Trinity, Incarnation—and of the history of our nearly two-thousand-year relationship. There is also the Shoah to confront, the State of Israel to consider, and the involvement of Jews and Christians in the public square to discern.

Transcending all of these things, however, is the reality of the One whom we worship. We cannot overemphasize the importance of the first statement by the authors of "Dabru Emet": "Jews and Christians worship the same God." In encountering each other, Jews and Christians see God through the eyes of another and are moved, as Nina Beth Cardin and Fayette Veverka write in the concluding essay, "beyond the limits of our own particularity to recognize the Infinite Mystery beyond human understanding."

Yet our worship of the same God neither solves all of our problems nor answers all of our questions, as Sharon Cohen Anisfeld

and Cynthia Terry show in their essay on Jewish and Christian responses to suffering. Suffering is a part of every life—and Jews and
Christians over time have wrestled with its meaning. Each community has approached this profound topic out of its distinctive experiences and theological frameworks. Neither has exhausted thinking
on the subject. Knowing how the other community strives to make
meaning out of suffering stimulates each of us to reflect more deeply
and challenges us to do whatever we can to ameliorate the suffering
in our midst.

Where to from Here?

Our reading of *Irreconcilable Differences?* leads us to believe that
this brief book will serve as a resource for many months of substan-
tive conversation. What might be the next steps when readers finally
lay this book aside? We suggest three: probing for personal implications, seeking further involvement in interreligious learning, and
creating opportunities for wider participation in Jewish–Christian
dialogue.

Probing for Personal Implications

It is our hope that the conversations this book engenders will moti-
vate readers to work through some of their previous (mis)under-
standings. The essay by Lawrence Farris and Isaac Serotta on Jewish
and Christian ethics provides an excellent resource for this work of
reconceptualizing. One of the most enduring caricatures many
Christians hold of Judaism is that it is a religion of vengeance—of
an "eye for an eye, a tooth for a tooth"—in contrast to the loving
way of Jesus Christ. One of the most persistent misconceptions Jews
hold about Christianity is that belief in Jesus is sentimental and individualistic, "Jesus and me." The Farris-Serotta essay shows how
rabbinic commentators over the ages have dealt with Exodus
21:23–24 ("The penalty shall be life for life, eye for eye, tooth for
tooth"), and thus how Jewish ethics developed over time. It also
shows that the Christian ethic grounded in the life of Jesus is far
from sentimental. Rather, "Jesus' teaching challenges the standards

and expectations of *all* Christians . . . because he overturns the logic of self-preservation."

Similarly, Jews and Christians readily talk past each other when making claims about the Messiah. The essay by Christine Blair, Jeff Marx, Christopher Leighton, Rosann Catalano, and David Fox Sandmel offers a rich resource for understanding how and why our two communities of faith hold different perspectives on messianism, and how these understandings connect to differing understandings of salvation and the afterlife.

Further Involvement in Interreligious Learning

Presumably, many readers of this study guide will have had little experience in sustained dialogue with the other. It is our hope that the mutual study stimulated by *Irreconcilable Differences?* will reshape attitudes and behaviors, as well as lead to continued contact and study. Study forces us to reconsider previous understandings of the other and, most likely, some oversimplified views we have held about our own tradition. It asks us to examine how we act toward the other and to use our newfound knowledge to build a genuinely pluralistic society.

As a concomitant of study, Jews might appropriately make it possible for Christians who have never had the opportunity to share a Shabbat meal or participate in a Seder to do so. Christians might invite Jews to be present for a sacramental event, such as a baptism, or to come to a typical worship service. Both might avail themselves of the many workshops, conferences, and public lectures on related topics. As we once did, they might choose to tour the United States Holocaust Memorial Museum together—an afternoon forever etched in our memories—or to go to Israel together. To stand together as Jew and Christian before Jerusalem's gates, or to walk together down the Avenue of the Righteous Gentiles at *Yad Vashem* (the Holocaust memorial) or to stroll together along the shore of Lake Kinneret (Sea of Galilee) . . . such moments reveal the presence of the Holy One in an extraordinary way.

To engage in dialogue at this level is life-changing. The risks of dialogue lead to transformation. As Sandra Lubarsky says so eloquently:

> In putting forward our beliefs and values for scrutiny and in opening ourselves to another worldview, we become vulnerable to our selves and our communities. It takes courage to enter the process, courage to redefine ourselves in response to new insights, courage to "side" at times with another tradition, courage to find ourselves sometimes marginalized in our own traditions. . . . Increased openness, sensitivity, and awareness cannot be confined; in opening ourselves to one person in dialogue, we open ourselves to many. . . . In crossing one barrier, we cross many.[3]

Creating Opportunities for Wider Participation

Dialogue between Christians and Jews remains largely peripheral in the church and synagogue. Yet in our experience those who partake in serious and sustained dialogue become "converts" to the cause, recognizing the importance of reconciliation between our two communities. It is our hope that readers of this book will themselves become advocates for dialogue and assume leadership roles. Such leadership might be expressed in convening and leading new dialogue groups; in creating opportunities for students and youth in our respective religious education programs to engage in interreligious learning; and in advocating for the study of the other's traditions in our respective educational institutions.

It is our hope that the work begun in these pages will be taken up into the lives of many Jews and Christians. May the work of dialogue—and it is indeed work—deepen our commitment to our own tradition, to one another, and to the healing of religious divisions in our world.

Notes

1. The Dutch bishops' 1995 statement, "Supported by One Root: Our Relationship to Judaism," may be found in *Catholics Remember the Holocaust* (Washington, D.C.: Secretariat for Ecumenical and Interreligious Affairs, National Confer-

ence of Catholic Bishops, 1998), 21–24. The term "still open wounds" comes from the French bishops' 1997 statement, "Declaration of Repentance," in the same volume, 31–37.

2. Rodger Kamenetz, *The Jew in the Lotus* (San Francisco: HarperSanFrancisco, 1994), 283.

3. Sandra Lubarsky, "Dialogue: 'Holy Insecurity,'" *Religious Education* 91, no. 4 (fall 1996): 543.

Glossary

This glossary presents brief, and therefore general, definitions of key terms that appear throughout the essays in this book. For more information, and for terms not included here, the reader should consult one or more of the following references: the *Encyclopedia Judaica,* the *Anchor Bible Dictionary,* and the *Encyclopedia of Religion.* Another useful resource is the glossary initiated by Robert Kraft (expanded and refined by others) for the University of Pennsylvania course "Religions of the West"; it can be found on the World Wide Web at http://ccat.sas.upenn.edu/~rs2/glossopt.html.

Apocrypha   From the Greek meaning "to hide" or "to uncover." Refers to certain Jewish books written in the Hellenistic-Roman period that came to be included in the Greek translation of Jewish scriptures (and thus in the eastern Christian biblical canon) and in the Roman Catholic canon (as "deuterocanonical") but not in the Jewish or Protestant biblical canons.

Apostle   Greek for "ambassador, legate." In early Christian circles, it was used to refer especially to the earliest missionaries sent out to preach the gospel message concerning Jesus; traditionally twelve of Jesus' close associates came to be called "the 12 Apostles" (also "the 12 disciples"). Paul considered himself an apostle of Jesus Christ, although he had not been an associate of Jesus during his life.

Aramaic   Semitic language closely related to Hebrew. Sections of the biblical books Daniel and Ezra are in Aramaic, as are many documents from the Second Temple period and later, including traditional Jewish biblical commentary, the Gemara (see below).

Augustine (354–430 C.E.)   One of the foremost philosophers and theologians of early Christianity. He had a profound influence on the subsequent development of Western thought and culture and first gave shape to the themes and defined the problems that have characterized the Western tradition of Christian theology.

B.C.E. (before the common era)   An attempt to use a neutral designation for the period traditionally labeled "B.C." (before Christ) by Christians. Thus 586 B.C.E. is identical to 586 B.C.

Baptism   In earliest Christianity, the rite of ritual immersion in water that initiated a person (usually an "adult") into the Christian church. Later, pouring or sprinkling with water, as well as the practice of baptizing infants, came into use in some churches.

Bar Kochba, Simon   Jewish leader of a failed revolt against Rome (132–135 C.E.).

Bar (Bat) Mitsvah (Hebrew, "son- (daughter-) of-the-commandment(s)") The phrase originally referred to a person responsible for performing the divine commandments of Judaism; it now also refers to the occasion when a boy or girl reaches the age of religious majority and responsibility (thirteen years for a boy; twelve years for a girl).

Ben (Hebrew) or Bar (Aramaic)   "Son," used frequently in "patronymics" (naming by identity of father); Akiba ben Joseph means Akiba son of Joseph.

C.E. (common era)   An attempt to use a neutral designation for the period traditionally labeled "A.D." (in Latin, *anno domini,* or "year of the Lord") by Christians. Thus 1992 C.E. is identical to 1992 A.D.

Church Fathers   Term used to describe the writers of early Christian literature (excluding the New Testament itself) whose works, written between the first and the sixth century, were considered correct and appropriate ("orthodox") by the church.

Church   The designation traditionally used for a specifically Christian assembly or body of people, and thus also for the building or location in which the assembled people meet. By extension it is also used for a specific organized denomination within Christianity (e.g., Roman Catholic Church, Methodist Church, etc.).

Communion   A term used especially in Protestant Christian circles for the sacrament (see below) of receiving bread and wine as the body and blood of Christ (or as symbols thereof), also known as the Lord's Supper or the Eucharist (see below).

Diaspora (Greek, "scattering")   Often used to refer to the Jewish communities living among the Gentiles outside the land Israel. In Hebrew, the term used is *galut,* "exile."

Easter   The most ancient Christian annual special day, commemorating the (death and) resurrection of Jesus in the spring, at the time of Jewish Passover (thus not a fixed day on the solar calendar). See also Lent.

Eucharist   The Christian sacrament of receiving bread (usually unleavened) and wine as the body and blood of Christ (or as symbols thereof). This term is more often used for the sacrament in the Roman Catholic and Eastern Orthodox churches, whereas "communion" or "Lord's Supper" is the term more common in the Protestant traditions.

Gemara (Aramaic, "completion")   See "Talmud."

Gnosticism   A form of mysticism found in Judaism, Christianity, and paganism in the Roman world. Although Gnosticism took many forms, it generally distinguished the Supreme Divine Being (usually seen as good) from the demiurge (usually seen as evil), a secondary power responsible for creation and involved in the material world. Dualism, the belief that the world is ruled by two opposing powers, was common to most forms of Gnosticism. Both rabbinic Judaism and classical Christianity were opposed to Gnosticism and viewed it as heretical.

Good Friday   The name given to the Friday of Holy Week, the week preceding Easter Sunday. It is the day on which Christians commemorate the death of Jesus.

Gospel (literally, "good news")   In the New Testament, it refers to four separate accounts of the life, death, and resurrection of Jesus Christ. In addition to the four canonical Gospels, there are other "lives of Jesus" from the same time period that were not included in the canon of the New Testament; these are sometimes referred to as noncanonical Gospels.

Grace   In Christian thought, unmerited divine assistance on one's spiritual path; often conceived as a special blessing received in an intense experience, but also may include a sense of special direction in one's life.

Halachah (Hebrew, "the way")   Law established or custom ratified by authoritative rabbinic jurists and teachers. Colloquially, if something is deemed halachic, it is considered proper and normative behavior.

Incarnation   A term in Christianity applied to the "becoming flesh" (human birth) of Jesus Christ.

Jerusalem Talmud   See "Talmud."

Kingdom of God   The state of the world in which God's will is fulfilled; expected to be brought into being at the end of time. In Judaism this occurs with the coming of the Messiah; in Christianity it occurs when Christ returns.

Lent   In the Christian liturgical calendar, the period of forty days beginning with "Ash Wednesday" (so called because penitents mark their heads with ashes) and Easter, the celebration of Jesus' resurrection.

Maimonides, Moses (1134–1205)   Premier medieval Jewish philosopher and legal expert also known as RaMBaM (acronym for Rabbi Moses ben Maimon).

Marcion   A second-century Christian who was considered heretical by his opponents because of certain dualistic and gnostic (see above) ideas. Marcion denied the sacred nature of the "Old Testament," viewing it as the book of an evil creator God.

Messiah   From the Hebrew meaning "anointed one" (in Greek, *christos*). Ancient priests and kings (and sometimes prophets) of Israel were anointed with oil. In early Judaism, the term came to mean a royal descendant of the dynasty of David who would restore the united kingdom of Israel and Judah and usher in an age of peace, justice, and plenty: the redeemer figure. The concept developed in many directions over the centuries. The messianic age was believed by some Jews to be a time of perfection of human institutions; others believed it to be a time of radical new beginnings, a new heaven and earth, after divine judgment and destruction. The title "Christos" came to be applied to Jesus of Nazareth by his followers, who were soon called "Christians" in Greek and Latin usage.

Midrash (Hebrew, "interpretation")   A general term for rabbinic interpretation of Scripture, as well as for specific collections of rabbinic literature.

Mishnah (Hebrew, "teaching")   An authorized compilation of rabbinic law, promulgated c. 210 C.E. by Rabbi Judah Ha-Nasi. See "Talmud."

Mitsvah (Hebrew, "commandment"), pl. mitsvot   A ritual or ethical duty or act of obedience to God's will. According to rabbinic Jewish tradition, there are 613 religious commandments referred to in the Torah (and elaborated upon by the rabbinic sages). In general, a mitsvah refers to any act of religious duty or obligation; more colloquially, a mitsvah refers to a "good deed."

Noahide Laws   According to rabbinic interpretation, seven laws were given to Noah (see Genesis 9) and were incumbent upon all humanity. A Gentile who followed the Noahide Laws was considered righteous (see Sanh. 105a).

Oral Torah   In traditional Jewish pharisaic/rabbinic thought, God revealed instructions for living through the Written Torah (Tanach) and through a parallel process of orally transmitted traditions. The Oral Torah was later written down as the Mishnah, Midrash, Tosefta, and the Talmuds (see entries above and below).

Origen (c. 185–251 C.E.)   One of the leading church fathers (see above).

Original Sin   In classical Christian thought, the term refers to the fundamental state of sinfulness and guilt inherited from the first man, Adam, that infects all of humanity but can be removed through depending on Christ and the grace he provides (e.g., in baptism).

Passion of Christ   A technical term in Christian circles for Jesus' suffering and crucifixion.

Pentecost   In Judaism, refers to the festival that occurs fifty days after Passover, known in Hebrew as Shavuot. In Christianity, it refers to the seventh Sunday after Easter, which commemorates the appearance of the Holy Spirit in Acts 2:1.

Pharisees (Hebrew *perushim*, "separatists" (?); adj. pharisaic) The name given to a group or movement in Second Temple Judaism, the origin and nature of which is unclear. Many scholars identify them with the later sages and rabbis who taught the oral and written law; others see them as a complex of pietistic and zealous separatists, distinct from the rabbis. According to the ancient Jewish historian Josephus, the Pharisees believed in the immortality of souls and resurrection of the dead, in a balance between predestination and free will, in angels as active divine agents, and in authoritative oral law. In the early Christian materials, Pharisees are often depicted as leading opponents of Jesus and his followers, and are often linked with "scribes" but distinguished from the Sadducees.

Philo Judaeus ("Philo the Jew") of Alexandria Greek speaking (and writing) prolific Jewish author in the first century C.E. Provides extensive evidence for Jewish thought in the Greco-Roman ("Hellenistic") world outside of Palestine. Philo's works were not preserved by the Jewish tradition but rather in Christianity, where they were influential in early Christian theology.

R. or Rabbi (Hebrew, "my master") An authorized teacher of the classical Jewish tradition (see oral law) after the fall of the Second Temple in 70 C.E. The role of the rabbi has changed considerably throughout the centuries. Traditionally, rabbis serve as the legal and spiritual guides of their congregations and communities. The title is conferred after considerable study of traditional Jewish sources. This conferral and its responsibilities are central to the chain of tradition in Judaism.

Rabbinic Judaism Term used to define the form of Judaism that emerged and became dominant after the destruction of the Second Temple in 70 C.E. See "R. or Rabbi" above.

Rashi Acronym of Rabbi Shlomo Yitzhaki (1040–1105), who wrote classical commentaries on both the Tanach and the Talmud (see below).

Sacrament Especially in classical Christianity, a formal religious rite (e.g., baptism, Eucharist; see above) regarded as sacred for its ability to convey divine blessing; in some traditions (especially Protestant), it is regarded as not effective in itself but as a sign or symbol of spiritual reality or truth.

Shema Title of the fundamental, monotheistic statement of Judaism, found in Deuteronomy 6:4 ("Hear, O Israel, the Lord is God, the Lord alone" *(shema Yisrael adonai elohenu adonai echad)*. This statement avers the unity of God and is recited daily in the liturgy (along with Deut. 6:5–9, 11.13–21; Num. 15.37–41, and other passages) and customarily before sleep at night. This proclamation also climaxes special liturgies (like Yom Kippur) and is central to the confession before death and to the ritual of martyrdom. The Shema is inscribed on the mezuzah and the tefilin (phylacteries). In public services, it is recited in unison.

Shoah (Hebrew, "destruction")   The term used for the destruction of European Jewry by the Nazis during World War II. The English term "holocaust" comes from the Greek meaning "wholly burnt," which is itself a translation of a Hebrew term, *olah*, found in the Tanach, referring to a sacrifice that was completely burnt. When applying the word "holocaust" to the Nazi destruction of European Jewry, the images of sacrifice and of being wholly burnt are troubling to Jews, who are increasingly using the term "Shoah," as are Christians who are sensitive to these same concerns.

Siddur   The standard daily Jewish prayer book.

Talmud (Hebrew, "study" or "learning")   Rabbinic Judaism produced two Talmuds: the one known as "Babylonian" is the most famous in the Western world and was completed around the fifth century C.E.; the other, known as the "Palestinian" or "Jerusalem" Talmud, was edited perhaps in the early fourth century C.E. Both have as their common core the Mishnah (see above), a collection of early rabbinic law, to which the *amoraim* (teachers) of the respective locales added commentary and discussion (gemara). Gemara has also become a colloquial, generic term for the Talmud and its study.

Tanach   A relatively modern acronym for the Jewish Bible, made up of the names of its three parts: Torah (Pentateuch or Law), Nevi'im (Prophets), and Ketuvim (Writings)—thus TNK, pronounced TaNaCh.

Temple   In the ancient world, temples were the centers of outward religious life, places at which public religious observances were normally conducted by the priestly professionals. In traditional Judaism, the only legitimate Temple was the one in Jerusalem, built first by King Solomon around 950 B.C.E., destroyed by the Babylonian king Nebuchadnezzar around 587/6 B.C.E., and rebuilt about seventy years later. The Second Temple was destroyed by the Romans in 70 C.E. The site of the ancient Jewish Temple is now occupied, in part, by the golden domed "Dome of the Rock" mosque. In recent times, "temple" has come to be used synonymously with synagogue in some Jewish usage.

Tosefta (Aramaic, "additional"): Early rabbinic work containing supplements to the Mishnah, called *beraita* (extraneous material) in the Talmud.

Virgin Birth   The belief that Mary, the mother of Jesus, was a virgin when Jesus was conceived and born. Often confused with Immaculate Conception.

YHVH   The sacred name of God in Jewish scriptures and tradition; also known as the tetragrammaton (Greek for "four letters"). Since Hebrew was written without vowels in ancient times, the four consonants YHVH contain no clue to their original pronunciation. They are generally rendered "Yahveh" in contemporary scholarship. In traditional Judaism, the name is not pronounced, but the Hebrew word *adonai* (Lord) or something similar is substituted. In most English versions of the Bible, the tetragrammaton is represented by "LORD."

For Further Study:
A Brief List of Print and
Internet Resources

There is an enormous wealth of material on Judaism, Christianity, and Jewish–Christian relations, both in print and on the World Wide Web. Basic information can be found in the *Anchor Bible Dictionary*, the *Encyclopedia Judaica*, and the *Encyclopedia of Religion* (edited by Mircea Eliade). The internet sites listed below provide access to many good resources. The bibliography that follows refers to works specifically on the relation between Jews and Christians. A useful bibliography, prepared by Jeffrey S. Siker, is found on pages 242–248 of *Jews and Christians: Exploring the Past, Present, and Future*, edited by James Charlesworth (see below).

Internet Resources

Institute for Christian and Jewish Studies (http://www.icjs.edu): The site for materials related to this book and the greater project of which it is part, as well as information about Jewish–Christian relations and an excellent list of related links.

Jewish Christian Relations (http://jcrelations.com): A substantial source of information about Jewish–Christian relations, with numerous links.

Internet Resources for the Study of Judaism and Christianity (http://ccat.sas.upenn.edu/rs/resources.html): This site, prepared by Dr. Jay Treat of the University of Pennsylvania, is a particularly rich set of links to academic sites that deal with a broad array of topics in the study of Judaism and Christianity.

Books

Allen, Ronald, and Clark M. Williamson. *Interpreting Difficult Texts: Anti-Judaism and Christian Preaching.* Philadelphia: Trinity Press International, 1989.

Beck, Norman A. *Mature Christianity in the Twenty-First Century.* New York: Crossroad, 1994.

Boadt, Lawrence, Helga Croner, and Leon Klenicki, eds. *Biblical Studies: Meeting Ground of Jews and Christians.* New York: Paulist Press, 1980.

Boys, Mary C. *Has God Only One Blessing? Judaism as a Source of Christian Self-Understanding.* New York: Paulist Press, 2000.

Braybrooke, Marcus. *Time to Meet: Toward a Deeper Relationship Between Jews and Christians.* Philadelphia: Trinity Press International, 1990.

Burrell, David, and Yehezkel Landau, eds. *Voices from Jerusalem: Jews and Christians Reflect on the Holy Land.* New York: Paulist Press, 1992.

Charlesworth, James, ed. *Jews and Christians: Exploring the Past, Present, and Future.* New York: Crossroad, 1990.

Charlesworth, James, ed. *Overcoming Fear Between Jews and Christians.* New York: Crossroad, 1992.

Cohen, Jeremy. *Living Letters of the Law: Ideas of the Jew in Medieval Christianity.* The S. Mark Taper Foundation Imprint in Jewish Studies. Berkeley: University of California Press, 1999.

Cohen, Martin A., and Helga Croner. *Christian Mission, Jewish Mission.* New York: Paulist Press, 1982.

Cohn, Sherbock. *A Dictionary of Judaism and Christianity.* Philadelphia: Trinity Press International, 1991.

Croner, Helga, and Leon Klenicki, eds. *Issues in the Jewish–Christian Dialogue: Jewish Perspectives on Covenant, Mission, and Witness.* New York: Paulist Press, 1979.

Cunningham, Philip A. *Education for Shalom.* Philadelphia: Liturgical Press, 1995.

Cunningham, Philip A., and Arthur F. Starr. *Sharing Shalom: A Process for Local Interfaith Dialogue Between Christians and Jews.* New York: Paulist Press, 1998.

Davies, W. D. *Christian Engagements with Judaism.* Harrisburg: Trinity Press International, 1999.

Dawe, Donald G., and Aurelia T. Fule. *Christians and Jews Together: Voices from the Conversation.* Presbyterian Publishing House, 1991.

Eakin, Frank E., Jr., *What Price Prejudice? Christian Anti-Semitism in America.* New York: Paulist Press, 1998.

Fisher, Eugene J. *Faith Without Prejudice: Rebuilding Christian Attitudes Toward Judaism.* Rev. and exp. ed. New York: Crossroad, 1993.

Fisher, Eugene J., ed. *Interwoven Destinies: Jews and Christians Throughout the Ages.* New York: Paulist Press, 1993.

Fisher, Eugene J., ed. *Visions of the Other: Jewish and Christian Theologians Assess the Dialogue.* New York: Paulist Press, 1994.

Fisher, Eugene J., and Leon Klenicki, eds. *In Our Time: The Flowering of Jewish–Catholic Dialogue.* With an annotated bibliography by Eugene J. Fisher. New York: Paulist Press, 1990.

Fisher, Eugene J., and Leon Klenicki, eds. *Spiritual Pilgrimage: Texts on Jews and Judaism, 1979–1995.* New York: Crossroad, 1995.

Flannery, Edward H. *The Anguish of the Jews: Twenty-Three Centuries of Anti-Semitism.* New York: Paulist Press, 1985.

Goldberg, Michael. *Jews and Christians: Getting Our Stories Straight.* Nashville: Abingdon Press, 1985.

Huck, Gabe, and Leon Klenicki, eds. *Spirituality and Prayer: Jewish and Christian Understandings.* New York: Paulist Press, 1983.

Interreligious Council of San Diego. *Bridging Our Faiths.* New York: Paulist Press, 1997.

Kee, Howard Clark, and Irvin J. Borowsky. *Removing Anti-Judaism from the Pulpit.* Philadelphia: American Interfaith Institute; New York: Continuum, 1996.

Kenny, Anthony. *Catholics, Jews, and the State of Israel.* New York: Paulist Press, 1993.

Klenicki, Leon, ed. *Toward a Theological Encounter: Jewish Understandings of Christianity.* New York: Paulist Press, 1991.

Klenicki, Leon, and Geoffrey Wigoder, eds. *A Dictionary of the Jewish–Christian Dialogue.* New York: Paulist Press, 1995.

Klenicki, Leon, and Michael Wyschogrod, eds. *Understanding Scripture: Explorations of Jewish and Christian Traditions of Interpretation.* New York: Paulist Press, 1987.

Lodahl, Michael E. *Shekhinah Spirit: Divine Presence in Jewish and Christian Religion.* New York: Paulist Press, 1992.

Neusner, Jacob. *A Rabbi Talks with Jesus: An Intermillennial, Interfaith Exchange.* New York: Doubleday, 1993.

Neusner, Jacob, and Bruce Chilton. *Jewish–Christian Debates: God, Kingdom, Messiah.* Minneapolis: Fortress Press, 1998.

Novak, David. *Jewish–Christian Dialogue: A Jewish Justification.* New York: Oxford University Press, 1989.

Ochs, Peter, ed. *The Return of Scripture in Judaism and Christianity: Essays in Postcritical Scriptural Interpretation.* New York: Paulist Press, 1993.

O'Hare, Padraic. *The Enduring Covenant: The Education of Christians and the End of Anti-Semitism.* Valley Forge: Trinity Press International, 1997.

Pawlikowski, John T. *Christ in the Light of the Christian–Jewish Dialogue.* New York: Paulist Press, 1982.

Pawlikowski, John T., and Hayim Goren Perelmuter, eds. *Reinterpreting Revelation and Tradition: Jews and Christians in Conversation.* Franklin, Wis.: Sheed and Ward, 2000.

Rothschild, Fritz A., ed. *Jewish Perspectives on Christianity: Leo Baeck, Martin Buber, Franz Rosenzweig, Will Herberg, and Abraham Joshua Heschel.* New York: Continuum, 1990.

Sandmel, Samuel. *We Jews and Jesus.* New York: Oxford University Press, 1965.

_____. *We Jews and You Christians: An Inquiry into Attitudes.* Philadelphia: Lippincott, 1967.

_____. *A Jewish Understanding of the New Testament.* Augmented ed. New York: KTAV Publishing House, 1974.

_____. *Anti-Semitism in the New Testament?* Philadelphia: Fortress Press, 1978.

Saperstein, Marc. *Moments of Crisis in Jewish–Christian Relations.* Philadelphia: Trinity Press International, 1989.

Shermis, Michael, and Arthur E. Zannoni. *Introduction to Jewish–Christian Relations.* New York: Paulist Press, 1991.

Soulen, R. Kendall. *The God of Israel and Christian Theology.* Minneapolis: Fortress Press, 1996.

Stimulus Foundation. *More Stepping Stones to Jewish–Christian Relations.* Compiled by Helga Croner. New York: Paulist Press, 1985.

Thoma, Clemens. *A Christian Theology of Judaism.* New York: Paulist Press, 1980.

van Buren, Paul M. *A Christian Theology of the People Israel: A Theology of the Jewish–Christian Reality.* New York: Seabury Press, 1983.

_____. *Discerning the Way: A Theology of the Jewish–Christian Reality, Part 2.* New York: The Seabury Press, 1980.

_____. *A Theology of the Jewish–Christian Reality, Part 3.* San Francisco: Harper and Row Publishers, 1988.

Williamson, Clark M. *A Guest in the House of Israel: Post-Holocaust Church Theology.* Louisville: Westminster/John Knox Press, 1993.

_____. *Way of Blessing, Way of Life: A Christian Theology.* St. Louis: Chalice Press, 1999.

Contributors

The Rev. Mary Katherine Allman is an ordained Episcopal priest working on a doctor of ministry degree at the Episcopal Divinity School in Cambridge, Massachusetts. She serves as an affiliate researcher of the Pluralism Project at Harvard University, which offers grants for research on the topic of religious pluralism, and also as assistant school minister at Brooks School, in North Andover, Massachusetts, teaching Old Testament and theology.

Rabbi Nina Beth Cardin is the director of Jewish life at the Jewish Community Center of Greater Baltimore. She is a writer and a lecturer. Her most recent book is *A Tapestry of Jewish Time: A Spiritual Guide to Holidays and Life Cycles*.

Rabbi Sharon Cohen Anisfeld is associate rabbi at Yale University's Hillel Foundation. She is also on the faculty of the Bronfman Youth Fellowships in Israel and is a graduate of the Reconstructionist Rabbinical College.

Dr. Christine Eaton Blair is associate professor of practical theology and director of the Doctor of Ministry Program for Austin Presbyterian Theological Seminary, Austin, Texas. She is an author of a book and numerous articles and has co-led, along with Rabbi Roy Walter of Congregation Emanu El in Houston, a Bible study on Christian–Jewish relations.

Mary C. Boys is the Skinner and McAlpin Professor of Practical Theology at Union Theological Seminary, New York City. Among her books are *Jewish–Christian Dialogue: One Woman's Experience* and *Has God Only One Blessing?: Judaism as a Source for Christian Self-Understanding*. A Roman Catholic, she is a member of the Sisters of the Holy Names of Jesus and Mary.

Dr. Rosann M. Catalano is the Roman Catholic theologian on the staff of the Institute for Christian & Jewish Studies in Baltimore, Maryland. She lectures widely to Protestant, Jewish, and Catholic audiences on theological and interfaith topics.

Dr. Philip A. Cunningham is executive director of the Center for Christian–Jewish Learning at Boston College. He is the author of several books concerning Jewish–Christian relations. He is also a member of the Advisory Committee on Catholic–Jewish Relations of the National Conference of Catholic Bishops and of the Christian Scholars Group on Jews and Judaism.

The Rev. Dr. Donald G. Dawe is the Robert L. Dabney Professor Emeritus of Systematic Theology at Union Theological Seminary in Virginia. He has published a number of books and articles, including ones on issues concerning interreligious studies.

The Rev. Lawrence W. Farris is a graduate of the University of Michigan and Princeton Theological Seminary and a Presbyterian minister who has pastored churches in Annapolis, Maryland, and in Okemos and Three Rivers, Michigan. He has published articles in a number of journals and the book *Dynamics of Small Town Ministry*.

Rabbi Jan Katzew serves as the director of the Union of American Hebrew Congregations Department of Jewish Education and as an adjunct member of the Hebrew Union College–Jewish Institute of Religion New York faculty. He has held leadership positions in supplementary and day schools as well as in a central agency for Jewish education.

Professor Sara S. Lee directs the Rhea Hirsch School of Education at the Hebrew Union College–Jewish Institute of Religion in Los Angeles. Together with Dr. Mary Boys she has directed two interreligious projects involving educators and academics: the Catholic–Jewish Colloquium and Educating for Religious Particularism and Pluralism. She received the Samuel Rothberg Prize in education from the Hebrew University in Jerusalem and a Doctor of Hebrew Letters honorary degree from the Jewish Theological Seminary for her contributions to Jewish education and to interreligious education.

Rabbi Daniel Lehmann is the founding headmaster of the New Jewish School of Greater Boston and serves as the scholar in residence at the Boston Synagogue. He is also the founder and president of the North American Association of Jewish High Schools. He has taught for the Institute of Jewish & Christian Studies, the National Jewish Center for Learning and Leadership, and the Wexner Heritage Foundation.

Dr. Christopher M. Leighton is an ordained Presbyterian minister and is the Executive Director of the Institute for Christian & Jewish Studies in Baltimore, Maryland. He has also served as adjunct professor at Johns Hopkins University and at the Ecumenical Institute of Theology at St. Mary's Seminary and University.

Rabbi Jeffrey A. Marx is rabbi of Sha'arei Am in Santa Monica, California. He is a member of the Academy of Family Mediators, specializing in interfaith issues. He has trained facilitators for the UAHC's various outreach programs for interfaith couples and has lectured and written on interfaith issues. He is the author of *What's Right, What's Wrong: A Guide to Talking About Values for Parents and Kids.*

The Rev. Dr. Kenneth J. Meyers is the associate pastor of Hendricks Avenue Baptist Church in Jacksonville, Florida. He also serves as moderator for *The Forum,* a weekly panel discussion of Bible lessons on local television. He is a board member of Inter-church Coalition of Action, Reconciliation, and Empowerment.

Amy Grossblatt Pessah graduated with honors from the Hebrew Union College–Jewish Institute of Religion with a master's degree in Jewish education. She now consults in the area of Jewish education, where her most recent projects have focused on program design and development for teachers, adults, and families.

Rabbi David Fox Sandmel served as the Jewish scholar at the Institute for Christian & Jewish Studies in Baltimore, Maryland, where he directed the National Jewish Scholars Project. He is coeditor of *Christianity in Jewish Terms.*

Rabbi Isaac (Ike) Serotta is rabbi of Lakeside Congregation for Reform Judaism in Highland Park, Illinois. Some of his interreligious work has included facilitating "Seminarians Interacting" for National Council of Christians and Jews; and, for American Jewish Committee, he pioneered an African American/Jewish Passover Seder and an interfaith/interracial discussion program.

The Rev. Cynthia Terry serves as associate university chaplain for Yale University. She is an ordained minister in the United Church of Christ and works on a variety of multifaith projects.

Dr. Fayette Breaux Veverka is assistant professor of theology and religious studies at Villanova University. She coordinates a program of Jewish Studies for Catholic educators, enabling them to explore the Jewish roots of Christian faith.

Jane West Walsh works nationally as an independent Jewish educational consultant. She is currently directing a qualitative research study, as part of doctoral work in adult education, on interreligious dialogue and adult learning that includes Christians, Muslims, and Jews.

Rabbi Avi Weinstein is the director of Hillel's Joseph Meyerhoff Center for Jewish Learning. He has written for and served as editor and translator for numerous publications in major U.S. and international companies and organizations.

Index

Irreconcilable
Differences?